# The DevOps 2.5 Toolkit

Monitoring, Logging, and Auto-Scaling Kubernetes: Making Resilient, Self-Adaptive, And Autonomous Kubernetes Clusters

**Viktor Farcic**

**BIRMINGHAM - MUMBAI**

# The DevOps 2.5 Toolkit

**Acquisition Editor:** Dominic Shakeshaft
**Technical Editor:** Aniket Shetty
**Indexer:** Manju Arasan
**Production Designer:** Sandip Tadge

First published: November 2019

Production reference: 1261119

Published by Packt Publishing Ltd.
Livery Place
35 Livery Street
Birmingham
B3 2PB, UK.

ISBN 978-1-83864-751-3

www.packt.com

`Packt.com`

Subscribe to our online digital library for full access to over 7,000 books and videos, as well as industry leading tools to help you plan your personal development and advance your career. For more information, please visit our website.

# Why subscribe?

- Spend less time learning and more time coding with practical eBooks and Videos from over 4,000 industry professionals

- Improve your learning with Skill Plans built especially for you

- Get a free eBook or video every month

- Fully searchable for easy access to vital information

- Copy and paste, print, and bookmark content

Did you know that Packt offers eBook versions of every book published, with PDF and ePub files available? You can upgrade to the eBook version at `www.packt.com` and as a print book customer, you are entitled to a discount on the eBook copy. Get in touch with us at `customercare@packtpub.com` for more details.

At `www.packt.com`, you can also read a collection of free technical articles, sign up for a range of free newsletters, and receive exclusive discounts and offers on Packt books and eBooks.

*To Sara and Eva.*

*–Viktor Farcic*

# Contributors

## About the author

Viktor Farcic is a Principal Consultant at CloudBees (`https://www.cloudbees.com/`), a member of the Docker Captains (`https://www.docker.com/community/docker-captains`) group, and author.

He coded using a plethora of languages starting with Pascal (yes, he is old), Basic (before it got Visual prefix), ASP (before it got .Net suffix), C, C++, Perl, Python, ASP.Net, Visual Basic, C#, JavaScript, Java, Scala, etc. He never worked with Fortran. His current favorite is Go.

His big passions are containers, distributed systems, microservices, continuous delivery and deployment (CD) and test-driven development (TDD).

He often speaks at community gatherings and conferences.

He wrote *The DevOps Toolkit Series* (`http://www.devopstoolkitseries.com/`) and Test-Driven Java Development (`https://www.packtpub.com/application-development/test-driven-java-development`).

His random thoughts and tutorials can be found in his blog TechnologyConversations.com (`https://technologyconversations.com/`).

# Table of Contents

# Preface

Kubernetes is probably the biggest project we know. It is vast, and yet many think that after a few weeks or months of reading and practice they know all there is to know about it. It's much bigger than that, and it is growing faster than most of us can follow. How far did you get in Kubernetes adoption?

From my experience, there are four main phases in Kubernetes adoption.

In the first phase, we create a cluster and learn intricacies of Kube API and different types of resources (for example, Pods, Ingress, Deployments, StatefulSets, and so on). Once we are comfortable with the way Kubernetes works, we start deploying and managing our applications. By the end of this phase, we can shout "**look at me, I have things running in my production Kubernetes cluster, and nothing blew up!**" I explained most of this phase in *The DevOps 2.3 Toolkit: Kubernetes* (`https://amzn.to/2GvzDjy`).

The second phase is often automation. Once we become comfortable with how Kubernetes works and we are running production loads, we can move to automation. We often adopt some form of continuous delivery (CD) or continuous deployment (CDP). We create Pods with the tools we need, we build our software and container images, we run tests, and we deploy to production. When we're finished, most of our processes are automated, and we do not perform manual deployments to Kubernetes anymore. We can say that **things are working and I'm not even touching my keyboard**. I did my best to provide some insights into CD and CDP with Kubernetes in *The DevOps 2.4 Toolkit: Continuous Deployment To Kubernetes* (`https://amzn.to/2NkIiVi`).

The third phase is in many cases related to monitoring, alerting, logging, and scaling. The fact that we can run (almost) anything in Kubernetes and that it will do its best to make it fault tolerant and highly available, does not mean that our applications and clusters are bulletproof. We need to monitor the cluster, and we need alerts that will notify us of potential issues. When we do discover that there is a problem, we need to be able to query metrics and logs of the whole system. We can fix an issue only once we know what the root cause is. In highly dynamic distributed systems like Kubernetes, that is not as easy as it looks.

Further on, we need to learn how to scale (and de-scale) everything. The number of Pods of an application should change over time to accommodate fluctuations in traffic and demand. Nodes should scale as well to fulfill the needs of our applications.

Kubernetes already has the tools that provide metrics and visibility into logs. It allows us to create auto-scaling rules. Yet, we might discover that Kuberentes alone is not enough and that we might need to extend our system with additional processes and tools. This phase is the subject of this book. By the time you finish reading it, you'll be able to say that **your clusters and applications are truly dynamic and resilient and that they require minimal manual involvement. We'll try to make our system self-adaptive.**

I mentioned the fourth phase. That, dear reader, is everything else. The last phase is mostly about keeping up with all the other goodies Kubernetes provides. It's about following its roadmap and adapting our processes to get the benefits of each new release.

Eventually, you might get stuck and will be in need of help. Or you might want to write a review or comment on the book's content. Please join the *DevOps20* (`http://slack.devops20toolkit.com/`) Slack workspace and post your thoughts, ask questions, or participate in a discussion. If you prefer a more one-on-one communication, you can use Slack to send me a private message or send an email to `viktor@farcic.com`. All the books I wrote are very dear to me, and I want you to have a good experience reading them. Part of that experience is the option to reach out to me. Don't be shy.

Please note that this one, just as the previous books, is self-published. I believe that having no intermediaries between the writer and the reader is the best way to go. It allows me to write faster, update the book more frequently, and have more direct communication with you. Your feedback is part of the process. No matter whether you purchased the book while only a few or all chapters were written, the idea is that it will never be truly finished. As time passes, it will require updates so that it is aligned with the change in technology or processes. When possible, I will try to keep it up to date and release updates whenever that makes sense. Eventually, things might change so much that updates are not a good option anymore, and that will be a sign that a whole new book is required. **I will keep writing as long as I continue getting your support.**

# Overview

We'll explore some of the skills and knowledge required for operating Kubernetes clusters. We'll deal with subjects that are often not studied at the very beginning but only after we get bored with Kubernetes' core features like Pod, ReplicaSets, Deployments, Ingress, PersistentVolumes, and so on. We'll master subjects we often dive into after we learn the basics and after we automate all the processes. We'll explore **monitoring**, **alerting**, **logging**, **auto-scaling**, and other subjects aimed at making our cluster **resilient**, **self-sufficient**, and **self-adaptive**.

# Audience

I assume that you are familiar with Kubernetes and that there is no need to explain how Kube API works, nor the difference between master and worker nodes, and especially not resources and constructs like Pods, Ingress, Deployments, StatefulSets, ServiceAccounts, and so on. If that is not you, this content might be too advanced, and I recommend you go through *The DevOps 2.3 Toolkit: Kubernetes* (https://amzn.to/2GvzDjy) first. I hope that you are already a Kubernetes ninja apprentice, and you are interested in how to make your cluster more resilient, scalable, and self-adaptive. If that's the case, this is the book for you. Read on.

# Requirements

The book assumes that you already know how to operate a Kubernetes cluster so we won't go into details how to create one nor we'll explore Pods, Deployments, StatefulSets, and other commonly used Kubernetes resources. If that assumption is not correct, you might want to read *The DevOps 2.3 Toolkit: Kubernetes* first.

Apart from assumptions based on knowledge, there are some technical requirements as well. If you are a **Windows user**, please run all the examples from **Git Bash**. It will allow you to run the same commands as MacOS and Linux users do through their terminals. Git Bash is set up during Git installation. If you don't have it already, please re-run Git setup.

Since we'll use a Kubernetes cluster, we'll need **kubectl** (https://kubernetes.io/docs/tasks/tools/install-kubectl/). Most of the applications we'll run inside the cluster will be installed using **Helm** (https://helm.sh/), so please make sure that you have the client installed as well. Finally, install **jq** (https://stedolan.github.io/jq/) as well. It's a tool that helps us format and filter JSON output.

Finally, we'll need a Kubernetes cluster. All the examples are tested using **Docker for Desktop**, **minikube**, **Google Kubernetes Engine (GKE)**, **Amazon Elastic Container Service for Kubernetes (EKS)**, and **Azure Kubernetes Service (AKS)**. I will provide requirements (for example, number of nodes, CPU, memory, Ingress, and so on.) for each of those Kubernetes flavors.

You're free to apply the lessons to any of the tested Kubernetes platforms, or you might choose to use a different one. There is no good reason why the examples from this book shouldn't work in every Kubernetes flavor. You might need to tweak them here and there, but I'm confident that won't be a problem.

If you run into any issue, please contact me through the *DevOps20* (`http://slack.`
`devops20toolkit.com/`) slack workspace or by sending me an email
to `viktor@farcic.com`. I'll do my best to help out. If you do use a Kuberentes cluster
other then one of those I tested, I'd appreciate your help in expanding the list.

Before you select a Kubernetes flavor, you should know that not all the features will be
available everywhere. In case of local clusters based on **Docker for Desktop** or **minikube**,
scaling nodes will not be possible since both are single-node clusters. Other clusters might
not be able to use more specific features. I'll use this opportunity to compare different
platforms and give you additional insights you might want to use if you're evaluating
which Kubernetes distribution to use and where to host it. Or, you can choose to run some
chapters with a local cluster and switch to a multi-node cluster only for the parts that do
not work in local. That way you'll save a few bucks by having a cluster in Cloud for very
short periods.

If you're unsure which Kubernetes flavor to select, choose GKE. It is currently the most
advanced and feature-rich managed Kubernetes on the market. On the other hand, if you're
already used to EKS or AKS, they are, more or less, OK as well. Most, if not all of the things
featured in this book will work. Finally, you might prefer to run a cluster locally, or you're
using a different (probably on-prem) Kubernetes platform. In that case, you'll learn what
you're missing and which things you'll need to build on top of "standard offerings" to
accomplish the same result.

# Download the example code files

You can download the example code files for this book from your account at
`www.packt.com`. If you purchased this book elsewhere, you can visit
`www.packtpub.com/support` and register to have the files emailed directly to you.

You can download the code files by following these steps:

1. Log in or register at `www.packt.com`.
2. Select the **Support** tab.
3. Click on **Code Downloads**.
4. Enter the name of the book in the **Search** box and follow the onscreen
   instructions.

Once the file is downloaded, please make sure that you unzip or extract the folder using the latest version of:

- WinRAR/7-Zip for Windows
- Zipeg/iZip/UnRarX for Mac
- 7-Zip/PeaZip for Linux

The code bundle for the book is also hosted on GitHub at `https://github.com/PacktPublishing/The-DevOps-2.5-Toolkit`. In case there's an update to the code, it will be updated on the existing GitHub repository.

We also have other code bundles from our rich catalog of books and videos available at `https://github.com/PacktPublishing/`. Check them out!

# Download the color images

We also provide a PDF file that has color images of the screenshots/diagrams used in this book. You can download it here: `https://static.packt-cdn.com/downloads/9781838647513_ColorImages.pdf`.

# Conventions used

There are a number of text conventions used throughout this book.

`CodeInText`: Indicates code words in text, database table names, folder names, filenames, file extensions, pathnames, dummy URLs, user input, and Twitter handles. Here is an example: "The definition uses `HorizontalPodAutoscaler` targeting the `api` Deployment. "

A block of code is set as follows:

```
1   sum(label_join(
2       rate(
3           container_cpu_usage_seconds_total{
4               namespace!="kube-system",
5               pod_name!=""
6           }[5m]
7       )
```

When we wish to draw your attention to a particular part of a code block, the relevant lines or items are set in bold:

```
1  sum(label_join(
2      rate(
3          container_cpu_usage_seconds_total{
4              namespace!="kube-system",
5              pod_name!=""
6          }[5m]
7      )
```

Any command-line input or output is written as follows:

```
1  cd k8s-specs
2
3  git pull
```

**Bold**: Indicates a new term, an important word, or words that you see onscreen. For example, words in menus or dialog boxes appear in the text like this. Here is an example: "Select **Prometheus**, and click the **Import** button."

 Warnings or important notes appear like this.

 Tips and tricks appear like this.

# Get in touch

Feedback from our readers is always welcome.

**General feedback**: If you have questions about any aspect of this book, mention the book title in the subject of your message and email us at customercare@packtpub.com.

**Errata**: Although we have taken every care to ensure the accuracy of our content, mistakes do happen. If you have found a mistake in this book, we would be grateful if you would report this to us. Please visit www.packtpub.com/support/errata, selecting your book, clicking on the Errata Submission Form link, and entering the details.

**Piracy**: If you come across any illegal copies of our works in any form on the Internet, we would be grateful if you would provide us with the location address or website name. Please contact us at copyright@packt.com with a link to the material.

**If you are interested in becoming an author**: If there is a topic that you have expertise in and you are interested in either writing or contributing to a book, please visit authors.packtpub.com.

# Reviews

Please leave a review. Once you have read and used this book, why not leave a review on the site that you purchased it from? Potential readers can then see and use your unbiased opinion to make purchase decisions, we at Packt can understand what you think about our products, and our authors can see your feedback on their book. Thank you!

For more information about Packt, please visit packt.com.

# 1

# Autoscaling Deployments and StatefulSets Based on Resource Usage

*Change is the essential process of all existence.*

*- Spock*

By now, you probably understood that one of the critical aspects of a system based on Kubernetes is a high level of dynamism. Almost nothing is static. We define Deployments or StatefulSets, and Kubernetes distributes the Pods across the cluster. In most cases, those Pods are rarely sitting in one place for a long time. Rolling updates result in Pods being re-created and potentially moved to other nodes. Failure of any kind provokes rescheduling of the affected resources. Many other events cause the Pods to move around. A Kubernetes cluster is like a beehive. It's full of life, and it's always in motion.

Dynamic nature of a Kubernetes cluster is not only due to our (human) actions or rescheduling caused by failures. Autoscaling is to be blamed as well. We should fully embrace Kubernetes' dynamic nature and move towards autonomous and self-sufficient clusters capable of serving the needs of our applications without (much) human involvement. To accomplish that, we need to provide sufficient information that will allow Kubernetes' to scale the applications as well as the nodes that constitute the cluster. In this chapter, we'll focus on the former case. We'll explore commonly used and basic ways to auto-scale Pods based on memory and CPU consumption. We'll accomplish that using HorizontalPodAutoscaler.

HorizontalPodAutoscaler's only function is to automatically scale the number of Pods in a Deployment, a StatefulSet, or a few other types of resources. It accomplishes that by observing CPU and memory consumption of the Pods and acting when they reach pre-defined thresholds.

HorizontalPodAutoscaler is implemented as a Kubernetes API resource and a controller. The resource determines the behavior of the controller. The controller periodically adjusts the number of replicas in a StatefulSet or a Deployment to match the observed average CPU utilization to the target specified by a user.

We'll see HorizontalPodAutoscaler in action soon and comment on its specific features through practical examples. But, before we get there, we need a Kubernetes cluster as well as a source of metrics.

# Creating a cluster

Before we create a cluster (or start using one you already have available), we'll clone the vfarcic/k8s-specs (https://github.com/vfarcic/k8s-specs) repository which contains most of the definitions we'll use in this book.

 **A note to Windows users**
Please execute all the commands from this book from Git Bash. That way, you'll be able to run them as they are instead of modifying their syntax to adapt them to Windows terminal or PowerShell.

 All the commands from this chapter are available in the 01-hpa.sh (https://gist.github.com/vfarcic/b46ca2eababb98d967e3e25748740d0 d) Gist.

```
1  git clone https://github.com/vfarcic/k8s-specs.git
2
3  cd k8s-specs
```

If you cloned the repository before, please make sure that you have the latest version by executing git pull.

The gists and the specifications that follow are used to test the commands in this chapter. Please use them as inspiration when creating your own test cluster or to validate that the one you're planning to use for the exercises meets the minimum requirements.

- `docker-scale.sh`: **Docker for Desktop** with 2 CPUs, 2 GB RAM and with **tiller** (https://gist.github.com/vfarcic/ca52ff97fc80565af0c46c37449babac).
- `minikube-scale.sh`: **minikube** with 2 CPUs, 2 GB RAM and with **tiller** (https://gist.github.com/vfarcic/5bc07d822f8825263245829715261a68).
- `gke-scale.sh`: **GKE** with 3 n1-standard-1 worker nodes and with **tiller** (https://gist.github.com/vfarcic/9c777487f7ebee6c09027d3a1df8663c).
- `eks-scale.sh`: **EKS** with 3 t2.small worker nodes and with **tiller** (https://gist.github.com/vfarcic/a94dffef7d6dc60f79570d351c92408d).
- `aks-scale.sh`: **AKS** with 3 Standard_B2s worker nodes and with **tiller** (https://gist.github.com/vfarcic/f1b05d33cc8a98e4ceab3d3770c2fe0b).

Please note that we will use Helm to install necessary applications, but we'll switch to "pure" Kubernetes YAML for experimenting with (probably new) resources used in this chapter and for deploying the demo application. In other words, we'll use Helm for one-time installations (for example, Metrics Server) and YAML for things we'll explore in more detail (for example, HorizontalPodAutoscaler).

Now, let's talk about Metrics Server.

# Observing Metrics Server data

The critical element in scaling Pods is the Kubernetes Metrics Server. You might consider yourself a Kubernetes ninja and yet never heard of the Metrics Server. Don't be ashamed if that's the case. You're not the only one.

If you started observing Kubernetes metrics, you might have used Heapster. It's been around for a long time, and you likely have it running in your cluster, even if you don't know what it is. Both serve the same purpose, with one being deprecated for a while, so let's clarify things a bit.

Early on, Kubernetes introduced Heapster as a tool that enables Container Cluster Monitoring and Performance Analysis for Kubernetes. It's been around since Kubernetes version 1.0.6. You can say that Heapster has been part of Kubernetes' life since its toddler age. It collects and interprets various metrics like resource usage, events, and so on. Heapster has been an integral part of Kubernetes and enabled it to schedule Pods appropriately. Without it, Kubernetes would be blind. It would not know which node has available memory, which Pod is using too much CPU, and so on. But, just as with most other tools that become available early, its design was a "failed experiment".

As Kubernetes continued growing, we (the community around Kubernetes) started realizing that a new, better, and, more importantly, a more extensible design is required. Hence, Metrics Server was born. Right now, even though Heapster is still in use, it is considered deprecated, even though today (September 2018) the Metrics Server is still in beta state.

So, what is Metrics Server? A simple explanation is that it collects information about used resources (memory and CPU) of nodes and Pods. It does not store metrics, so do not think that you can use it to retrieve historical values and predict tendencies. There are other tools for that, and we'll explore them later. Instead, Metrics Server's goal is to provide an API that can be used to retrieve current resource usage. We can use that API through `kubectl` or by sending direct requests with, let's say, `curl`. In other words, Metrics Server collects cluster-wide metrics and allows us to retrieve them through its API. That, by itself, is very powerful, but it is only the part of the story.

I already mentioned extensibility. We can extend Metrics Server to collect metrics from other sources. We'll get there in due time. For now, we'll explore what it provides out of the box and how it interacts with some other Kubernetes resources that will help us make our Pods scalable and more resilient.

If you read my other books, you know that I do not go into much theory and, instead, prefer demonstrating features and principles through practical examples. This book is no exception, and we'll dive straight into Metrics Server hands-on exercises. The first step is to install it.

Helm makes installation of almost any publicly available software very easy if there is a Chart available. If there isn't, you might want to consider an alternative since that is a clear indication that the vendor or the community behind it does not believe in Kubernetes. Or, maybe they do not have the skills necessary to develop a Chart. Either way, the best course of action is to run away from it and adopt an alternative. If that's not an option, develop a Helm Chart yourself. In our case, there won't be a need for such measures. Metrics Server does have a Helm Chart, and all we need to do is to install it.

**A note to GKE and AKS users**
Google and Microsoft already ship Metrics Server as part of their managed Kubernetes clusters (GKE and AKS). There is no need to install it, so please skip the commands that follow.

**A note to minikube users**
Metrics Server is available as one of the plugins. Please execute `minikube addons enable metrics-server` and `kubectl -n kube-system rollout status deployment metrics-server` commands instead of those following.

**A note to Docker for Desktop users**
Recent updates to the Metrics Server do not work with self-signed certificates by default. Since Docker for Desktop uses such certificates, you'll need to allow insecure TLS. Please add `--set args={"--kubelet-insecure-tls=true"}` argument to the `helm install` command that follows.

```
1  helm install stable/metrics-server \
2      --name metrics-server \
3      --version 2.0.2 \
4      --namespace metrics
5
6  kubectl -n metrics \
7      rollout status \
8      deployment metrics-server
```

We used Helm to install Metrics Server, and we waited until it rolled out.

Metrics Server will periodically fetch metrics from Kubeletes running on the nodes. Those metrics, for now, contain memory and CPU utilization of the Pods and the nodes. Other entities can request data from the Metrics Server through the API Server which has the Master Metrics API. An example of those entities is the Scheduler that, once Metrics Server is installed, uses its data to make decisions.

As you will see soon, the usage of the Metrics Server goes beyond the Scheduler but, for now, the explanation should provide an image of the basic flow of data.

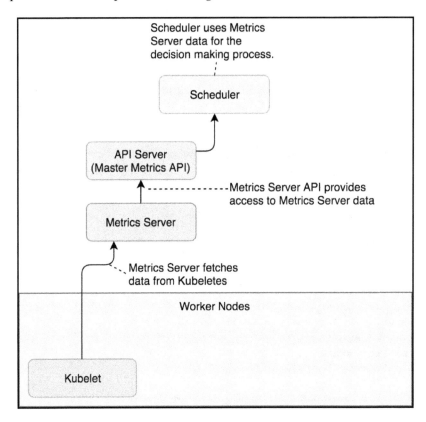

Figure 1-1: The basic flow of the data to and from the Metrics Server (arrows show directions of data flow)

Now we can explore one of the ways we can retrieve the metrics. We'll start with those related to nodes.

```
1  kubectl top nodes
```

If you were fast, the output should state that `metrics are not available yet`. That's normal. It takes a few minutes before the first iteration of metrics retrieval is executed. The exception is GKE and AKS that already come with the Metrics Server baked in.

Fetch some coffee before we repeat the command.

```
1  kubectl top nodes
```

This time, the output is different.

In this chapter, I'll show the outputs from Docker for Desktop. Depending on the Kubernetes flavor you're using, your outputs will be different. Still, the logic is the same and you should not have a problem to follow along.

My output is as follows.

```
NAME                   CPU(cores) CPU% MEMORY(bytes) MEMORY%
docker-for-desktop 248m          12%  1208Mi        63%
```

We can see that I have one node called `docker-for-desktop`. It is using 248 CPU milliseconds. Since the node has two cores, that's 12% of the total available CPU. Similarly, 1.2 GB of RAM is used, which is 63% of the total available memory of 2 GB.

Resource usage of the nodes is useful but is not what we're looking for. In this chapter, we're focused on auto-scaling Pods. But, before we get there, we should observe how much memory each of our Pods is using. We'll start with those running in the `kube-system` Namespace.

```
1  kubectl -n kube-system top pod
```

The output (on Docker for Desktop) is as follows.

```
NAME                                          CPU(cores) MEMORY(bytes)
etcd-docker-for-desktop                       16m        74Mi
kube-apiserver-docker-for-desktop             33m        427Mi
kube-controller-manager-docker-for-desktop 44m         63Mi
kube-dns-86f4d74b45-c47nh                     1m         39Mi
kube-proxy-r56kd                              2m         22Mi
kube-scheduler-docker-for-desktop             13m        23Mi
tiller-deploy-5c688d5f9b-2pspz                0m         21Mi
```

We can see resource usage (CPU and memory) for each of the Pods currently running in `kube-system`. If we do not find better tools, we could use that information to adjust `requests` of those Pods to be more accurate. However, there are better ways to get that info, so we'll skip adjustments for now. Instead, let's try to get current resource usage of all the Pods, no matter the Namespace.

```
1  kubectl top pods --all-namespaces
```

The output (on Docker for Desktop) is as follows.

```
NAMESPACE     NAME                              CPU(cores)
MEMORY(bytes)
docker        compose-7447646cf5-wqbwz          0m          11Mi
docker        compose-api-6fbc44c575-gwhxt      0m          14Mi
```

```
kube-system etcd-docker-for-desktop                     16m      74Mi
kube-system kube-apiserver-docker-for-desktop           33m      427Mi
kube-system kube-controller-manager-docker-for-desktop  46m      63Mi
kube-system kube-dns-86f4d74b45-c47nh                   1m       38Mi
kube-system kube-proxy-r56kd                            3m       22Mi
kube-system kube-scheduler-docker-for-desktop           14m      23Mi
kube-system tiller-deploy-5c688d5f9b-2pspz              0m       21Mi
metrics     metrics-server-5d78586d76-pbqj8             0m       10Mi
```

That output shows the same information as the previous one, only extended to all Namespaces. There should be no need to comment it.

Often, metrics of a Pod are not granular enough, and we need to observe the resources of each of the containers that constitute a Pod. All we need to do to get container metrics is to add `--containers` argument.

```
1  kubectl top pods \
2    --all-namespaces \
3    --containers
```

The output (on Docker for Desktop) is as follows.

```
NAMESPACE    POD                                                    NAME
CPU(cores)  MEMORY(bytes)
docker       compose-7447646cf5-wqbwz                               compose
0m           11Mi
docker       compose-api-6fbc44c575-gwhxt                           compose
0m           14Mi
kube-system etcd-docker-for-desktop                                 etcd
16m          74Mi
kube-system kube-apiserver-docker-for-desktop                       kube-apiserver
33m          427Mi
kube-system kube-controller-manager-docker-for-desktop kube-controller-
manager 46m        63Mi
kube-system kube-dns-86f4d74b45-c47nh                                kubedns
0m           13Mi
kube-system kube-dns-86f4d74b45-c47nh                                dnsmasq
0m           10Mi
kube-system kube-dns-86f4d74b45-c47nh                                sidecar
1m           14Mi
kube-system kube-proxy-r56kd                                         kube-proxy
3m           22Mi
kube-system kube-scheduler-docker-for-desktop                        kube-scheduler
14m          23Mi
kube-system tiller-deploy-5c688d5f9b-2pspz                           tiller
0m           21Mi
metrics      metrics-server-5d78586d76-pbqj8                        metrics-server
0m           10Mi
```

We can see that, this time, the output shows each container separately. We can, for example, observe metrics of the `kube-dns-*` Pod separated into three containers (`kubedns`, `dnsmasq`, `sidecar`).

When we request metrics through `kubectl top`, the flow of data is almost the same as when the scheduler makes requests. A request is sent to the API Server (Master Metrics API), which gets data from the Metrics Server which, in turn, was collecting information from Kubeletes running on the nodes of the cluster.

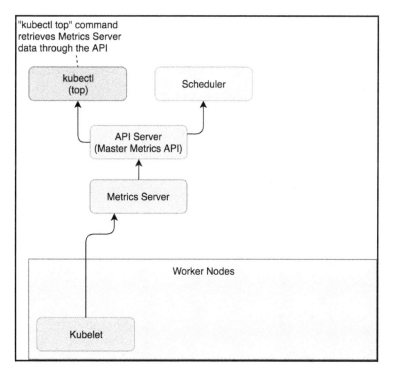

Figure 1-2: The flow of the data to and from the Metrics Server (arrows show directions of data flow)

While `kubectl top` command is useful to observe current metrics, it is pretty useless if we'd like to access them from other tools. After all, the goal is not for us to sit in front of a terminal with `watch "kubectl top pods"` command. That would be a waste of our (human) talent. Instead, our goal should be to scrape those metrics from other tools and create alerts and (maybe) dashboards based on both real-time and historical data. For that, we need output in JSON or some other machine-parsable format. Luckily, `kubectl` allows us to invoke its API directly in raw format and retrieve the same result as if a tool would query it.

```
1  kubectl get \
2      --raw "/apis/metrics.k8s.io/v1beta1" \
3      | jq '.'
```

The output is as follows.

```
{
  "kind": "APIResourceList",
  "apiVersion": "v1",
  "groupVersion": "metrics.k8s.io/v1beta1",
  "resources": [
    {
      "name": "nodes",
      "singularName": "",
      "namespaced": false,
      "kind": "NodeMetrics",
      "verbs": [
        "get",
        "list"
      ]
    },
    {
      "name": "pods",
      "singularName": "",
      "namespaced": true,
      "kind": "PodMetrics",
      "verbs": [
        "get",
        "list"
      ]
    }
  ]
}
```

We can see that the /apis/metrics.k8s.io/v1beta1 endpoint is an index API that has two resources (nodes and pods).

Let's take a closer look at the pods resource of the metrics API.

```
1  kubectl get \
2      --raw "/apis/metrics.k8s.io/v1beta1/pods" \
3      | jq '.'
```

The output is too big to be presented in a book, so I'll leave it up to you to explore it. You'll notice that the output is JSON equivalent of what we observed through the kubectl top pods --all-namespaces --containers command.

That was a rapid overview of the Metrics Server. There are two important things to note. First of all, it provides current (or short-term) memory and CPU utilization of the containers running inside a cluster. The second and the more important note is that we will not use it directly. Metrics Server was not designed for humans but for machines. We'll get there later. For now, remember that there is a thing called Metrics Server and that you should not use it directly (once you adopt a tool that will scrape its metrics).

Now that we explored Metrics Server, we'll try to put it to good use and learn how to auto-scale our Pods based on resource utilization.

# Auto-scaling Pods based on resource utilization

Our goal is to deploy an application that will be automatically scaled (or de-scaled) depending on its use of resources. We'll start by deploying an app first, and discuss how to accomplish auto-scaling later.

 I already warned you that I assume that you are familiar with Kubernetes and that in this book we'll explore a particular topic of monitoring, alerting, scaling, and a few other things. We will not discuss Pods, StatefulSets, Deployments, Services, Ingress, and other "basic" Kubernetes resources. This is your last chance to admit that you do NOT understand Kubernetes' fundamentals, to take a step back, and to read *The DevOps 2.3 Toolkit: Kubernetes* (`https://www.devopstoolkitseries.com/posts/devops-23/`) and *The DevOps 2.4 Toolkit: Continuous Deployment To Kubernetes* (`https://www.devopstoolkitseries.com/posts/devops-24/`).

Let's take a look at a definition of the application we'll use in our examples.

```
1  cat scaling/go-demo-5-no-sidecar-mem.yml
```

If you are familiar with Kubernetes, the YAML definition should be self-explanatory. We'll comment only the parts that are relevant for auto-scaling.

The output, limited to the relevant parts, is as follows.

```
...
apiVersion: apps/v1
kind: StatefulSet
metadata:
  name: db
  namespace: go-demo-5
```

```
spec:
  ...
  template:
    ...
    spec:
      ...
      containers:
      - name: db
        ...
        resources:
          limits:
            memory: "150Mi"
            cpu: 0.2
          requests:
            memory: "100Mi"
            cpu: 0.1
        ...
      - name: db-sidecar
        ...

apiVersion: apps/v1
kind: Deployment
metadata:
  name: api
  namespace: go-demo-5
spec:
  ...
  template:
    ...
    spec:
      containers:
      - name: api
        ...
        resources:
          limits:
            memory: 15Mi
            cpu: 0.1
          requests:
            memory: 10Mi
            cpu: 0.01
  ...
```

We have two Pods that form an application. The `api` Deployment is a backend API that uses `db` StatefulSet for its state.

The essential parts of the definition are `resources`. Both the `api` and the `db` have `requests` and `limits` defined for memory and CPU. The database uses a sidecar container that will join MongoDB replicas into a replica set. Please note that, unlike other containers, the sidecar does not have `resources`. The importance behind that will be revealed later. For now, just remember that two containers have the `requests` and the `limits` defined, and that one doesn't.

Now, let's create those resources.

```
1  kubectl apply \
2      -f scaling/go-demo-5-no-sidecar-mem.yml \
3      --record
```

The output should show that quite a few resources were created and our next action is to wait until the `api` Deployment is rolled out thus confirming that the application is up-and-running.

```
1  kubectl -n go-demo-5 \
2      rollout status \
3      deployment api
```

After a few moments, you should see the message stating that `deployment "api" was successfully rolled out`.

To be on the safe side, we'll list the Pods in the `go-demo-5` Namespace and confirm that one replica of each is running.

```
1  kubectl -n go-demo-5 get pods
```

The output is as follows.

```
NAME      READY STATUS  RESTARTS AGE
api-...   1/1   Running 0        1m
db-0      2/2   Running 0        1m
```

So far, we did not yet do anything beyond the ordinary creation of the StatefulSet and the Deployment.

They, in turn, created ReplicaSets, which resulted in the creation of the Pods.

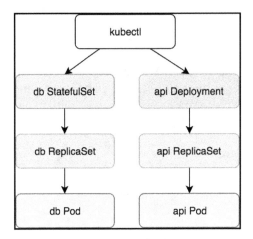

Figure 1-3: Creation of the StatefulSet and the Deployment

As you hopefully know, we should aim at having at least two replicas of each Pod, as long as they are scalable. Still, neither of the two had `replicas` defined. That is intentional. The fact that we can specify the number of replicas of a Deployment or a StatefulSet does not mean that we should. At least, not always.

 If the number of replicas is static and you have no intention to scale (or de-scale) your application over time, set `replicas` as part of your Deployment or StatefulSet definition. If, on the other hand, you plan to change the number of replicas based on memory, CPU, or other metrics, use HorizontalPodAutoscaler resource instead.

Let's take a look at a simple example of a HorizontalPodAutoscaler.

```
1   cat scaling/go-demo-5-api-hpa.yml
```

The output is as follows.

```
apiVersion: autoscaling/v2beta1
kind: HorizontalPodAutoscaler
metadata:
  name: api
  namespace: go-demo-5
spec:
  scaleTargetRef:
    apiVersion: apps/v1
    kind: Deployment
```

```
      name: api
minReplicas: 2
maxReplicas: 5
metrics:
- type: Resource
  resource:
    name: cpu
    targetAverageUtilization: 80
- type: Resource
  resource:
    name: memory
    targetAverageUtilization: 80
```

The definition uses `HorizontalPodAutoscaler` targeting the `api` Deployment. Its boundaries are the minimum of two and the maximum of five replicas. Those limits are fundamental. Without them, we'd run a risk of scaling up into infinity or scaling down to zero replicas. The `minReplicas` and `maxReplicas` fields are a safety net.

The key section of the definition is `metrics`. It provides formulas Kubernetes should use to decide whether it should scale (or de-scale) a resource. In our case, we're using the `Resource` type entries. They are targeting average utilization of eighty percent for memory and CPU. If the actual usage of the either of the two deviates, Kubernetes will scale (or de-scale) the resource.

Please note that we used `v2beta1` version of the API and you might be wondering why we chose that one instead of the stable and production ready `v1`. After all, `beta1` releases are still far from being polished enough for general usage. The reason is simple. HorizontalPodAutoscaler `v1` is too basic. It only allows scaling based on CPU. Even our simple example goes beyond that by adding memory to the mix. Later on, we'll extend it even more. So, while `v1` is considered stable, it does not provide much value, and we can either wait until `v2` is released or start experimenting with `v2beta` releases right away. We're opting for the latter option. By the time you read this, more stable releases are likely to exist and to be supported in your Kubernetes cluster. If that's the case, feel free to change `apiVersion` before applying the definition.

Now let's apply it.

```
1  kubectl apply \
2      -f scaling/go-demo-5-api-hpa.yml \
3      --record
```

We applied the definition that created the **HorizontalPodAutoscaler** (**HPA**). Next, we'll take a look at the information we'll get by retrieving the HPA resources.

```
1  kubectl -n go-demo-5 get hpa
```

If you were quick, the output should be similar to the one that follows.

```
NAME REFERENCE       TARGETS                        MINPODS MAXPODS REPLICAS
AGE
api  Deployment/api <unknown>/80%, <unknown>/80% 2     5       0
20s
```

We can see that Kubernetes does not yet have the actual CPU and memory utilization and that it output <unknown> instead. We need to give it a bit more time until the next iteration of data gathering from the Metrics Server. Get yourself some coffee before we repeat the same query.

```
1  kubectl -n go-demo-5 get hpa
```

This time, the output is without unknowns.

```
NAME REFERENCE       TARGETS        MINPODS MAXPODS REPLICAS AGE
api  Deployment/api 38%/80%, 10%/80% 2     5       2        1m
```

We can see that both CPU and memory utilization are way below the expected utilization of 80%. Still, Kubernetes increased the number of replicas from one to two because that's the minimum we defined. We made the contract stating that the api Deployment should never have less than two replicas, and Kubernetes complied with that by scaling up even if the resource utilization is way below the expected average utilization. We can confirm that behavior through the events of the HorizontalPodAutoscaler.

```
1  kubectl -n go-demo-5 describe hpa api
```

The output, limited to the event messages, is as follows.

```
...
Events:
... Message
... -------
... New size: 2; reason: Current number of replicas below Spec.MinReplicas
```

The message of the event should be self-explanatory. The HorizontalPodAutoscaler changed the number of replicas to 2 because the current number (1) was below the MinReplicas value.

Finally, we'll list the Pods to confirm that the desired number of replicas is indeed running.

```
1  kubectl -n go-demo-5 get pods
```

The output is as follows.

```
NAME     READY STATUS  RESTARTS AGE
```

```
api-... 1/1   Running 0        2m
api-... 1/1   Running 0        6m
db-0    2/2   Running 0        6m
```

So far, the HPA did not yet perform auto-scaling based on resource usage. Instead, it only increased the number of Pod to meet the specified minimum. It did that by manipulating the Deployment.

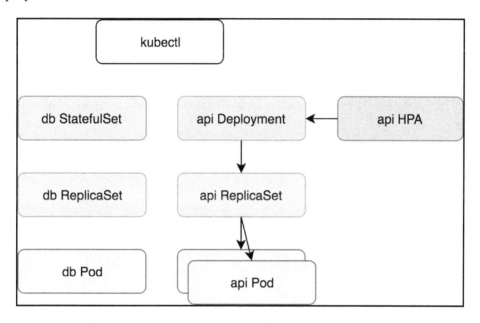

Figure 1-4: Scaling of the Deployment based on minimum number of replicas specified in the HPA

Next, we'll try to create another HorizontalPodAutoscaler but, this time, we'll target the StatefulSet that runs our MongoDB. So, let's take a look at yet another YAML definition.

```
1  cat scaling/go-demo-5-db-hpa.yml
```

The output is as follows.

```
apiVersion: autoscaling/v2beta1
kind: HorizontalPodAutoscaler
metadata:
  name: db
  namespace: go-demo-5
spec:
  scaleTargetRef:
    apiVersion: apps/v1
    kind: StatefulSet
```

```
        name: db
   minReplicas: 3
   maxReplicas: 5
   metrics:
   - type: Resource
     resource:
       name: cpu
       targetAverageUtilization: 80
   - type: Resource
     resource:
       name: memory
       targetAverageUtilization: 80
```

That definition is almost the same as the one we used before. The only difference is that this time we're targeting StatefulSet called db and that the minimum number of replicas should be 3.

Let's apply it.

```
1   kubectl apply \
2       -f scaling/go-demo-5-db-hpa.yml \
3       --record
```

Let's take another look at the HorizontalPodAutoscaler resources.

```
1   kubectl -n go-demo-5 get hpa
```

The output is as follows.

```
NAME REFERENCE        TARGETS                       MINPODS MAXPODS REPLICAS
AGE
api  Deployment/api 41%/80%, 0%/80%                 2       5       2
5m
db   StatefulSet/db <unknown>/80%, <unknown>/80% 3  5       0
20s
```

We can see that the second HPA was created and that the current utilization is unknown. That must be a similar situation as before. Should we give it some time for data to start flowing in? Wait for a few moments and retrieve HPAs again. Are the targets still unknown?

There might be something wrong since the resource utilization continued being unknown. Let's describe the newly created HPA and see whether we'll be able to find the cause behind the issue.

```
1   kubectl -n go-demo-5 describe hpa db
```

The output, limited to the event messages, is as follows.

```
...
Events:
... Message
... -------
... New size: 3; reason: Current number of replicas below Spec.MinReplicas
... missing request for memory on container db-sidecar in pod go-
demo-5/db-0
... failed to get memory utilization: missing request for memory on
container db-sidecar in pod go-demo-5/db-0
```

 Please note that your output could have only one event, or even none of those. If that's the case, please wait for a few minutes and repeat the previous command.

If we focus on the first message, we can see that it started well. HPA detected that the current number of replicas is below the limit and increased them to three. That is the expected behavior, so let's move to the other two messages.

HPA could not calculate the percentage because we did not specify how much memory we are requesting for the `db-sidecar` container. Without `requests`, HPA cannot calculate the percentage of the actual memory usage. In other words, we missed specifying resources for the `db-sidecar` container and HPA could not do its work. We'll fix that by applying `go-demo-5-no-hpa.yml`.

Let's take a quick look at the new definition.

```
1   cat scaling/go-demo-5-no-hpa.yml
```

The output, limited to the relevant parts, is as follows.

```
...
apiVersion: apps/v1
kind: StatefulSet
metadata:
  name: db
  namespace: go-demo-5
spec:
  ...
  template:
    ...
    spec:
      ...
      - name: db-sidecar
        ...
```

```
resources:
  limits:
    memory: "100Mi"
    cpu: 0.2
  requests:
    memory: "50Mi"
    cpu: 0.1
...
```

The only noticeable difference, when compared with the initial definition, is that this time we defined the resources for the db-sidecar container. Let's apply it.

```
1   kubectl apply \
2       -f scaling/go-demo-5-no-hpa.yml \
3       --record
```

Next, we'll wait for a few moments for the changes to take effect, before we retrieve the HPAs again.

```
1   kubectl -n go-demo-5 get hpa
```

This time, the output is more promising.

| NAME | REFERENCE | TARGETS | MINPODS | MAXPODS | REPLICAS | AGE |
|------|-----------|---------|---------|---------|----------|-----|
| api | Deployment/api | 66%/80%, 10%/80% | 2 | 5 | 2 | 16m |
| db | StatefulSet/db | 60%/80%, 4%/80% | 3 | 5 | 3 | 10m |

Both HPAs are showing the current and the target resource usage. Neither reached the target values, so HPA is maintaining the minimum number of replicas. We can confirm that by listing all the Pods in the go-demo-5 Namespace.

```
1   kubectl -n go-demo-5 get pods
```

The output is as follows.

| NAME | READY | STATUS | RESTARTS | AGE |
|------|-------|--------|----------|-----|
| api-... | 1/1 | Running | 0 | 42m |
| api-... | 1/1 | Running | 0 | 46m |
| db-0 | 2/2 | Running | 0 | 33m |
| db-1 | 2/2 | Running | 0 | 33m |
| db-2 | 2/2 | Running | 0 | 33m |

We can see that there are two Pods for the api Deployment and three replicas of the db StatefulSet. Those numbers are equivalent to the spec.minReplicas entries in the HPA definitions.

Let's see what happens when the actual memory usage is above the target value.

We'll modify the definition of one of the HPAs by lowering one of the targets as a way to reproduce the situation in which our Pods are consuming more resources than desired.

Let's take a look at a modified HPA definition.

```
1  cat scaling/go-demo-5-api-hpa-low-mem.yml
```

The output, limited to the relevant parts, is as follows.

```
apiVersion: autoscaling/v2beta1
kind: HorizontalPodAutoscaler
metadata:
  name: api
  namespace: go-demo-5
spec:
  ...
  metrics:
  ...
  - type: Resource
    resource:
      name: memory
      targetAverageUtilization: 10
```

We decreased `targetAverageUtilization` to `10`. That will surely be below the current memory utilization, and we'll be able to witness HPA in action. Let's apply the new definition.

```
1  kubectl apply \
2      -f scaling/go-demo-5-api-hpa-low-mem.yml \
3      --record
```

Please wait a few moments for the next iteration of data gathering to occur, and retrieve the HPAs.

```
1  kubectl -n go-demo-5 get hpa
```

The output is as follows.

```
NAME REFERENCE        TARGETS            MINPODS MAXPODS REPLICAS AGE
api  Deployment/api   49%/10%, 10%/80%  2       5       2        44m
db   StatefulSet/db   64%/80%, 5%/80%   3       5       3        39m
```

We can see that the actual memory of the `api` HPA (`49%`) is way above the threshold (`10%`). However, the number of replicas is still the same (`2`). We'll have to wait for a few more minutes before we retrieve HPAs again.

```
1  kubectl -n go-demo-5 get hpa
```

This time, the output is slightly different.

```
NAME REFERENCE       TARGETS        MINPODS MAXPODS REPLICAS AGE
api  Deployment/api 49%/10%, 10%/80% 2       5       4        44m
db   StatefulSet/db 64%/80%, 5%/80%  3       5       3        39m
```

We can see that the number of replicas increased to 4. HPA changed the Deployment, and that produced the cascading effect that resulted in the increased number of Pods.

Let's describe the `api` HPA.

```
1  kubectl -n go-demo-5 describe hpa api
```

The output, limited to the messages of the events, is as follows.

```
...
Events:
... Message
... -------
... New size: 2; reason: Current number of replicas below Spec.MinReplicas
... New size: 4; reason: memory resource utilization (percentage of
request) above target
```

We can see that the HPA changed the size to 4 because `memory resource utilization (percentage of request)` was `above target`.

Since, in this case, increasing the number of replicas did not reduce memory consumption below the HPA target, we should expect that the HPA will continue scaling up the Deployment until it reaches the limit of 5. We'll confirm that assumption by waiting for a few minutes and describing the HPA one more time.

```
1  kubectl -n go-demo-5 describe hpa api
```

The output, limited to the messages of the events, is as follows.

```
...
Events:
... Message
... -------
... New size: 2; reason: Current number of replicas below Spec.MinReplicas
... New size: 4; reason: memory resource utilization (percentage of
request) above target
... New size: 5; reason: memory resource utilization (percentage of
request) above target
```

We got the message stating that the new size is now 5, thus proving that the HPA will continue scaling up until the resources are below the target or, as in our case, it reaches the maximum number of replicas.

We can confirm that scaling indeed worked by listing all the Pods in the `go-demo-5` Namespace.

```
1  kubectl -n go-demo-5 get pods
```

The output is as follows.

```
NAME       READY  STATUS    RESTARTS  AGE
api-...    1/1    Running   0         47m
api-...    1/1    Running   0         51m
api-...    1/1    Running   0         4m
api-...    1/1    Running   0         4m
api-...    1/1    Running   0         24s
db-0       2/2    Running   0         38m
db-1       2/2    Running   0         38m
db-2       2/2    Running   0         38m
```

As we can see, there are indeed five replicas of the `api` Deployment.

HPA retrieved data from the Metrics Server, concluded that the actual resource usage is higher than the threshold, and manipulated the Deployment with the new number of replicas.

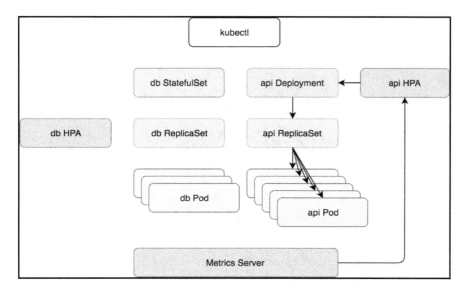

Figure 1-5: HPA scaling through manipulation of the Deployment

Next, we'll validate that de-scaling works as well. We'll do that by re-applying the initial definition that has both the memory and the CPU set to eighty percent. Since the actual memory usage is below that, the HPA should start scaling down until it reaches the minimum number of replicas.

```
1  kubectl apply \
2      -f scaling/go-demo-5-api-hpa.yml \
3      --record
```

Just as before, we'll wait for a few minutes before we describe the HPA.

```
1  kubectl -n go-demo-5 describe hpa api
```

The output, limited to the events messages, is as follows.

```
...
Events:
... Message
... -------
... New size: 2; reason: Current number of replicas below Spec.MinReplicas
... New size: 4; reason: memory resource utilization (percentage of
request) above target
... New size: 5; reason: memory resource utilization (percentage of
request) above target
... New size: 3; reason: All metrics below target
```

As we can see, it changed the size to 3 since all the `metrics` are `below target`.

A while later, it will de-scale again to two replicas and stop since that's the limit we set in the HPA definition.

# To replicas or not to replicas in Deployments and StatefulSets?

Knowing that HorizontalPodAutoscaler (HPA) manages auto-scaling of our applications, the question might arise regarding replicas. Should we define them in our Deployments and StatefulSets, or should we rely solely on HPA to manage them? Instead of answering that question directly, we'll explore different combinations and, based on results, define the strategy.

First, let's see how many Pods we have in our cluster right now.

```
1  kubectl -n go-demo-5 get pods
```

The output is as follows.

```
NAME      READY STATUS   RESTARTS AGE
api-...   1/1   Running  0        27m
api-...   1/1   Running  2        31m
db-0      2/2   Running  0        20m
db-1      2/2   Running  0        20m
db-2      2/2   Running  0        21m
```

We can see that there are two replicas of the api Deployment, and three replicas of the db StatefulSets.

Let's say that we want to roll out a new release of our go-demo-5 application. The definition we'll use is as follows.

```
1   cat scaling/go-demo-5-replicas-10.yml
```

The output, limited to the relevant parts, is as follows.

```
...
apiVersion: apps/v1
kind: Deployment
metadata:
  name: api
  namespace: go-demo-5
spec:
  replicas: 10
...

apiVersion: autoscaling/v2beta1
kind: HorizontalPodAutoscaler
metadata:
  name: api
  namespace: go-demo-5
spec:
  scaleTargetRef:
    apiVersion: apps/v1
    kind: Deployment
    name: api
  minReplicas: 2
  maxReplicas: 5
  metrics:
  - type: Resource
    resource:
      name: cpu
      targetAverageUtilization: 80
  - type: Resource
    resource:
```

```
    name: memory
    targetAverageUtilization: 80
```

The important thing to note is that our `api` Deployment has `10` replicas and that we have the HPA. Everything else is the same as it was before.

What will happen if we apply that definition?

```
1  kubectl apply \
2    -f scaling/go-demo-5-replicas-10.yml
3
4  kubectl -n go-demo-5 get pods
```

We applied the new definition and retrieved all the Pods from the `go-demo-5` Namespace. The output of the latter command is as follows.

```
NAME      READY STATUS            RESTARTS AGE
api-...   1/1   Running           0        9s
api-...   0/1   ContainerCreating 0        9s
api-...   0/1   ContainerCreating 0        9s
api-...   1/1   Running           2        41m
api-...   1/1   Running           0        22s
api-...   0/1   ContainerCreating 0        9s
api-...   0/1   ContainerCreating 0        9s
api-...   1/1   Running           0        9s
api-...   1/1   Running           0        9s
api-...   1/1   Running           0        9s
db-0      2/2   Running           0        31m
db-1      2/2   Running           0        31m
db-2      2/2   Running           0        31m
```

Kubernetes complied with our desire to have ten replicas of the `api` and created eight Pods (we had two before). At the first look, it seems that HPA does not have any effect. Let's retrieve the Pods one more time.

```
1  kubectl -n go-demo-5 get pods
```

The output is as follows.

```
NAME      READY STATUS  RESTARTS AGE
api-...   1/1   Running 0        30s
api-...   1/1   Running 2        42m
api-...   1/1   Running 0        43s
api-...   1/1   Running 0        30s
api-...   1/1   Running 0        30s
db-0      2/2   Running 0        31m
db-1      2/2   Running 0        32m
db-2      2/2   Running 0        32m
```

Our Deployment de-scaled from ten to five replicas. HPA detected that there are more replicas then the maximum threshold and acted accordingly. But what did it do? Did it simply remove five replicas? That could not be the case since that would only have a temporary effect. If HPA removes or adds Pods, Deployment would also remove or add Pods, and the two would be fighting with each other. The number of Pods would be fluctuating indefinitely. Instead, HPA modified the Deployment.

Let's describe the `api`.

```
1  kubectl -n go-demo-5 \
2    describe deployment api
```

The output, limited to the relevant parts, is as follows.

```
. . .
Replicas: 5 desired | 5 updated | 5 total | 5 available | 0 unavailable
. . .
Events:
. . . Message
. . . -------
. . .
. . . Scaled up replica set api-5bbfd85577 to 10
. . . Scaled down replica set api-5bbfd85577 to 5
```

The number of replicas is set to `5 desired`. HPA modified our Deployment. We can observe that better through the event messages. The second to last states that the number of replicas was scaled up to `10`, while the last message indicates that it scaled down to `5`. The former is the result of us executing rolling update by applying the new Deployment, while the latter was produced by HPA modifying the Deployment by changing its number of replicas.

So far, we observed that HPA modifies our Deployments. No matter how many replicas we defined in a Deployment (or a StatefulSets), HPA will change it to fit its own thresholds and calculations. In other words, when we update a Deployment, the number of replicas will be temporarily changed to whatever we have defined, only to be modified again by HPA a few moments later. That behavior is unacceptable.

If HPA changed the number of replicas, there is usually a good reason for that. Resetting that number to whatever is set in a Deployment (or a StatetefulSet) can produce serious side-effect.

Let's say that we have three replicas defined in a Deployment and that HPA scaled it to thirty because there is an increased load on that application. If we `apply` the Deployment because we want to roll out a new release, for a brief period, there will be three replicas, instead of thirty.

As a result, our users would experience slow response times from our application, or some other effect caused by too few replicas serving too much traffic. We must try to avoid such a situation. The number of replicas should be controlled by HPA at all times. That means we'll need to change our strategy.

If specifying the number of replicas in a Deployment does not produce the effect we want, we might just as well remove them altogether. Let's see what happens in that case.

We'll use `go-demo-5.yml` definition, so let's see how it differs from `go-demo-5-replicas-10.yml` that we used previously.

```
1  diff \
2    scaling/go-demo-5-replicas-10.yml \
3    scaling/go-demo-5.yml
```

The output shows that the only difference is that, this time, we are not specifying the number of replicas.

Let's apply the change and see what happens.

```
1  kubectl apply \
2    -f scaling/go-demo-5.yml
3
4  kubectl -n go-demo-5 \
5    describe deployment api
```

The output of the latter command, limited to the relevant parts, is as follows.

```
. . .
Replicas: 1 desired | 5 updated | 5 total | 5 available | 0 unavailable
. . .
Events:
... Message
... -------
. . .
... Scaled down replica set api-5bbfd85577 to 5
... Scaled down replica set api-5bbfd85577 to 1
```

Applying the Deployment without `replicas` resulted in 1 desired. Sure, HPA will scale it up to 2 (its minimum) soon enough, but we still failed in our mission to maintain the number of replicas defined by HPA at all times.

What else can we do? No matter whether we define our Deployment with or without `replicas`, the result is the same. Applying the Deployment always cancels the effect of the HPA, even when we do NOT specify `replicas`.

Actually, that statement is incorrect. We can accomplish the desired behavior without `replicas` if we know how the whole process works.

 If `replicas` is defined for a Deployment, it will be used every time we `apply` a definition. If we change the definition by removing `replicas`, the Deployment will think that we want to have one, instead of the number of replicas we had before. But, if we never specify the number of `replicas`, they will be entirely controlled by HPA.

Let's test it out.

```
1   kubectl delete -f scaling/go-demo-5.yml
```

We deleted everything related to the `go-demo-5` application. Now, let's test how the Deployment behaves if `replicas` is not defined from the start.

```
1   kubectl apply \
2     -f scaling/go-demo-5.yml
3
4   kubectl -n go-demo-5 \
5     describe deployment api
```

The output of the latter command, limited to the relevant parts, is as follows.

```
...
Replicas: 1 desired | 1 updated | 1 total | 0 available | 1 unavailable
...
```

Seems that we failed. The Deployment did set the number of replicas to 1. But, what you cannot see, is that replicas are not defined internally.

Nevertheless, a few moments later, our Deployment will be scaled up by HPA to two replicas. That is the expected behavior, but we'll confirm it anyway.

```
1   kubectl -n go-demo-5 \
2     describe deployment api
```

You should see from the output that the number of replicas was changed (by HPA) to 2.

Now comes the final test. If we make a new release of the Deployment, will it scale down to 1 replica, or will it stay on 2?

We'll apply a new definition. The only difference, when compared with the one currently running, is in the tag of the image. That way we'll guarantee that the Deployment will be indeed updated.

```
1  kubectl apply \
2     -f scaling/go-demo-5-2-5.yml
3
4  kubectl -n go-demo-5 \
5     describe deployment api
```

The output of the latter command, limited to the relevant parts, is as follows.

```
...
Replicas: 2 desired | 1 updated | 3 total | 2 available | 1 unavailable
...
Events:
... Message
... -------
... Scaled up replica set api-5bbfd85577 to 1
... Scaled up replica set api-5bbfd85577 to 2
... Scaled up replica set api-745bc9fc6d to 1
```

We can see that the number of replicas, set by the HPA, is preserved.

Don't be alarmed if you see in the `events` that the number of replicas was scaled to `1`. That's the second ReplicaSet spin up by the Deployment. You can see that by observing the name of the ReplicaSet. The Deployment is doing rolling updates by joggling two ReplicaSets in the attempt to roll out the new release without downtime. That is unrelated to auto-scaling, and I assume that you already know how rolling updates work. If you don't, you know where to learn it.

Now comes the critical question. How should we define replicas in Deployments and StatefulSets?

 If you plan to use HPA with a Deployment or a StatefulSet, do NOT declare replicas. If you do, each rolling update will cancel the effect of the HPA for a while. Define replicas only for the resources that are NOT used in conjunction with HPA.

# What now?

We explored the simplest way to scale our Deployments and StatefulSets. It's simple because the mechanism is baked into Kubernetes. All we had to do is define a HorizontalPodAutoscaler with target memory and CPU. While this method for auto-scaling is commonly used, it is often not sufficient. Not all applications increase memory or CPU usage when under stress. Even when they do, those two metrics might not be enough.

In one of the following chapters, we'll explore how to extend HorizontalPodAutoscaler to use a custom source of metrics. For now, we'll destroy what we created, and we'll start the next chapter fresh.

If you are planning to keep the cluster running, please execute the commands that follow to remove the resources we created.

```
1   # If NOT GKE or AKS
2   helm delete metrics-server --purge
3
4   kubectl delete ns go-demo-5
```

Otherwise, please delete the whole cluster if you created it only for the purpose of this book and you're not planning to dive into the next chapter right away.

Before you leave, you might want to go over the main points of this chapter.

- HorizontalPodAutoscaler's only function is to automatically scale the number of Pods in a Deployment, a StatefulSet, or a few other types of resources. It accomplishes that by observing CPU and memory consumption of the Pods and acting when they reach pre-defined thresholds.
- Metrics Server collects information about used resources (memory and CPU) of nodes and Pods.
- Metrics Server periodically fetches metrics from Kubeletes running on the nodes.
- If the number of replicas is static and you have no intention to scale (or de-scale) your application over time, set replicas as part of your Deployment or StatefulSet definition. If, on the other hand, you plan to change the number of replicas based on memory, CPU, or other metrics, use HorizontalPodAutoscaler resource instead.
- If replicas is defined for a Deployment, it will be used every time we apply a definition. If we change the definition by removing replicas, the Deployment will think that we want to have one, instead of the number of replicas we had before. But, if we never specify the number of replicas, they will be entirely controlled by HPA.
- If you plan to use HPA with a Deployment or a StatefulSet, do NOT declare replicas. If you do, each rolling update will cancel the effect of the HPA for a while. Define replicas only for the resources that are NOT used in conjunction with HPA.

# 2
# Auto-scaling Nodes of a Kubernetes Cluster

*May I say that I have not thoroughly enjoyed serving with humans? I find their illogic and foolish emotions a constant irritant.*

*- Spock*

Usage of **HorizontalPodAutoscaler** (**HPA**) is one of the most critical aspects of making a resilient, fault-tolerant, and highly-available system. However, it is of no use if there are no nodes with available resources. When Kubernetes cannot schedule new Pods because there's not enough available memory or CPU, new Pods will be unschedulable and in the pending status. If we do not increase the capacity of our cluster, pending Pods might stay in that state indefinitely. To make things more complicated, Kubernetes might start removing other Pods to make room for those that are in the pending state. That, as you might have guessed, might lead to worse problems than the issue of our applications not having enough replicas to serve the demand.

Kubernetes solves the problem of scaling nodes through Cluster Autoscaler.

Cluster Autoscaler has a single purpose to adjust the size of the cluster by adding or removing worker nodes. It adds new nodes when Pods cannot be scheduled due to insufficient resources. Similarly, it eliminates nodes when they are underutilized for a period of time and when Pods running on one such node can be rescheduled somewhere else.

The logic behind Cluster Autoscaler is simple to grasp. We are yet to see whether it is simple to use as well.

Let's create a cluster (unless you already have one) and prepare it for autoscaling.

# Creating a cluster

We'll continue using definitions from the `vfarcic/k8s-specs` (`https://github.com/vfarcic/k8s-specs`) repository. To be on the safe side, we'll pull the latest version first.

 All the commands from this chapter are available in the `02-ca.sh` (`https://gist.github.com/vfarcic/a6b2a5132aad6ca05b8ff5033c61a88 f`) Gist.

```
1  cd k8s-specs
2
3  git pull
```

Next, we need a cluster. Please use the Gists below as inspiration to create a new cluster or to validate that the one you already fulfills all the requirements.

 **A note to AKS users**
At the time of this writing (October 2018), Cluster Autoscaler does not (always) work in **Azure Kubernetes Service** (**AKS**). Please jump to *Setting up Cluster Autoscaler in AKS* section for more info and the link to instructions how to set it up.

- `gke-scale.sh`: **GKE** with 3 n1-standard-1 worker nodes, with **tiller**, and with the `--enable-autoscaling` argument (`https://gist.github.com/vfarcic/9c777487f7ebee6c09027d3a1df8663c`).
- `eks-ca.sh`: **EKS** with 3 t2.small worker nodes, with **tiller**, and with **Metrics Server** (`https://gist.github.com/vfarcic/3dfc71dc687de3ed98e8f804d7abba0b`).
- `aks-scale.sh`: **AKS** with 3 Standard_B2s worker nodes and with **tiller** (`https://gist.github.com/vfarcic/f1b05d33cc8a98e4ceab3d3770c2fe0b`).

When examining the Gists, you'll notice a few things. First of all, Docker for Desktop and minikube are not there. Both are single-node clusters that cannot be scaled. We need to run a cluster in a place where we can add and remove the nodes on demand. We'll have to use one of the cloud vendors (for example, AWS, Azure, GCP). That does not mean that we cannot scale on-prem clusters.

We can, but that depends on the vendor we're using. Some do have a solution, while others don't. For simplicity, we'll stick with one of the big three. Please choose between **Google Kuberentes Engine** (**GKE**), Amazon **Elastic Container Service** for Kubernetes (**EKS**), or **Azure Kubernetes Service** (**AKS**). If you're not sure which one to pick, I suggest GKE, since it's the most stable and feature-rich managed Kubernetes cluster.

You'll also notice that GKE and AKS Gists are the same as in the previous chapter, while EKS changed. As you already know, the former already have the Metrics Server baked in. EKS doesn't, so I copied the Gist we used before and added the instructions to install Metrics Server. We might not need it in this chapter but we will use it heavily later on, and I want you to get used to having it at all times.

If you prefer running the examples locally, you might be devastated by the news that we won't use a local cluster in this chapter. Don't despair. The costs will be kept to a minimum (probably a few dollars in total), and we'll be back to local clusters in the next chapter (unless you choose to stay in clouds).

Now that we have a cluster in GKE, EKS, or AKS, our next step is to enable cluster auto-scaling.

# Setting up Cluster Autoscaling

We might need to install Cluster Autoscaler before we start using it. I said that we *might*, instead of saying that we *have to* because some Kubernetes flavors do come with Cluster Autoscaler baked in, while others don't. We'll go through each of the "big three" managed Kubernetes clusters. You might choose to explore all three of them, or to jump to the one you prefer. As a learning experience, I believe that it is beneficial to experience running Kubernetes in all three providers. Nevertheless, that might not be your view and you might prefer using only one. The choice is yours.

# Setting up Cluster Autoscaler in GKE

This will be the shortest section ever written. There's nothing to do in GKE if you specified the `--enable-autoscaling` argument when creating the cluster. It already comes with Cluster Autoscaler pre-configured and ready.

# Setting up Cluster Autoscaler in EKS

Unlike GKE, EKS does not come with Cluster Autoscaler. We'll have to configure it ourselves. We'll need to add a few tags to the Autoscaling Group dedicated to worker nodes, to put additional permissions to the Role we're using, and to install Cluster Autoscaler.

Let's get going.

We'll add a few tags to the Autoscaling Group dedicated to worker nodes. To do that, we need to discover the name of the group. Since we created the cluster using **eksctl**, names follow a pattern which we can use to filter the results. If, on the other hand, you created your EKS cluster without eksctl, the logic should still be the same as the one that follows, even though the commands might differ slightly.

First, we'll retrieve the list of the AWS Autoscaling Groups, and filter the result with jq so that only the name of the matching group is returned.

```
 1   export NAME=devops25
 2
 3   ASG_NAME=$(aws autoscaling \
 4       describe-auto-scaling-groups \
 5       | jq -r ".AutoScalingGroups[] \
 6       | select(.AutoScalingGroupName \
 7       | startswith(\"eksctl-$NAME-nodegroup\")) \
 8       .AutoScalingGroupName")
 9
10   echo $ASG_NAME
```

The output of the latter command should be similar to the one that follows.

```
eksctl-devops25-nodegroup-0-NodeGroup-1KWSL5SEH9L1Y
```

We stored the name of the cluster in the environment variable NAME. Further on, we retrieved the list of all the groups and filtered the output with jq so that only those with names that start with eksctl-$NAME-nodegroup are returned. Finally, that same jq command retrieved the AutoScalingGroupName field and we stored it in the environment variable ASG_NAME. The last command output the group name so that we can confirm (visually) that it looks correct.

Next, we'll add a few tags to the group. Kubernetes Cluster Autoscaler will work with the one that has the k8s.io/cluster-autoscaler/enabled and kubernetes.io/cluster/[NAME_OF_THE_CLUSTER] tags. So, all we have to do to let Kubernetes know which group to use is to add those tags.

```
1  aws autoscaling \
2      create-or-update-tags \
3      --tags \
4      ResourceId=$ASG_NAME,ResourceType=auto-scaling-group,Key=k8s.io/
   clusterautoscaler/enabled,Value=true,PropagateAtLaunch=true \
5      ResourceId=$ASG_NAME,ResourceType=auto-scaling-
   group,Key=kubernetes.io/cluster/$NAME,Value=true,PropagateAtLaunch=true
```

The last change we'll have to do in AWS is to add a few additional permissions to the role created through eksctl. Just as with the Autoscaling Group, we do not know the name of the role, but we do know the pattern used to create it. Therefore, we'll retrieve the name of the role, before we add a new policy to it.

```
1  IAM_ROLE=$(aws iam list-roles \
2      | jq -r ".Roles[] \
3      | select(.RoleName \
4      | startswith(\"eksctl-$NAME-nodegroup-0-NodeInstanceRole\")) \
5      .RoleName")
6
7  echo $IAM_ROLE
```

The output of the latter command should be similar to the one that follows.

**eksctl-devops25-nodegroup-0-NodeInstanceRole-UU6CKXYESUES**

We listed all the roles, and we used `jq` to filter the output so that only the one with the name that starts with `eksctl-$NAME-nodegroup-0-NodeInstanceRole` is returned. Once we filtered the roles, we retrieved the `RoleName` and stored it in the environment variable `IAM_ROLE`.

Next, we need JSON that describes the new policy. I already prepared one, so let's take a quick look at it.

```
1  cat scaling/eks-autoscaling-policy.json
```

The output is as follows.

```
{
  "Version": "2012-10-17",
  "Statement": [
    {
      "Effect": "Allow",
      "Action": [
        "autoscaling:DescribeAutoScalingGroups",
        "autoscaling:DescribeAutoScalingInstances",
        "autoscaling:DescribeLaunchConfigurations",
        "autoscaling:DescribeTags",
```

```
            "autoscaling:SetDesiredCapacity",
            "autoscaling:TerminateInstanceInAutoScalingGroup"
        ],
        "Resource": "*"
      }
   ]
}
```

If you're familiar with AWS (I hope you are), that policy should be straightforward. It allows a few additional actions related to autoscaling.

Finally, we can put the new policy to the role.

```
1  aws iam put-role-policy \
2      --role-name $IAM_ROLE \
3      --policy-name $NAME-AutoScaling \
4      --policy-document file://scaling/eks-autoscaling-policy.json
```

Now that we added the required tags to the Autoscaling Group and that we created the additional permissions that will allow Kubernetes to interact with the group, we can install Cluster Autoscaler Helm Chart.

```
 1  helm install stable/cluster-autoscaler \
 2      --name aws-cluster-autoscaler \
 3      --namespace kube-system \
 4      --set autoDiscovery.clusterName=$NAME \
 5      --set awsRegion=$AWS_DEFAULT_REGION \
 6      --set sslCertPath=/etc/kubernetes/pki/ca.crt \
 7      --set rbac.create=true
 8
 9  kubectl -n kube-system \
10      rollout status \
11      deployment aws-cluster-autoscaler
```

Once the Deployment is rolled out, the autoscaler should be fully operational.

# Setting up Cluster Autoscaler in AKS

At the time of this writing (October 2018), Cluster Autoscaler does not work in AKS. At least, not always. It is still in beta stage, and I cannot recommend it just yet. Hopefully, it will be fully operational and stable soon. When that happens, I will update this chapter with AKS-specific instructions. If you feel adventurous or you are committed to Azure, please follow the instructions from the *Cluster Autoscaler on Azure Kubernetes Service (AKS) - Preview* (https://docs.microsoft.com/en-in/azure/aks/cluster-autoscaler) article. If it works, you should be able to follow the rest of this chapter.

# Scaling up the cluster

The objective is to scale the nodes of our cluster to meet the demand of our Pods. We want not only to increase the number of worker nodes when we need additional capacity, but also to remove them when they are underused. For now, we'll focus on the former, and explore the latter afterward.

Let's start by taking a look at how many nodes we have in the cluster.

```
1  kubectl get nodes
```

The output, from GKE, is as follows.

```
NAME              STATUS ROLES   AGE    VERSION
gke-devops25-... Ready  <none> 5m27s v1.9.7-gke.6
gke-devops25-... Ready  <none> 5m28s v1.9.7-gke.6
gke-devops25-... Ready  <none> 5m24s v1.9.7-gke.6
```

In your case, the number of nodes might differ. That's not important. What matters is to remember how many you have right now since that number will change soon.

Let's take a look at the definition of the `go-demo-5` application before we roll it out.

```
1  cat scaling/go-demo-5-many.yml
```

The output, limited to the relevant parts, is as follows.

```
apiVersion: apps/v1
kind: Deployment
metadata:
  name: api
  namespace: go-demo-5
spec:
  ...
  template:
    ...
    spec:
      containers:
      - name: api
        ...
        resources:
          limits:
            memory: 1Gi
            cpu: 0.1
          requests:
            memory: 500Mi
            cpu: 0.01
```

```
. . .
apiVersion: autoscaling/v2beta1
kind: HorizontalPodAutoscaler
metadata:
  name: api
  namespace: go-demo-5
spec:
  scaleTargetRef:
    apiVersion: apps/v1
    kind: Deployment
    name: api
  minReplicas: 15
  maxReplicas: 30
. . .
```

In this context, the only important part of the definition we are about to apply is the HPA connected to the `api` Deployment. Its minimum number of replicas is `15`. Given that each `api` container requests 500 MB RAM, fifteen replicas (7.5 GB RAM) should be more than our cluster can sustain, assuming that it was created using one of the Gists. Otherwise, you might need to increase the minimum number of replicas.

Let's apply the definition and take a look at the HPAs.

```
1  kubectl apply \
2      -f scaling/go-demo-5-many.yml \
3      --record
4
5  kubectl -n go-demo-5 get hpa
```

The output of the latter command is as follows.

| NAME | REFERENCE | TARGETS | MINPODS | MAXPODS | REPLICAS | AGE |
|------|-----------|---------|---------|---------|----------|-----|
| api | Deployment/api | <unknown>/80%, <unknown>/80% | 15 | 30 | 1 | 38s |
| db | StatefulSet/db | <unknown>/80%, <unknown>/80% | 3 | 5 | 1 | 40s |

It doesn't matter if the targets are still unknown. They will be calculated soon, but we do not care for them right now. What matters is that the api HPA will scale the Deployment to at least 15 replicas.

Next, we need to wait for a few seconds before we take a look at the Pods in the go-demo-5 Namespace.

```
1  kubectl -n go-demo-5 get pods
```

The output is as follows.

```
NAME       READY  STATUS            RESTARTS AGE
api-...    0/1    ContainerCreating 0        2s
api-...    0/1    Pending           0        2s
api-...    0/1    Pending           0        2s
api-...    0/1    ContainerCreating 0        2s
api-...    0/1    ContainerCreating 0        2s
api-...    0/1    ContainerCreating 1        32s
api-...    0/1    Pending           0        2s
api-...    0/1    ContainerCreating 0        2s
api-...    0/1    ContainerCreating 0        2s
api-...    0/1    ContainerCreating 0        2s
api-...    0/1    ContainerCreating 0        2s
api-...    0/1    ContainerCreating 0        2s
api-...    0/1    Pending           0        2s
api-...    0/1    ContainerCreating 0        2s
api-...    0/1    ContainerCreating 0        2s
db-0       2/2    Running           0        34s
db-1       0/2    ContainerCreating 0        34s
```

We can see that some of the api Pods are being created, while others are pending. There can be quite a few reasons why a Pod would enter into the pending state.

In our case, there are not enough available resources to host all the Pods.

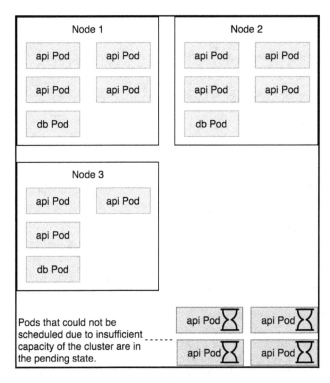

Figure 2-1: Unschedulable (pending) Pods waiting for the cluster capacity to increase

Let's see whether Cluster Autoscaler did anything to help with our lack of capacity. We'll explore the ConfigMap that contains Cluster Autoscaler status.

```
1  kubectl -n kube-system get cm \
2      cluster-autoscaler-status \
3      -o yaml
```

The output is too big to be presented in its entirety, so we'll focus on the parts that matter.

```
apiVersion: v1
data:
  status: |+
    Cluster-autoscaler status at 2018-10-03 ...
    Cluster-wide:
      ...
      ScaleUp: InProgress (ready=3 registered=3)
            ...

    NodeGroups:
      Name:    ...gke-devops25-default-pool-ce277413-grp
      ...
      ScaleUp: InProgress (ready=1 cloudProviderTarget=2)
            ...
```

The status is split into two sections; `Cluster-wide` and `NodeGroups`. The `ScaleUp` section of the cluster-wide status shows that scaling is `InProgress`. At the moment, there are 3 ready nodes.

If we move down to the `NodeGroups`, we'll notice that there is one for each group that hosts our nodes. In AWS those groups map to Autoscaling Groups, in case of Google to Instance Groups, and in Azure to Autoscale. One of the `NodeGroups` in the config has the `ScaleUp` section `InProgress`. Inside that group, 1 node is `ready`. The `cloudProviderTarget` value should be set to a number higher than the number of `ready` nodes, and we can conclude that Cluster Autoscaler already increased the desired amount of nodes in that group.

 Depending on the provider, you might see three groups (GKE) or one (EKS) node group. That depends on how each provider organizes its node groups internally.

Now that we know that Cluster Autoscaler is in progress of scaling up the nodes, we might explore what triggered that action.

Let's describe the `api` Pods and retrieve their events. Since we want only those related to `cluster-autoscaler`, we'll limit the output using `grep`.

```
1  kubectl -n go-demo-5 \
2      describe pods \
3      -l app=api \
4      | grep cluster-autoscaler
```

The output, on GKE, is as follows.

```
   Normal TriggeredScaleUp 85s cluster-autoscaler pod triggered scale-up:
[{... 1->2 (max: 3)}]
   Normal TriggeredScaleUp 86s cluster-autoscaler pod triggered scale-up:
[{... 1->2 (max: 3)}]
   Normal TriggeredScaleUp 87s cluster-autoscaler pod triggered scale-up:
[{... 1->2 (max: 3)}]
   Normal TriggeredScaleUp 88s cluster-autoscaler pod triggered scale-up:
[{... 1->2 (max: 3)}]
```

We can see that several Pods triggered `scale-up` event. Those are the Pods that were in the pending state. That does not mean that each trigger created a new node. Cluster Autoscaler is intelligent enough to know that it should not create new nodes for each trigger, but that, in this case, one or two nodes (depending on the missing capacity) should be enough. If that proves to be false, it will scale up again a while later.

Let's retrieve the nodes that constitute the cluster and see whether there are any changes.

```
1  kubectl get nodes
```

The output is as follows.

```
NAME                                      STATUS     ROLES    AGE
VERSION
gke-devops25-default-pool-7d4b99ad-...    Ready      <none>   2m45s
v1.9.7-gke.6
gke-devops25-default-pool-cb207043-...    Ready      <none>   2m45s
v1.9.7-gke.6
gke-devops25-default-pool-ce277413-...    NotReady   <none>   12s
v1.9.7-gke.6
gke-devops25-default-pool-ce277413-...    Ready      <none>   2m48s
v1.9.7-gke.6
```

We can see that a new worker node was added to the cluster. It is not yet ready, so we'll need to wait for a few moments until it becomes fully operational.

Please note that the number of new nodes depends on the required capacity to host all the Pods. You might see one, two, or more new nodes.

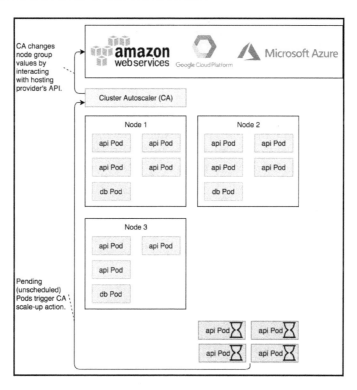

Figure 2-2: The Cluster Autoscaler process of scaling up nodes

Now, let's see what happened to out Pods. Remember, the last time we checked them, there were quite a few in the pending state.

```
1   kubectl -n go-demo-5 get pods
```

The output is as follows.

```
NAME      READY STATUS   RESTARTS AGE
api-...   1/1   Running  1        75s
api-...   1/1   Running  0        75s
api-...   1/1   Running  0        75s
api-...   1/1   Running  1        75s
api-...   1/1   Running  1        75s
api-...   1/1   Running  3        105s
api-...   1/1   Running  0        75s
api-...   1/1   Running  0        75s
api-...   1/1   Running  1        75s
```

```
api-... 1/1   Running 1     75s
api-... 1/1   Running 0     75s
api-... 1/1   Running 1     75s
api-... 1/1   Running 0     75s
api-... 1/1   Running 1     75s
api-... 1/1   Running 0     75s
db-0   2/2   Running 0     107s
db-1   2/2   Running 0     67s
db-2   2/2   Running 0     28s
```

Cluster Autoscaler increased the desired number of nodes in the node group (for example, Autoscaling Group in AWS) which, in turn, created a new node. Once the scheduler noticed the increase in cluster's capacity, it scheduled the pending Pods into the new node. Within a few minutes, our cluster expanded and all the scaled Pods are running.

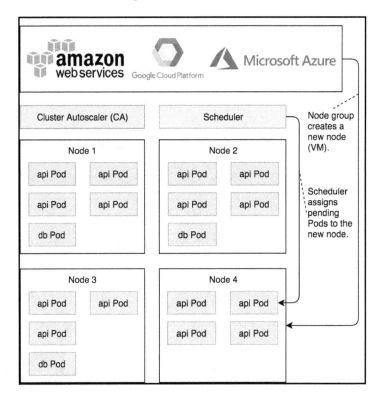

Figure 2-3: Creation of the new node through node groups and rescheduling of the pending Pods

So, what are the rules Cluster Autoscaler uses to decide when to scale up the nodes?

# The rules governing nodes scale-up

Cluster Autoscaler monitors Pods through a watch on Kube API. It checks every 10 seconds whether there are any unschedulable Pods (configurable through the `--scan-interval` flag). In that context, a Pod is unschedulable when the Kubernetes Scheduler is unable to find a node that can accommodate it. For example, a Pod can request more memory than what is available on any of the worker nodes.

 Cluster Autoscaler assumes that the cluster is running on top of some kind of node groups. As an example, in the case of AWS, those groups are **Autoscaling Groups (ASGs)**. When there is a need for additional nodes, Cluster Autoscaler creating a new node by increasing the size of a node group.

Cluster Autoscaler assumes that requested nodes will appear within 15 minutes (configurable through the `--max-node-provision-time` flag). If that period expires and a new node was not registered, it will attempt to scale up a different group if the Pods are still in pending state. It will also remove unregistered nodes after 15 minutes (configurable through the `--unregistered-node-removal-time` flag).

Next, we'll explore how to scale down the cluster.

# Scaling down the cluster

Scaling up the cluster to meet the demand is essential since it allows us to host all the replicas we need to fulfill (some of) our SLAs. When the demand drops and our nodes become underutilized, we should scale down. That is not essential given that our users will not experience problems caused by having too much hardware in our cluster. Nevertheless, we shouldn't have underutilized nodes if we are to reduce expenses. Unused nodes result in wasted money. That is true in all situations, especially when running in Cloud and paying only for the resources we used. Even on-prem, where we already purchased hardware, it is essential to scale down and release resources so that they can be used by other clusters.

We'll simulate a decrease in demand by applying a new definition that will redefine the HPAs threshold to 2 (min) and 5 (max).

```
1   kubectl apply \
2       -f scaling/go-demo-5.yml \
3       --record
4
5   kubectl -n go-demo-5 get hpa
```

The output of the latter command is as follows.

```
NAME REFERENCE        TARGETS            MINPODS MAXPODS REPLICAS AGE
api  Deployment/api  0%/80%, 0%/80%     2       5       15       2m56s
db   StatefulSet/db  56%/80%, 10%/80% 3       5       3        2m57s
```

We can see that the min and max values of the api HPA changed to 2 and 5. The current number of replicas is still 15, but that will drop to 5 soon. The HPA already changed the replicas of the Deployment, so let's wait until it rolls out and take another look at the Pods.

```
1   kubectl -n go-demo-5 rollout status \
2       deployment api
3
4   kubectl -n go-demo-5 get pods
```

The output of the latter command is as follows.

```
NAME       READY STATUS   RESTARTS AGE
api-...    1/1   Running  0        104s
api-...    1/1   Running  0        104s
api-...    1/1   Running  0        104s
api-...    1/1   Running  0        94s
api-...    1/1   Running  0        104s
db-0       2/2   Running  0        4m37s
db-1       2/2   Running  0        3m57s
db-2       2/2   Running  0        3m18s
```

Let's see what happened to the nodes.

```
1   kubectl get nodes
```

The output shows that we still have four nodes (or whatever was your number before we de-scaled the Deployment).

Given that we haven't yet reached the desired state of only three nodes, we might want to take another look at the `cluster-autoscaler-status` ConfigMap.

```
1  kubectl -n kube-system \
2      get configmap \
3      cluster-autoscaler-status \
4      -o yaml
```

The output, limited to the relevant parts, is as follows.

```
apiVersion: v1
data:
  status: |+
    Cluster-autoscaler status at 2018-10-03 ...
    Cluster-wide:
      Health: Healthy (ready=4 ...)
      ...
      ScaleDown: CandidatesPresent (candidates=1)
              ...

    NodeGroups:
      Name:        ...gke-devops25-default-pool-f4c233dd-grp
      ...
      ScaleDown: CandidatesPresent (candidates=1)
              LastProbeTime:      2018-10-03 23:06:...
              LastTransitionTime: 2018-10-03 23:05:...

    ...
```

If your output does not contain `ScaleDown: CandidatesPresent`, you might need to wait a bit and repeat the previous command.

If we focus on the `Health` section of the cluster-wide status, all four nodes are still ready.

Judging by the cluster-wide section of the status, we can see that there is one candidate to `ScaleDown` (it might be more in your case). If we move to the `NodeGroups`, we can observe that one of them has `CandidatesPresent` set to `1` in the `ScaleDown` section (or whatever was your initial value before scaling up).

In other words, one of the nodes is the candidate for removal. If it remains so for ten minutes, the node will be drained first to allow graceful shutdown of the Pods running inside it. After that, it will be physically removed through manipulation of the scaling group.

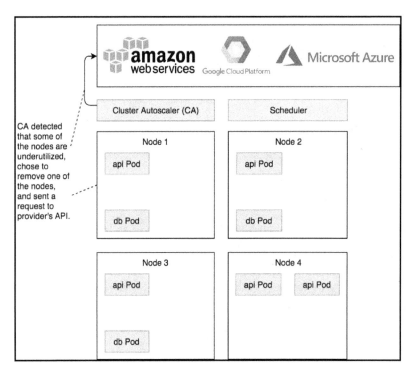

Figure 2-4: Cluster Autoscaler processes of scaling-down

We should wait for ten minutes before we proceed, so this is an excellent opportunity to grab some coffee (or tea).

Now that enough time passed, we'll take another look at the `cluster-autoscaler-status` ConfigMap.

```
1  kubectl -n kube-system \
2      get configmap \
3      cluster-autoscaler-status \
4      -o yaml
```

The output, limited to the relevant parts, is as follows.

```
apiVersion: v1
data:
```

```
status: |+
  Cluster-autoscaler status at 2018-10-03 23:16:24...
  Cluster-wide:
    Health:    Healthy (ready=3 ... registered=4 ...)
               . . .
    ScaleDown: NoCandidates (candidates=0)
               . . .
  NodeGroups:
    Name:      ...gke-devops25-default-pool-f4c233dd-grp
    Health:    Healthy (ready=1 ... registered=2 ...)
               . . .
    ScaleDown: NoCandidates (candidates=0)
               . . .
```

From the cluster-wide section, we can see that now there are 3 ready nodes, but that there are still 4 (or more) registered. That means that one of the nodes was drained, but it was still not destroyed. Similarly, one of the node groups shows that there is 1 ready node, even though 2 are registered (your numbers might vary).

From Kubernetes perspective, we are back to three operational worker nodes, even though the fourth is still physically present.

Now we need to wait a bit more before we retrieve the nodes and confirm that only three are available.

```
1  kubectl get nodes
```

The output, from GKE, is as follows.

```
NAME       STATUS ROLES  AGE VERSION
gke-... Ready  <none> 36m v1.9.7-gke.6
gke-... Ready  <none> 36m v1.9.7-gke.6
gke-... Ready  <none> 36m v1.9.7-gke.6
```

We can see that the node was removed and we already know from past experience that Kube Scheduler moved the Pods that were in that node to those that are still operational. Now that you experienced scaling down of your nodes, we'll explore the rule that governs the process.

# The rules governing nodes scale-down

Cluster Autoscaler iterates every 10 seconds (configurable through the `--scan-interval` flag). If the conditions for scaling up are not met, it checks whether there are unneeded nodes.

It will consider a node eligible for removal when all of the following conditions are met.

- The sum of CPU and memory requests of all Pods running on a node is less than 50% of the node's allocatable resources (configurable through the `--scale-down-utilization-threshold` flag).
- All Pods running on the node can be moved to other nodes. The exceptions are those that run on all the nodes like those created through DaemonSets.

Whether a Pod might not be eligible for rescheduling to a different node when one of the following conditions are met.

- A Pod with affinity or anti-affinity rules that tie it to a specific node.
- A Pod that uses local storage.
- A Pod created directly instead of through controllers like Deployment, StatefulSet, Job, or ReplicaSet.

All those rules boil down to a simple one. If a node contains a Pod that cannot be safely evicted, it is not eligible for removal.

Next, we should speak about cluster scaling boundaries.

# Can we scale up too much or de-scale to zero nodes?

If we let Cluster Autoscaler do its "magic" without defining any thresholds, our cluster or our wallet might be at risk.

We might, for example, misconfigure HPA and end up scaling Deployments or StatefulSets to a huge number of replicas. As a result, Cluster Autoscaler might add too many nodes to the cluster. As a result, we could end up paying for hundreds of nodes, even though we need much less. Luckily, AWS, Azure, and GCP limit how many nodes we can have so we cannot scale to infinity. Nevertheless, we should not allow Cluster Autoscaler to go over some limits.

Similarly, there is a danger that Cluster Autoscaler will scale down to too few nodes. Having zero nodes is almost impossible since that would mean that we have no Pods in the cluster. Still, we should maintain a healthy minimum of nodes, even if that means sometimes being underutilized.

A reasonable minimum of nodes is three. That way, we have a worker node in each zone (datacenter) of the region. As you already know, Kubernetes requires three zones with master nodes to maintain quorum. In some cases, especially on-prem, we might have only one geographically collocated datacenter with low latency. In that case, one zone (datacenter) is better than none. But, in the case of Cloud providers, three zones is the recommended distribution, and having a minimum of one worker node in each makes sense. That is especially true if we use block storage.

By its nature, block storage (for example, EBS in AWS, Persistent Disk in GCP, and Block Blob in Azure) cannot move from one zone to another. That means that we have to have a worker node in each zone so that there is (most likely) always a place for it in the same zone as the storage. Of course, we might not use block storage in which case this argument is unfounded.

How about the maximum number of worker nodes? Well, that differs from one use case to another. You do not have to stick with the same maximum for all eternity. It can change over time.

As a rule of thumb, I'd recommend having a maximum double from the actual number of nodes. However, don't take that rule seriously. It truly depends on the size of your cluster. If you have only three worker nodes, your maximum size might be nine (three times bigger). On the other hand, if you have hundreds or even thousands of nodes, it wouldn't make sense to double that number as the maximum. That would be too much. Just make sure that the maximum number of nodes reflects the potential increase in demand.

In any case, I'm sure that you'll figure out what should be your minimum and your maximum number of worker nodes. If you make a mistake, you can correct it later. What matters more is how to define those thresholds.

Luckily, setting up min and max values is easy in EKS, GKE, and AKS. For EKS, if you're using `eksctl` to create the cluster, all we have to do is add `--nodes-min` and `--nodes-max` arguments to the `eksctl create cluster` command. GKE is following a similar logic with `--min-nodes` and `--max-nodes` arguments of the `gcloud container clusters create` command. If one of the two is your preference, you already used those arguments if you followed the Gists. Even if you forget to specify them, you can always modify Autoscaling Groups (AWS) or Instance Groups (GCP) since that's where the limits are actually applied.

Azure takes a bit different approach. We define its limits directly in the `cluster-autoscaler` Deployment, and we can change them just by applying a new definition.

# Cluster Autoscaler compared in GKE, EKS, and AKS

Cluster Autoscaler is a prime example of the differences between different managed Kubernetes offerings. We'll use it to compare the three major Kubernetes-as-a-Service providers.

 I'll limit the comparison between the vendors only to the topics related to Cluster Autoscaling.

GKE is a no-brainer for those who can use Google to host their cluster. It is the most mature and feature-rich platform. They started **Google Kubernetes Engine** (**GKE**) long before anyone else. When we combine their head start with the fact that they are the major contributor to Kubernetes and hence have the most experience, it comes as no surprise that their offering is way above others.

When using GKE, everything is baked into the cluster. That includes Cluster Autoscaler. We do not have to execute any additional commands. It simply works out of the box. Our cluster scales up and down without the need for our involvement, as long as we specify the `--enable-autoscaling` argument when creating the cluster. On top of that, GKE brings up new nodes and joins them to the cluster faster than the other providers. If there is a need to expand the cluster, new nodes are added within a minute.

There are many other reasons I would recommend GKE, but that's not the subject right now. Still, Cluster Autoscaling alone should be the proof that GKE is the solution others are trying to follow.

Amazon's **Elastic Container Service** for Kubernetes (**EKS**) is somewhere in the middle. Cluster Autoscaling works, but it's not baked in. It's as if Amazon did not think that scaling clusters is important and left it as an optional add-on.

EKS installation is too complicated (when compared to GKE and AKS) but thanks to eksctl (`https://eksctl.io/`) from the folks from Weaveworks, we have that, more or less, solved. Still, there is a lot left to be desired from eksctl. For example, we cannot use it to upgrade our clusters.

The reason I'm mentioning eksctl in the context of auto-scaling lies in the Cluster Autoscaler setup.

I cannot say that setting up Cluster Autoscaler in EKS is hard. It's not. And yet, it's not as simple as it should be. We have to tag the Autoscaling Group, put additional privileges to the role, and install Cluster Autoscaler. That's not much. Still, those steps are much more complicated than they should be. We can compare it with GKE. Google understands that auto-scaling Kuberentes clusters is a must and it provides that with a single argument (or a checkbox if you prefer UIs). AWS, on the other hand, did not deem auto-scaling important enough to give us that much simplicity. On top of the unnecessary setup in EKS, the fact is that AWS added the internal pieces required for scaling only recently. Metrics Server can be used only since September 2018.

My suspicion is that AWS does not have the interest to make EKS great by itself and that they are saving the improvements for Fargate. If that's the case (we'll find that out soon), I'd characterize it as "sneaky business." Kubernetes has all the tools required for scaling Pod and nodes and they are designed to be extensible. The choice not to include Cluster Autoscaler as an integral part of their managed Kubernetes service is a big minus.

What can I say about AKS? I admire the improvements Microsoft made in Azure as well as their contributions to Kubernetes. They do recognize the need for a good managed Kubernetes offering. Yet, Cluster Autoscaler is still in beta. Sometimes it works, more often than not it doesn't. Even when it does work as it should, it is slow. Waiting for a new node to join the cluster is an exercise in patience.

The steps required to install Cluster Autoscaler in AKS are sort of ridiculous. We are required to define a myriad of arguments that were supposed to be already available inside the cluster. It should know what is the name of the cluster, what is the resource group, and so on and so forth. And yet, it doesn't. At least, that's the case at the time of this writing (October 2018). I hope that both the process and the experience will improve over time. For now, from the perspective of auto-scaling, AKS is at the tail of the pack.

You might argue that the complexity of the setup does not really matter. You'd be right. What matters is how reliable Cluster Autoscaling is and how fast it adds new nodes to the cluster. Still, the situation is the same. GKE leads in reliability and the speed. EKS is the close second, while AKS is trailing behind.

# What now?

There's not much left to say about Cluster Autoscaler.

We finished exploring fundamental ways to auto-scale Pods and nodes. Soon we'll dive into more complicated subjects and explore things that are not "baked" into a Kubernetes cluster. We'll go beyond the core project and introduce a few new tools and processes.

This is the moment when you should destroy your cluster if you're not planning to move into the next chapter right away and if your cluster is disposable (for example, not on bare-metal). Otherwise, please delete the `go-demo-5` Namespace to remove the resources we created in this chapter.

```
1  kubectl delete ns go-demo-5
```

Before you leave, you might want to go over the main points of this chapter.

- Cluster Autoscaler has a single purpose to adjust the size of the cluster by adding or removing worker nodes. It adds new nodes when Pods cannot be scheduled due to insufficient resources. Similarly, it eliminates nodes when they are underutilized for a period of time and when Pods running on one such node can be rescheduled somewhere else.
- Cluster Autoscaler assumes that the cluster is running on top of some kind of node groups. As an example, in the case of AWS, those groups are Autoscaling Groups (ASGs). When there is a need for additional nodes, Cluster Autoscaler creating a new node by increasing the size of a node group.
- The cluster will be scaled down when the sum of CPU and memory requests of all Pods running on a node is less than 50% of the node's allocatable resources and when all Pods running on the node can be moved to other nodes (DamonSets are the exception).

# 3
# Collecting and Querying Metrics and Sending Alerts

*Insufficient facts always invite danger.*

*- Spock*

So far, we explored how to leverage some of Kubernetes core features. We used HorizontalPodAutoscaler and Cluster Autoscaler. While the former relies on Metrics Server, the latter is not based on metrics, but on Scheduler's inability to place Pods within the existing cluster capacity. Even though Metrics Server does provide some basic metrics, we are in desperate need for more.

We have to be able to monitor our cluster and Metrics Server is just not enough. It contains a limited amount of metrics, it keeps them for a very short period, and it does not allow us to execute anything but simplest queries. I can't say that we are blind if we rely only on Metrics Server, but that we are severely impaired. Without increasing the number of metrics we're collecting, as well as their retention, we get only a glimpse into what's going on in our Kubernetes clusters.

Being able to fetch and store metrics cannot be the goal by itself. We also need to be able to query them in search for a cause of an issue. For that, we need metrics to be "rich" with information, and we need a powerful query language.

Finally, being able to find the cause of a problem is not worth much without being able to be notified that there is an issue in the first place. That means that we need a system that will allow us to define alerts that, when certain thresholds are reached, will send us notifications or, when appropriate, send them to other parts of the system that can automatically execute steps that will remedy issues.

If we accomplish that, we'll be a step closer to having not only a self-healing (Kubernetes already does that) but also a self-adaptive system that will react to changed conditions. We might go even further and try to predict that "bad things" will happen in the future and be proactive in resolving them before they even arise.

All in all, we need a tool, or a set of tools, that will allow us to fetch and store "rich" metrics, that will allow us to query them, and that will notify us when an issue happens or, even better, when a problem is about to occur.

We might not be able to build a self-adapting system in this chapter, but we can try to create a foundation. But, first things first, we need a cluster that will allow us to "play" with some new tools and concepts.

# Creating a cluster

We'll continue using definitions from the `vfarcic/k8s-specs` (`https://github.com/vfarcic/k8s-specs`) repository. To be on the safe side, we'll pull the latest version first.

 All the commands from this chapter are available in the `03-monitor.sh` (`https://gist.github.com/vfarcic/718886797a247f2f9ad4002f17e9ebd9`) Gist.

```
1  cd k8s-specs
2
3  git pull
```

In this chapter, we'll need a few things that were not requirements before, even though you probably already used them.

We'll start using UIs so we'll need NGINX Ingress Controller that will route traffic from outside the cluster. We'll also need environment variable `LB_IP` with the IP through which we can access worker nodes. We'll use it to configure a few Ingress resources.

The Gists used to test the examples in this chapters are below. Please use them as they are, or as inspiration to create your own cluster or to confirm whether the one you already have meets the requirements. Due to new requirements (Ingress and `LB_IP`), all the cluster setup Gists are new.

**A note to Docker for Desktop users**
You'll notice `LB_IP=[...]` command at the end of the Gist. You'll have to replace `[...]` with the IP of your cluster. Probably the easiest way to find it is through the `ifconfig` command. Just remember that it cannot be `localhost`, but the IP of your laptop (for example, `192.168.0.152`).

**A note to minikube and Docker for Desktop users**
We have to increase memory to 3 GB. Please have that in mind in case you were planning only to skim through the Gist that matches your Kubernetes flavor.

The Gists are as follows.

- `gke-monitor.sh`: **GKE** with 3 n1-standard-1 worker nodes, **nginx Ingress**, **tiller**, and cluster IP stored in environment variable **LB_IP** (https://gist.github.com/vfarcic/10e14bfbec466347d70d11a78fe7eec4).
- `eks-monitor.sh`: **EKS** with 3 t2.small worker nodes, **nginx Ingress**, **tiller**, **Metrics Server**, and cluster IP stored in environment variable **LB_IP** (https://gist.github.com/vfarcic/211f8dbe204131f8109f417605dbddd5).
- `aks-monitor.sh`: **AKS** with 3 Standard_B2s worker nodes, **nginx Ingress**, and **tiller**, and cluster IP stored in environment variable **LB_IP** (https://gist.github.com/vfarcic/5fe5c238047db39cb002cdfdadcfbad2).
- `docker-monitor.sh`: **Docker for Desktop** with **2 CPUs, 3 GB RAM, nginx Ingress, tiller, Metrics Server**, and cluster IP stored in environment variable **LB_IP** (https://gist.github.com/vfarcic/4d9ab04058cf00b9dd0faac11bda8f13).
- `minikube-monitor.sh`: **minikube** with **2 CPUs, 3 GB RAM, ingress, storage-provisioner, default-storageclass**, and **metrics-server** addons enabled, **tiller**, and cluster IP stored in environment variable **LB_IP** (https://gist.github.com/vfarcic/892c783bf51fc06dd7f31b939bc90248).

Now that we have a cluster, we'll need to choose the tools we'll use to accomplish our goals.

# Choosing the tools for storing and querying metrics and alerting

**HorizontalPodAutoscaler (HPA)** and **Cluster Autoscaler (CA)** provide essential, yet very rudimentary mechanisms to scale our Pods and clusters.

While they do scaling decently well, they do not solve our need to be alerted when there's something wrong, nor do they provide enough information required to find the cause of an issue. We'll need to expand our setup with additional tools that will allow us to store and query metrics as well as to receive notifications when there is an issue.

If we focus on tools that we can install and manage ourselves, there is very little doubt about what to use. If we look at the list of *Cloud Native Computing Foundation (CNCF)* projects (`https://www.cncf.io/projects/`), only two graduated so far (October 2018). Those are *Kubernetes* and *Prometheus* (`https://prometheus.io/`). Given that we are looking for a tool that will allow us to store and query metrics and that Prometheus fulfills that need, the choice is straightforward. That is not to say that there are no other similar tools worth considering. There are, but they are all service based. We might explore them later but, for now, we're focused on those that we can run inside our cluster. So, we'll add Prometheus to the mix and try to answer a simple question. What is Prometheus?

 Prometheus is a database (of sorts) designed to fetch (pull) and store highly dimensional time series data.

Time series are identified by a metric name and a set of key-value pairs. Data is stored both in memory and on disk. Former allows fast retrieval of information, while the latter exists for fault tolerance.

Prometheus' query language allows us to easily find data that can be used both for graphs and, more importantly, for alerting. It does not attempt to provide "great" visualization experience. For that, it integrates with *Grafana* (`https://grafana.com/`).

Unlike most other similar tools, we do not push data to Prometheus. Or, to be more precise, that is not the common way of getting metrics. Instead, Prometheus is a pull-based system that periodically fetches metrics from exporters. There are many third-party exporters we can use. But, in our case, the most crucial exporter is baked into Kubernetes. Prometheus can pull data from an exporter that transforms information from Kube API. Through it, we can fetch (almost) everything we might need. Or, at least, that's where the bulk of the information will be coming from.

Finally, storing metrics in Prometheus would not be of much use if we are not notified when there's something wrong. Even when we do integrate Prometheus with Grafana, that will only provide us with dashboards. I assume that you have better things to do than to stare at colorful graphs. So, we'll need a way to send alerts from Prometheus to, let's say, Slack. Luckily, *Alertmanager* (`https://prometheus.io/docs/alerting/alertmanager/`) allows us just that. It is a separate application maintained by the same community.

We'll see how all those pieces fit together through hands-on exercises. So, let's get going and install Prometheus, Alertmanager, and a few other applications.

# A quick introduction to Prometheus and Alertmanager

We'll continue the trend of using Helm as the installation mechanism. Prometheus' Helm Chart is maintained as one of the official Charts. You can find more info in the project's *README* (`https://github.com/helm/charts/tree/master/stable/prometheus`). If you focus on the variables in the *Configuration section* (`https://github.com/helm/charts/tree/master/stable/prometheus#configuration`), you'll notice that there are quite a few things we can tweak. We won't go through all the variables. You can check the official documentation for that. Instead, we'll start with a basic setup, and extend it as our needs increase.

Let's take a look at the variables we'll use as a start.

```
1   cat mon/prom-values-bare.yml
```

The output is as follows.

```
server:
  ingress:
    enabled: true
    annotations:
      ingress.kubernetes.io/ssl-redirect: "false"
      nginx.ingress.kubernetes.io/ssl-redirect: "false"
  resources:
    limits:
      cpu: 100m
      memory: 1000Mi
    requests:
      cpu: 10m
      memory: 500Mi
alertmanager:
  ingress:
    enabled: true
    annotations:
      ingress.kubernetes.io/ssl-redirect: "false"
      nginx.ingress.kubernetes.io/ssl-redirect: "false"
  resources:
    limits:
      cpu: 10m
```

```
        memory: 20Mi
      requests:
        cpu: 5m
        memory: 10Mi
kubeStateMetrics:
  resources:
    limits:
      cpu: 10m
      memory: 50Mi
    requests:
      cpu: 5m
      memory: 25Mi
nodeExporter:
  resources:
    limits:
      cpu: 10m
      memory: 20Mi
    requests:
      cpu: 5m
      memory: 10Mi
pushgateway:
  resources:
    limits:
      cpu: 10m
      memory: 20Mi
        requests:
      cpu: 5m
      memory: 10Mi
```

All we're doing for now is defining `resources` for all five applications we'll install, as well as enabling Ingress with a few annotations that will make sure that we are not redirected to HTTPS version since we do not have certificates for our ad-hoc domains. We'll dive into the applications that'll be installed later. For now, we'll define the addresses for Prometheus and Alertmanager UIs.

```
1  PROM_ADDR=mon.$LB_IP.nip.io
2
3  AM_ADDR=alertmanager.$LB_IP.nip.io
```

Let's install the Chart.

```
1  helm install stable/prometheus \
2      --name prometheus \
3      --namespace metrics \
4      --version 7.1.3 \
5      --set server.ingress.hosts={$PROM_ADDR} \
6      --set alertmanager.ingress.hosts={$AM_ADDR} \
7      -f mon/prom-values-bare.yml
```

The command we just executed should be self-explanatory, so we'll jump into the relevant parts of the output.

```
. . .
RESOURCES:
==> v1beta1/DaemonSet
NAME                        DESIRED  CURRENT  READY  UP-TO-DATE  AVAILABLE  NODE
SELECTOR AGE
prometheus-node-exporter 3        3        0      3           0          <none>
3s

==> v1beta1/Deployment
NAME                          DESIRED  CURRENT  UP-TO-DATE  AVAILABLE  AGE
prometheus-alertmanager       1        1        1           0          3s
prometheus-kube-state-metrics 1        1        1           0          3s
prometheus-pushgateway        1        1        1           0          3s
prometheus-server             1        1        1           0          3s
. . .
```

We can see that the Chart installed one DeamonSet and four Deployments.

The DeamonSet is Node Exporter, and it'll run a Pod on every node of the cluster. It provides node-specific metrics that will be pulled by Prometheus. The second exporter (Kube State Metrics) runs as a single replica Deployment. It fetches data from Kube API and transforms them into the Prometheus-friendly format. The two will provide most of the metrics we'll need. Later on, we might choose to expand them with additional exporters. For now, those two together with metrics fetched directly from Kube API should provide more metrics than we can absorb in a single chapter.

Further on, we got the Server, which is Prometheus itself. Alertmanager will forward alerts to their destination. Finally, there is Pushgateway that we might explore in one of the following chapters.

While waiting for all those apps to become operational, we might explore the flow between them.

Prometheus Server pulls data from exporters. In our case, those are Node Exporter and Kube State Metrics. The job of those exporters is to fetch data from the source and transform it into the Prometheus-friendly format. Node Exporter gets the data from /proc and /sys volumes mounted on the nodes, while Kube State Metrics gets it from Kube API. Metrics are stored internally in Prometheus.

Apart from being able to query that data, we can define alerts. When an alert reaches its threshold, it is forwarded to Alertmanager that acts as a crossroad.

Depending on its internal rules, it can forward those alerts further to various destinations like Slack, email, and HipChat (only to name a few).

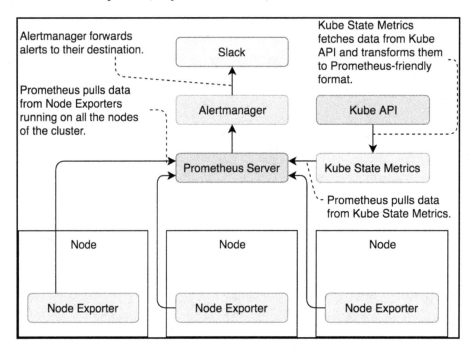

Figure 3-1: The flow of data to and from Prometheus (arrows indicate the direction)

By now, Prometheus Server probably rolled out. We'll confirm that just in case.

```
1   kubectl -n metrics \
2       rollout status \
3       deploy prometheus-server
```

Let's take a look at what is inside the Pod created through the `prometheus-server` Deployment.

```
1   kubectl -n metrics \
2       describe deployment \
3       prometheus-server
```

The output, limited to the relevant parts, is as follows.

```
Containers:
  prometheus-server-configmap-reload:
    Image: jimmidyson/configmap-reload:v0.2.2
    ...
```

```
prometheus-server:
  Image: prom/prometheus:v2.4.2
  . . .
```

Besides the container based on the prom/prometheus image, we got another one created from jimmidyson/configmap-reload. The job of the latter is to reload Prometheus whenever we change the configuration stored in a ConfigMap.

Next, we might want to take a look at the prometheus-server ConfigMap, since it stores all the configuration Prometheus needs.

```
1  kubectl -n metrics \
2      describe cm prometheus-server
```

The output, limited to the relevant parts, is as follows.

```
. . .
Data
====
alerts:
----
{}

prometheus.yml:
----
global:
  evaluation_interval: 1m
  scrape_interval: 1m
  scrape_timeout: 10s

rule_files:
- /etc/config/rules
- /etc/config/alerts
scrape_configs:
- job_name: prometheus
  static_configs:
  - targets:
    - localhost:9090
- bearer_token_file: /var/run/secrets/kubernetes.io/serviceaccount/token
  job_name: kubernetes-apiservers
  kubernetes_sd_configs:
  - role: endpoints
  relabel_configs:
  - action: keep
    regex: default;kubernetes;https
    source_labels:
    - __meta_kubernetes_namespace
    - __meta_kubernetes_service_name
```

```
      - __meta_kubernetes_endpoint_port_name
  scheme: https
  tls_config:
    ca_file: /var/run/secrets/kubernetes.io/serviceaccount/ca.crt
    insecure_skip_verify: true
...
```

We can see that the `alerts` are still empty. We'll change that soon.

Further down is the `prometheus.yml` config with `scrape_configs` taking most of the space. We could spend a whole chapter explaining the current config and the ways we could modify it. We will not do that because the config in front of you is bordering insanity. It's the prime example of how something can be made more complicated than it should be. In most cases, you should keep it as-is. If you do want to fiddle with it, please consult the official documentation.

Next, we'll take a quick look at Prometheus' screens.

**A note to Windows users**
Git Bash might not be able to use the `open` command. If that's the case, replace `open` with `echo`. As a result, you'll get the full address that should be opened directly in your browser of choice.

```
1  open "http://$PROM_ADDR/config"
```

The config screen reflects the same information we already saw in the `prometheus-server` ConfigMap, so we'll move on.

Next, let's take a look at the targets.

```
1  open "http://$PROM_ADDR/targets"
```

That screen contains seven targets, each providing different metrics. Prometheus is periodically pulling data from those targets.

All the outputs and screenshots in this chapter are taken from AKS. You might see some differences depending on your Kubernetes flavor.

You might notice that this chapter contains much more screenshots than any other. Even though it might look like there are too many, I wanted to make sure that you can compare your results with mine, since there will be inevitable differences that might sometimes look confusing if you do not have a reference (my screenshots).

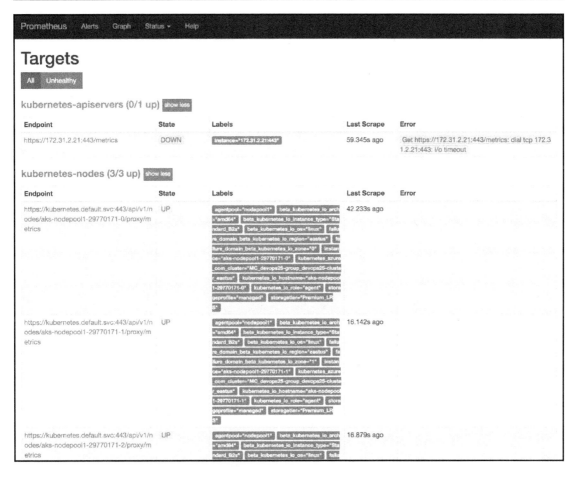

Figure 3-2: Prometheus' targets screen

**A note to AKS users**

The *kubernetes-apiservers* target might be red indicating that Prometheus
cannot connect to it. That's OK since we won't use its metrics.

**A note to minikube users**

The *kubernetes-service-endpoints* target might have a few sources in red.
There's no reason for alarm. Those are not reachable, but that won't affect
our exercises.

We cannot find out what each of those targets provides from that screen. We'll try to query
the exporters in the same way as Prometheus pulls them.

To do that, we'll need to find out the Services through which we can access the exporters.

```
1  kubectl -n metrics get svc
```

The output, from AKS, is as follows.

| NAME AGE | TYPE | CLUSTER-IP | EXTERNAL-IP | PORT(S) |
|---|---|---|---|---|
| prometheus-alertmanager 41d | ClusterIP | 10.23.245.165 | \<none\> | 80/TCP |
| prometheus-kube-state-metrics 41d | ClusterIP | None | \<none\> | 80/TCP |
| prometheus-node-exporter 41d | ClusterIP | None | \<none\> | 9100/TCP |
| prometheus-pushgateway 41d | ClusterIP | 10.23.244.47 | \<none\> | 9091/TCP |
| prometheus-server 41d | ClusterIP | 10.23.241.182 | \<none\> | 80/TCP |

We are interested in `prometheus-kube-state-metrics` and `prometheus-node-exporter` since they provide access to data from the exporters we'll use in this chapter.

Next, we'll create a temporary Pod through which we'll access the data available through the exporters behind those Services.

```
1  kubectl -n metrics run -it test \
2      --image=appropriate/curl \
3      --restart=Never \
4      --rm \
5      -- prometheus-node-exporter:9100/metrics
```

We created a new Pod based on `appropriate/curl`. That image serves a single purpose of providing `curl`. We specified `prometheus-node-exporter:9100/metrics` as the command, which is equivalent to running `curl` with that address. As a result, a lot of metrics were output. They are all in the same `key/value` format with optional labels surrounded by curly braces (`{` and `}`). On top of each metric, there is a `HELP` entry that explains its function as well as `TYPE` (for example, `gauge`). One of the metrics is as follows.

```
1  # HELP node_memory_MemTotal_bytes Memory information field
   MemTotal_bytes.
2  # TYPE node_memory_MemTotal_bytes gauge
3  node_memory_MemTotal_bytes 3.878477824e+09
```

We can see that it provides `Memory information field MemTotal_bytes` and that the type is `gauge`. Below the `TYPE` is the actual metric with the key (`node_memory_MemTotal_bytes`) and value `3.878477824e+09`.

Most of Node Exporter metrics are without labels. So, we'll have to look for an example in the `prometheus-kube-state-metrics` exporter.

```
1  kubectl -n metrics run -it test \
2      --image=appropriate/curl \
3      --restart=Never \
4      --rm \
5      -- prometheus-kube-state-metrics:8080/metrics
```

As you can see, the Kube State metrics follow the same pattern as those from the Node Exporter. The major difference is that most of them do have labels. An example is as follows.

```
1  kube_deployment_created{deployment="prometheus-
   server",namespace="metrics"} 1.535566512e+09
```

That metric represents the time the Deployment `prometheus-server` was created inside the `metrics` Namespace.

I'll leave it to you to explore those metrics in more detail. We'll use quite a few of them soon.

For now, just remember that with the combination of the metrics coming from the Node Exporter, Kube State Metrics, and those coming from Kubernetes itself, we can cover most of our needs. Or, to be more precise, those provide data required for most of the basic and common use cases.

Next, we'll take a look at the alerts screen.

```
1  open "http://$PROM_ADDR/alerts"
```

The screen is empty. Do not despair. We'll get back to that screen quite a few times. The alerts we'll be increasing as we progress. For now, just remember that's where you can find your alerts.

Finally, we'll open the graph screen.

```
1  open "http://$PROM_ADDR/graph"
```

That is where you'll spend your time debugging issues you'll discover through alerts.

As our first task, we'll try to retrieve information about our nodes. We'll use `kube_node_info` so let's take a look at its description (help) and its type.

```
1   kubectl -n metrics run -it test \
2       --image=appropriate/curl \
3       --restart=Never \
4       --rm \
5       -- prometheus-kube-state-metrics:8080/metrics \
6       | grep "kube_node_info"
```

The output, limited to the HELP and TYPE entries, is as follows.

```
1   # HELP kube_node_info Information about a cluster node.
2   # TYPE kube_node_info gauge
3   ...
```

You are likely to see variations between your results and mine. That's normal since our clusters probably have different amounts of resources, my bandwidth might be different, and so on. In some cases, my alerts will fire, and yours won't, or the other way around. I'll do my best to explain my experience and provide screenshots that accompany them. You'll have to compare that with what you see on your screen.

Now, let's try using that metric in Prometheus.

Please type the following query in the expression field.

```
1   kube_node_info
```

Click the **Execute** button to retrieve the values of the `kube_node_info` metric.

Unlike previous chapters, the Gist from this one (`03-monitor.sh` (`https://gist.github.com/vfarcic/718886797a247f2f9ad4002f17e9ebd9`)) contains not only the commands but also Prometheus expressions. They are all commented (with #). If you're planning to copy and paste the expressions from the Gist, please exclude the comments. Each expression has `# Prometheus expression` comment on top to help you identify it. As an example, the one you just executed is written in the Gist as follows.
`# Prometheus expression # kube_node_info`

If you check the HELP entry of the `kube_node_info`, you'll see that it provides `information about a cluster node` and that it is a `gauge`. A **gauge** (`https://prometheus.io/docs/concepts/metric_types/#gauge`) is a metric that represents a single numerical value that can arbitrarily go up and down.

That makes sense for information about nodes since their number can increase or decrease over time.

 A Prometheus gauge is a metric that represents a single numerical value that can arbitrarily go up and down.

If we focus on the output, you'll notice that there are as many entries as there are worker nodes in the cluster. The value (1) is useless in this context. Labels, on the other hand, can provide some useful information. For example, in my case, operating system (os_image) is Ubuntu 16.04.5 LTS. Through that example, we can see that we can use the metrics not only to calculate values (for example, available memory) but also to get a glimpse into the specifics of our system.

Figure 3-3: Prometheus' console output of the kube_node_info metric

Let's see if we can get a more meaningful query by combining that metric with one of the Prometheus' functions. We'll count the number of worker nodes in our cluster. The count is one of Prometheus' *aggregation operators* (https://prometheus.io/docs/prometheus/latest/querying/operators/#aggregation-operators).

Please execute the expression that follows.

```
1   count(kube_node_info)
```

The output should show the total number of worker nodes in your cluster. In my case (AKS) there are 3. On the first look, that might not be very helpful. You might think that you should know without Prometheus how many nodes you have in your cluster. But that might not be true. One of the nodes might have failed, and it did not recuperate. That is especially true if you're running your cluster on-prem without scaling groups. Or maybe Cluster Autoscaler increased or decreased the number of nodes. Everything changes over time, either due to failures, through human actions, or through a system that adapts itself. No matter the reasons for volatility, we might want to be notified when something reaches a threshold. We'll use nodes as the first example.

Our mission is to define an alert that will notify us if there are more than three or less than one nodes in the cluster. We'll imagine that those are our limits and that we want to know if the lower or the upper thresholds are reached due to failures or Cluster Autoscaling.

We'll take a look at a new definition of the Prometheus Chart's values. Since the definition is big and it will grow with time, from now on, we'll only look at the differences.

```
1   diff mon/prom-values-bare.yml \
2       mon/prom-values-nodes.yml
```

The output is as follows.

```
> serverFiles:
>   alerts:
>     groups:
>     - name: nodes
>       rules:
>       - alert: TooManyNodes
>         expr: count(kube_node_info) > 3
>         for: 15m
>         labels:
>           severity: notify
>         annotations:
>           summary: Cluster increased
>           description: The number of the nodes in the cluster increased
>       - alert: TooFewNodes
>         expr: count(kube_node_info) < 1
>         for: 15m
>         labels:
>           severity: notify
>         annotations:
>           summary: Cluster decreased
```

```
>        description: The number of the nodes in the cluster decreased
```

We added a new entry `serverFiles.alerts`. If you check Prometheus' Helm documentation, you'll see that it allows us to define alerts (hence the name). Inside it, we're using the "standard" Prometheus syntax for defining alerts.

 Please consult *Alerting Rules documentation* (`https://prometheus.io/docs/prometheus/latest/configuration/alerting_rules/`) for more info about the syntax.

We defined only one group of rules called `nodes`. Inside it are two `rules`. The first one (`TooManyNodes`) will notify us if there are more than 3 nodes `for` more than 15 minutes. The other (`TooFewNodes`) will do the opposite. It'll tell us if there are no nodes (<1) for 15 minutes. Both `rules` have `labels` and `annotations` that, for now, serve only informational purposes. Later on, we'll see their real usage.

Let's upgrade our Prometheus' Chart and see the effect of the new alerts.

```
1    helm upgrade -i prometheus \
2      stable/prometheus \
3      --namespace metrics \
4      --version 7.1.3 \
5      --set server.ingress.hosts={$PROM_ADDR} \
6      --set alertmanager.ingress.hosts={$AM_ADDR} \
7      -f mon/prom-values-nodes.yml
```

It'll take a few moments until the new configuration is "discovered" and Prometheus is reloaded. After a while, we can open the Prometheus alerts screen and check whether we got our first entries.

 From now on, I won't comment (much) on the need to wait for a while until next config is propagated. If what you see on the screen does not coincide with what you're expecting, please wait for a while and refresh it.

```
1    open "http://$PROM_ADDR/alerts"
```

You should see two alerts.

Both alerts are green since none evaluates to `true`. Depending on the Kuberentes flavor you choose, you either have only one node (for example, Docker for Desktop and minikube) or you have three nodes (for example, GKE, EKS, AKS). Since our alerts are checking whether we have less than one, or more than three nodes, neither of the conditions are met, no matter which Kubernetes flavor you're using.

If your cluster was not created through one of the Gists provided at the beginning of this chapter, then you might have more than three nodes in your cluster, and the alert will fire. If that's the case, I suggest you modify the `mon/prom-values-nodes.yml` file to adjust the threshold of the alert.

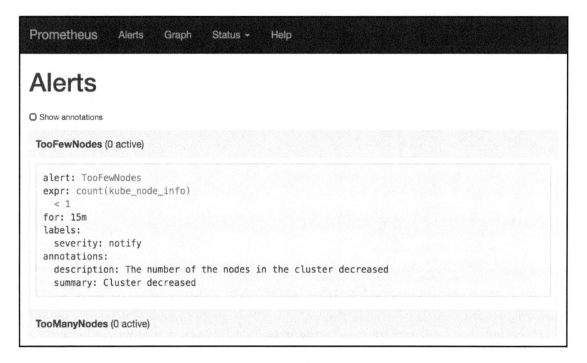

Figure 3-4: Prometheus' alerts screen

Seeing inactive alerts is boring, so I want to show you one that fires (becomes red). To do that, we can add more nodes to the cluster (unless you're using a single node cluster like Docker for Desktop and minikube). However, it would be easier to modify the expression of one of the alerts, so that's what we'll do next.

```
1  diff mon/prom-values-nodes.yml \
2      mon/prom-values-nodes-0.yml
```

The output is as follows.

```
57,58c57,58
< expr: count(kube_node_info) > 3
< for: 15m
---
> expr: count(kube_node_info) > 0
> for: 1m
66c66
< for: 15m
---
> for: 1m
```

The new definition changed the condition of the TooManyNodes alert to fire if there are more than zero nodes. We also changed the for statement so that we do not need to wait for 15 minutes before the alert fires.

Let's upgrade the Chart one more time.

```
1  helm upgrade -i prometheus \
2      stable/prometheus \
3      --namespace metrics \
4      --version 7.1.3 \
5      --set server.ingress.hosts={$PROM_ADDR} \
6      --set alertmanager.ingress.hosts={$AM_ADDR} \
7      -f mon/prom-values-nodes-0.yml
```

... and we'll go back to the alerts screen.

```
1  open "http://$PROM_ADDR/alerts"
```

A few moments later (don't forget to refresh the screen), the alert will switch to the pending state, and the color will change to yellow. That means that the conditions for the alert are met (we do have more than zero nodes) but the for period did not yet expire.

Wait for a minute (duration of the `for` period) and refresh the screen. The alert's state switched to firing and the color changed to red. Prometheus sent our first alert.

Figure 3-5: Prometheus' alerts screen with one of the alerts firing

Where was the alert sent? Prometheus Helm Chart deployed Alertmanager and pre-configured Prometheus to send its alerts there. Let's take a look at it's UI.

```
1  open "http://$AM_ADDR"
```

We can see that one alert reached Alertmanager. If we click the **+ info** button next to the `TooManyNodes` alert, we'll see the annotations (**summary** and **description**) as well as the labels (**severity**).

Figure 3-6: Alertmanager UI with one of the alerts expanded

We are likely not going to sit in front of the Alertmanager waiting for issues to appear. If that would be our goal, we could just as well wait for the alerts in Prometheus.

Displaying alerts is indeed not the reason why we have Alertmanager. It is supposed to receive alerts and dispatch them further. It is not doing anything of that sort simply because we did not yet define the rules it should use to forward alerts. That's our next task.

We'll take a look at yet another update of the Prometheus Chart values.

```
1  diff mon/prom-values-nodes-0.yml \
2      mon/prom-values-nodes-am.yml
```

The output is as follows.

```
71a72,93
> alertmanagerFiles:
>   alertmanager.yml:
>     global: {}
>     route:
>       group_wait: 10s
>       group_interval: 5m
>       receiver: slack
>       repeat_interval: 3h
>       routes:
>       - receiver: slack
>         repeat_interval: 5d
>         match:
>           severity: notify
>           frequency: low
>     receivers:
>     - name: slack
>       slack_configs:
>       - api_url:
"https://hooks.slack.com/services/T308SC7HD/BD8BU8TUH/a1jt08DeRJUaNUF3t2ax4
GsQ"
>         send_resolved: true
>         title: "{{ .CommonAnnotations.summary }}"
>         text: "{{ .CommonAnnotations.description }}"
>         title_link: http://my-prometheus.com/alerts
```

When we apply that definition, we'll add `alertmanager.yml` file to Alertmanager. If contains the rules it should use to dispatch alerts. The `route` section contains general rules that will be applied to all alerts that do not match one of the `routes`. The `group_wait` value makes Alertmanager wait for 10 seconds in case additional alerts from the same group arrive. That way, we'll avoid receiving multiple alerts of the same type.

When the first alert of a group is dispatched, it'll use the value of the `group_interval` field (5m) before sending the next batch of the new alerts from the same group.

The `receiver` field in the `route` section defines the default destination of the alerts. Those destinations are defined in the `receivers` section below. In our case, we're sending the alerts to the `slack` receiver by default.

The `repeat_interval` (set to `3h`) defines the period after which alerts will be resent if Alertmanager continues receiving them.

The `routes` section defines specific rules. Only if none of them match, those in the `route` section above will be used. The `routes` section inherits properties from above so only those that we define in this section will change. We'll keep sending matching `routes` to `slack`, and the only change is the increase of the `repeat_interval` from `3h` to `5d`.

The critical part of the `routes` is the `match` section. It defines filters that are used to decide whether an alert is a match or not. In our case, only those with the labels `severity:` `notify` and `frequency: low` will be considered a match.

All in all, the alerts with `severity` label set to `notify` and `frequency` set to `low` will be resent every five days. All the other alerts will have a frequency of three hours.

The last section of our Alertmanager config is `receivers`. We have only one receiver named `slack`. Below the `name` is `slack_config`. It contains Slack-specific configuration. We could have used `hipchat_config`, `pagerduty_config`, or any other of the supported ones. Even if our destination is not one of those, we could always fall back to `webhook_config` and send a custom request to the API of our tool of choice.

For the list of all the supported `receivers`, please consult *Alertmanager Configuration* page (`https://prometheus.io/docs/alerting/configuration/`).

Inside `slack_configs` section, we have the `api_url` that contains the Slack address with the token from one of the rooms in the *devops20* channel.

For information how to general an incoming webhook address for your Slack channel, please visit the *Incoming Webhooks* page (`https://api.slack.com/incoming-webhooks`).

Next is the `send_resolved` flag. When set to `true`, Alertmanager will send notifications not only when an alert is fired, but also when the issue that caused it is resolved.

We're using `summary` annotation as the `title` of the message, and the `description` annotation for the `text`. Both are using *Go Templates* (`https://golang.org/pkg/text/template/`). Those are the same annotations we defined in the Prometheus' alerts.

Finally, the `title_link` is set to `http://my-prometheus.com/alerts`. That is indeed not the address of your Prometheus UI but, since I could not know in advance what will be your domain, I put a non-existing one. Feel free to change `my-prometheus.com` to the value of the environment variable `$PROM_ADDR`. Or just leave it as-is knowing that if you click the link, it will not take you to your Prometheus UI.

Now that we explored Alertmanager configuration, we can proceed and upgrade the Chart.

```
1  helm upgrade -i prometheus \
2    stable/prometheus \
3    --namespace metrics \
4    --version 7.1.3 \
5    --set server.ingress.hosts={$PROM_ADDR} \
6    --set alertmanager.ingress.hosts={$AM_ADDR} \
7    -f mon/prom-values-nodes-am.yml
```

A few moments later, Alertmanager will be reconfigured, and the next time it receives the alert from Prometheus, it'll dispatch it to Slack. We can confirm that by visiting the `devops20.slack.com` workspace. If you did not register already, please go to `slack.devops20toolkit.com`. Once you are a member, we can visit the `devops25-tests` channel.

```
1  open "https://devops20.slack.com/messages/CD8QJA8DS/"
```

You should see the `Cluster increased` notification. Don't get confused if you see other messages. You are likely not the only one running the exercises from this book.

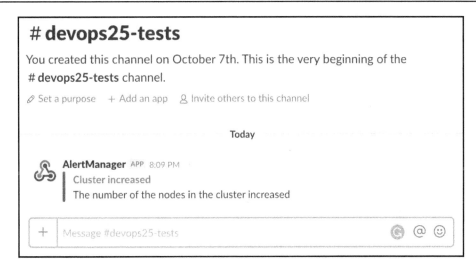

Figure 3-7: Slack with an alert message received from Alertmanager

 Sometimes, for reasons I could not figure out, Slack receives empty notifications from Alertmanager. For now, I'm ignoring the issue out of laziness.

Now that we went through the basic usage of Prometheus and Alertmanager, we'll take a break from hands-on exercises and discuss the types of metrics we might want to use.

# Which metric types should we use?

If this is the first time you're using Prometheus hooked into metrics from Kube API, the sheer amount might be overwhelming. On top of that, consider that the configuration excluded many of the metrics offered by Kube API and that we could extend the scope even further with additional exporters.

While every situation is different and you are likely to need some metrics specific to your organization and architecture, there are some guidelines that we should follow. In this section, we'll discuss the key metrics. Once you understand them through a few examples, you should be able to extend their use to your specific use-cases.

 The four key metrics everyone should utilize are latency, traffic, errors, and saturation.

Those four metrics been championed by Google **Site Reliability Engineers** (**SREs**) as the most fundamental metrics for tracking performance and health of a system.

**Latency** represents the time it takes to service to respond to a request. The focus should not be only on duration but also on distinguishing between the latency of successful requests and the latency of failed requests.

**Traffic** is a measure of demand that is being placed on services. An example would be the number of HTTP requests per second.

**Errors** are measured by the rate of requests that fail. Most of the time those failures are explicit (for example, HTTP 500 errors) but they can be implicit as well (for example, an HTTP 200 response with the body describing that the query did not return any results).

**Saturation** can be described by "fullness" of a service or a system. A typical example would be lack of CPU that results in throttling and, consequently, degrades the performance of the applications.

Over time, different monitoring methods were developed. We got, for example, the **USE** method that states that for every resource, we should check **utilization**, **saturation**, and **errors**. Another one is the **RED** method that defines **rate**, **errors**, and **duration** as the key metrics. Those and many others are similar in their essence and do not differ significantly from SREs demand to measure latency, traffic, errors, and saturation.

We'll go through each of the four types of measurements described by SREs and provide a few examples. We might even extend them with metrics that do not necessarily fit into any of the four categories. The first in line is latency.

# Alerting on latency-related issues

We'll use the `go-demo-5` application to measure latency, so our first step is to install it.

```
1  GD5_ADDR=go-demo-5.$LB_IP.nip.io
2
3  helm install \
4      https://github.com/vfarcic/go-demo-5/releases/download/
   0.0.1/go-demo-5-0.0.1.tgz \
5      --name go-demo-5 \
6      --namespace go-demo-5 \
7      --set ingress.host=$GD5_ADDR
```

We generated an address that we'll use as Ingress entry-point, and we deployed the application using Helm. Now we should wait until it rolls out.

```
1  kubectl -n go-demo-5 \
2      rollout status \
3      deployment go-demo-5
```

Before we proceed, we'll check whether the application is indeed working correctly by sending an HTTP request.

```
1  curl "http://$GD5_ADDR/demo/hello"
```

The output should be the familiar `hello, world!` message.

Now, let's see whether we can, for example, get the duration of requests entering the system through Ingress.

```
1  open "http://$PROM_ADDR/graph"
```

If you click on the **- insert metrics at cursor -** drop-down list, you'll be able to browse through all the available metrics. The one we're looking for is `nginx_ingress_controller_request_duration_seconds_bucket`. As its name implies, the metric comes from NGINX Ingress Controller, and provide request durations in seconds and grouped in buckets.

Please type the expression that follows and click the **Execute** button.

```
1   nginx_ingress_controller_request_duration_seconds_bucket
```

In this case, seeing the raw values might not be very useful, so please click the **Graph** tab.

You should see graphs, one for each Ingress. Each is increasing because the metric in question is a counter (`https://prometheus.io/docs/concepts/metric_types/#counter`). Its value is growing with each request.

> A Prometheus counter is a cumulative metric whose value can only increase, or be reset to zero on restart.

What we need is to calculate the rate of requests over a period of time. We'll accomplish that by combining `sum` and `rate` (`https://prometheus.io/docs/prometheus/latest/querying/functions/#rate()`) functions. The former should be self-explanatory.

> Prometheus' rate function calculates the per-second average rate of increase of the time series in the range vector.

Please type the expression that follows, and press the **Execute** button.

```
1   sum(rate(
2     nginx_ingress_controller_request_duration_seconds_count[5m]
3   ))
4   by (ingress)
```

The resulting graph shows us the per-second rate of all the requests entering the system through Ingress. The rate is calculated based on five minutes intervals. If you hover one of the lines, you'll see the additional information like the value and the Ingress. The `by` statement allows us to group the results by `ingress`.

Still, the result by itself is not very useful, so let's redefine our requirement. We should be able to find out how many of the requests are slower than 0.25 seconds. We cannot do that directly. Instead, we can retrieve all those that are 0.25 second or faster.

Please type the expression that follows, and press the **Execute** button.

```
1   sum(rate(
2     nginx_ingress_controller_request_duration_seconds_bucket{
```

```
3        le="0.25"
4      }[5m]
5  ))
6  by (ingress)
```

What we really want is to find the percentage of requests that fall into 0.25 seconds bucket. To accomplish that, we'll get the rate of the requests faster than or equal to 0.25 seconds, and divide the result with the rate of all the requests.

Please type the expression that follows, and press the **Execute** button.

```
 1  sum(rate(
 2    nginx_ingress_controller_request_duration_seconds_bucket{
 3      le="0.25"
 4    }[5m]
 5  ))
 6  by (ingress) /
 7  sum(rate(
 8    nginx_ingress_controller_request_duration_seconds_count[5m]
 9  ))
10  by (ingress)
```

You probably won't see much in the graph since we did not yet generate much traffic, beyond occasional interaction with Prometheus and Alertmanager and a single request we sent to go-demo-5. Nevertheless, the few lines you can see display the percentage of the requests that responded within 0.25 seconds.

For now, we are interested only in go-demo-5 requests, so we'll refine the expression further, to limit the results only to go-demo-5 Ingress.

Please type the expression that follows, and press the **Execute** button.

```
 1  sum(rate(
 2    nginx_ingress_controller_request_duration_seconds_bucket{
 3      le="0.25",
 4      ingress="go-demo-5"
 5    }[5m]
 6  ))
 7  by (ingress) /
 8  sum(rate(
 9    nginx_ingress_controller_request_duration_seconds_count{
10      ingress="go-demo-5"
11    }[5m]
12  ))
13  by (ingress)
```

The graph should be almost empty since we sent only one request. Or, maybe you received the no datapoints found message. It's time to generate some traffic.

```
1  for i in {1..30}; do
2    DELAY=$[ $RANDOM % 1000 ]
3    curl "http://$GD5_ADDR/demo/hello?delay=$DELAY"
4  done
```

We sent thirty requests to go-demo-5. The application has a "hidden" feature to delay response to a request. Given that we want to generate traffic with random response time, we used DELAY variable with a random value up to thousand milliseconds. Now we can re-run the same query and see whether we can get some more meaningful data.

Please wait for a while until data from new requests is gathered, then type the expression that follows (in Prometheus), and press the **Execute** button.

```
1   sum(rate(
2     nginx_ingress_controller_request_duration_seconds_bucket{
3       le="0.25",
4       ingress="go-demo-5"
5     }[5m]
6   ))
7   by (ingress) /
8   sum(rate(
9     nginx_ingress_controller_request_duration_seconds_count{
10      ingress="go-demo-5"
11    }[5m]
12  ))
13  by (ingress)
```

This time, we can see the emergence of a new line. In my case (screenshot following), around twenty-five percent of requests have durations that are within 0.25 seconds. Or, to put it into different words, around a quarter of the requests are slower than expected.

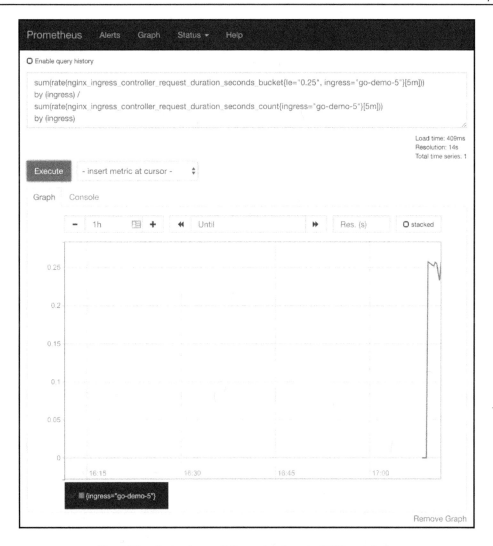

Figure 3-8: Prometheus' graph screen with the percentage of requests with 0.25 seconds duration

Filtering metrics for a specific application (Ingress) is useful when we do know that there is a problem and we want to dig further into it. However, we still need an alert that will tell us that there is an issue. For that, we'll execute a similar query, but this time without limiting the results to a specific application (Ingress). We'll also have to define a condition that will fire the alert, so we'll set the threshold to ninety-five percent (0.95). Without such a threshold, we'd get a notification every time a single request is slow. As a result, we'd get swarmed with alarms and would probably start ignoring them soon afterward. After all, no system is in danger if a single request is slow, but only if a considerable number of them is. In our case, that is five percent of slow requests or, to be more precise, less than ninety-five percent of fast requests.

Please type the expression that follows, and press the **Execute** button.

```
 1  sum(rate(
 2    nginx_ingress_controller_request_duration_seconds_bucket{
 3      le="0.25"
 4    }[5m]
 5  ))
 6  by (ingress) /
 7  sum(rate(
 8    nginx_ingress_controller_request_duration_seconds_count[5m]
 9  ))
10  by (ingress) < 0.95
```

We can see occasional cases when less than ninety-five percent of requests are within 0.25 second. In my case (screenshot following), we can see that Prometheus, Alertmanager, and `go-demo-5` are occasionally slow.

Figure 3-9: Prometheus' graph screen with the percentage of requests within 0.25 seconds duration and limited only to results higher than ninety-five percent

The only thing missing is to define an alert based on the previous expression. As a result, we should get a notification whenever less than ninety-five percent of requests have a duration less than 0.25 seconds.

I prepared an updated set of Prometheus' Chart values, so let's take a look at the differences when compared with the one we're using currently.

```
1   diff mon/prom-values-nodes-am.yml \
2       mon/prom-values-latency.yml
```

The output is as follows.

```
53a54,62
>  - name: latency
>    rules:
>    - alert: AppTooSlow
>      expr:
sum(rate(nginx_ingress_controller_request_duration_seconds_bucket{le=
"0.25"}[5m])) by (ingress) /
sum(rate(nginx_ingress_controller_request_duration_seconds_count[5m])) by
(ingress) < 0.95
>      labels:
>        severity: notify
>      annotations:
>        summary: Application is too slow
>        description: More then 5% of requests are slower than 0.25s
57c66
<      expr: count(kube_node_info) > 0
---
>      expr: count(kube_node_info) > 3
```

We added a new alert `AppTooSlow`. It'll trigger if the percentage of requests with the duration of 0.25 seconds or less is smaller than ninety-five percent (`0.95`).

We also we reverted the threshold of the `TooManyNodes` back to its original value of `3`.

Next, we'll update the `prometheus` Chart with the new values and open the alerts screen to confirm whether the new alert was indeed added.

```
1   helm upgrade -i prometheus \
2       stable/prometheus \
3       --namespace metrics \
4       --version 7.1.3 \
5       --set server.ingress.hosts={$PROM_ADDR} \
6       --set alertmanager.ingress.hosts={$AM_ADDR} \
7       -f mon/prom-values-latency.yml
8
```

```
9   open "http://$PROM_ADDR/alerts"
```

If the `AppTooSlow` alert is still not available, please wait a few moments and refresh the screen.

Figure 3-10: Prometheus' alerts screen

The newly added alert is (probably) green (not triggering). We need to generate a few slow requests to see it in action.

Please execute the command that follows to send thirty requests with a random response time of up to ten thousand milliseconds (ten seconds).

```
1   for i in {1..30}; do
2     DELAY=$[ $RANDOM % 10000 ]
3     curl "http://$GD5_ADDR/demo/hello?delay=$DELAY"
4   done
```

It'll take a few moments until Prometheus scrapes new metrics and for the alert to detect that the threshold is reached. After a while, we can open the alerts screen again and check whether the alert is indeed firing.

```
1   open "http://$PROM_ADDR/alerts"
```

We can see that the state of the alert is firing. If that's not your case, please wait a while longer and refresh the screen. In my case (screenshot following), the value is 0.125, meaning that only 12.5 percent of requests have a duration of 0.25 seconds or less.

There might be two or more active alerts inside `AppTooSlow` if `prometheus-server`, `prometheus-alertmanager`, or some other application is responding slow.

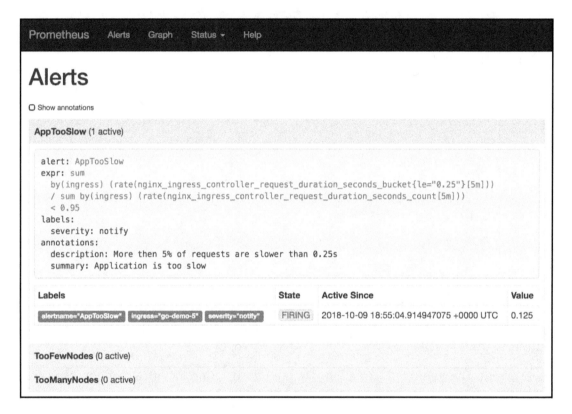

Figure 3-11: Prometheus' alerts screen with one alert firing

The alert is red meaning that Prometheus sent it to Alertmanager which, in turn, forwarded it to Slack. Let's confirm that.

```
1  open "https://devops20.slack.com/messages/CD8QJA8DS/"
```

As you can see (screenshot following), we received two notification. Since we reverted the threshold of the `TooManyNodes` alert back to greater than three nodes, and our cluster has less, Prometheus sent a notification to Alertmanager that the problem is resolved. As a result, we got a new notification in Slack. This time, the color of the message is green.

Further on, a new red message appeared indicating that an `Application is too slow`.

Figure 3-12: Slack with alerts firing (red) and resolved (green) messages

We often cannot rely on a single rule that will fit all the applications. Prometheus and, for example, Jenkins would be a good candidate of internal applications which we cannot expect to have less than five percent of response times above 0.25 seconds. So, we might want to filter further the alerts. We can use any number of labels for that. To keep it simple, we'll continue leveraging `ingress` label but, this time, we'll use regular expressions to exclude some applications (Ingresses) from the alert.

Let's open the graph screen one more time.

```
1   open "http://$PROM_ADDR/graph"
```

Please type the expression that follows, press the **Execute** button, and switch to the *Graph* tab.

```
1    sum(rate(
2      nginx_ingress_controller_request_duration_seconds_bucket{
3        le="0.25",
4        ingress!~"prometheus-server|jenkins"
5      }[5m]
6    ))
7    by (ingress) /
8    sum(rate(
9      nginx_ingress_controller_request_duration_seconds_count{
10       ingress!~"prometheus-server|jenkins"
11     }[5m]
12   ))
13   by (ingress)
```

The addition to the previous query is the `ingress!~"prometheus-server|jenkins"` filter. The `!~` is used to select metrics with labels that do NOT regex match the `prometheus-server|jenkins` string. Since `|` is equivalent to the `or` statement, we can translate that filter as "everything that is NOT `prometheus-server` or is NOT `jenkins`." We do not have Jenkins in our cluster. I just wanted to show you a way to exclude multiple values.

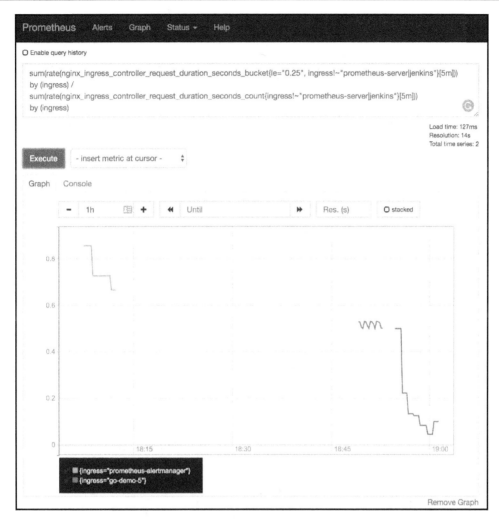

Figure 3-13: Prometheus graph screen with the percentage of requests with 0.25 seconds duration and the results excluding prometheus-server and jenkins

We could have complicated it a bit more and specified
`ingress!~"prometheus.+|jenkins.+` as the filter. In that case, it would exclude all
Ingresses with the name that starts with `prometheus` and `jenkins`. The key is in the `.+`
addition that, in RegEx, matches one or more entries (+) of any character (`.`).

We won't go into an explanation of RegEx syntax. I expect you to be already familiar with
it. If you're not, you might want to Google it or to visit *Regular expression Wiki* page
(`https://en.wikipedia.org/wiki/Regular_expression`).

The previous expression retrieves only the results that are NOT `prometheus-server` and
`jenkins`. We would probably need to create another one that includes only those two.

Please type the expression that follows, and press the **Execute** button.

```
 1  sum(rate(
 2    nginx_ingress_controller_request_duration_seconds_bucket{
 3      le="0.5",
 4      ingress=~"prometheus-server|jenkins"
 5    }[5m]
 6  ))
 7  by (ingress) /
 8  sum(rate(
 9    nginx_ingress_controller_request_duration_seconds_count{
10      ingress=~"prometheus-server|jenkins"
11    }[5m]
12  ))
13  by (ingress)
```

The only difference, when compared with the previous expression, is that this time we used
the `=~` operator. It selects labels that regex-match the provided string. Also, the bucket (`le`)
is now set to `0.5` seconds, given that both applications might need more time to respond
and we are OK with that.

In my case, the graph shows `prometheus-server` as having one hundred percent requests
with durations within 0.5 seconds (in your case that might not be true).

Figure 3-14: Prometheus graph screen with the percentage of requests with 0.5 seconds duration and the results including only prometheus-server and jenkins

The few latency examples should be enough to get you going with that type of metrics, so we'll move to traffic.

# Alerting on traffic-related issues

So far, we measured the latency of our applications, and we created alerts that fire when certain thresholds based on request duration are reached. Those alerts are not based on the number of requests coming in (traffic), but on the percentage of slow requests. The `AppTooSlow` would fire even if only one single request enters an application, as long as the duration is above the threshold. For completeness, we need to start measuring traffic or, to be more precise, the number of requests sent to each application and the system as a whole. Through that, we can know if our system is under a lot of stress and make a decision on whether to scale our applications, add more workers, or apply some other solution to mitigate the problem. We might even choose to block part of the incoming traffic if the number of requests reaches abnormal numbers providing a clear indication that we are under **Denial of Service (DoS)** attack
(`https://en.wikipedia.org/wiki/Denial-of-service_attack`).

We'll start by creating a bit of traffic that we can use to visualize requests.

```
1  for i in {1..100}; do
2      curl "http://$GD5_ADDR/demo/hello"
3  done
4
5  open "http://$PROM_ADDR/graph"
```

We sent a hundred requests to the `go-demo-5` application and opened Prometheus' graph screen.

We can retrieve the number of requests coming into the Ingress controller through the `nginx_ingress_controller_requests`. Since it is a counter, we can continue using `rate` function combined with `sum`. Finally, we probably want to know the rate of requests grouped by the `ingress` label.

Please type the expression that follows, press the **Execute** button, and switch to the *Graph* tab.

```
1  sum(rate(
2    nginx_ingress_controller_requests[5m]
3  ))
4  by (ingress)
```

We can see a spike on the right side of the graph. It shows the requests that went to the `go-demo-5` applications through the Ingress with the same name.

In my case (screenshot following), the peak is close to one request per second (yours will be different).

Figure 3-15: Prometheus' graph screen with the rate of the number of requests

We are probably more interested in the number of requests per second per replica of an application, so our next task is to find a way to retrieve that data. Since `go-demo-5` is a Deployment, we can use `kube_deployment_status_replicas`.

Please type the expression that follows, and press the **Execute** button.

```
1   kube_deployment_status_replicas
```

We can see the number of replicas of each Deployment in the system. The `go-demo-5` application, in my case painted in red (screenshot following), has three replicas.

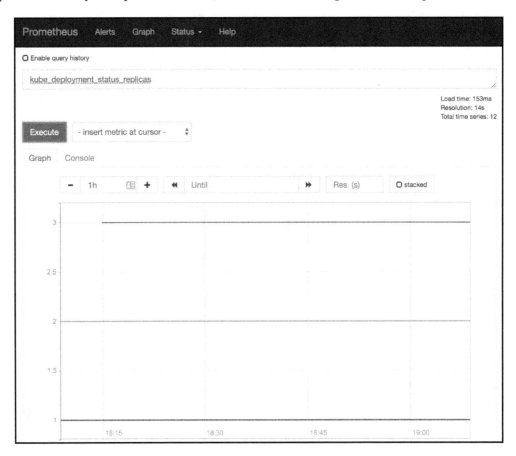

Figure 3-16: Prometheus' graph screen with the number of replicas of Deployments

Next, we should combine the two expressions, to get the number of requests per second per replica. However, we are facing a problem. For two metrics to join, they need to have matching labels. Both the Deployment and the Ingress of `go-demo-5` have the same name so we can use that to our benefit, given that we can rename one of the labels. We'll do that with the help of the `label_join` (`https://prometheus.io/docs/prometheus/latest/querying/functions/#label_join()`) function.

 For each timeseries in v, `label_join(v instant-vector, dst_label string, separator string, src_label_1 string, src_label_2 string, ...)` joins all the values of all the `src_labels` using the separator and returns the timeseries with the label `dst_label` containing the joined value.

If the previous explanation of the `label_join` function was confusing, you're not alone. Instead, let's go through the example that will transform `kube_deployment_status_replicas` by adding `ingress` label that will contain values from the `deployment` label. If we are successful, we'll be able to combine the result with `nginx_ingress_controller_requests` since both will have the same matching labels (`ingress`).

Please type the expression that follows, and press the **Execute** button.

```
1  label_join(
2    kube_deployment_status_replicas,
3    "ingress",
4    ",",
5    "deployment"
6  )
```

Since we are, this time, interested mostly in values of the labels, please switch to the **Console** view by clicking the tab.

As you can see from the output, each metric now contains an additional label `ingress` with the same value as `deployment`.

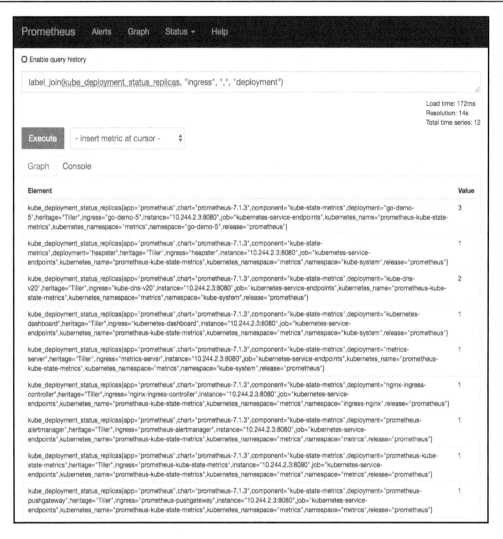

Figure 3-17: Prometheus' console view of Deployment replicas status and a new label ingress created from the deployment label

Now we can combine the two metrics.

Please type the expression that follows, and press the **Execute** button.

```
 1  sum(rate(
 2    nginx_ingress_controller_requests[5m]
 3  ))
 4  by (ingress) /
 5  sum(label_join(
 6    kube_deployment_status_replicas,
 7    "ingress",
 8    ",",
 9    "deployment"
10  ))
11  by (ingress)
```

Switch back to the *Graph* view.

We calculated the rate of the number of requests per application (ingress) and divided it with the total number of replicas per application (ingress). The end result is the rate of the number of requests per application (ingress) per replica.

It might be worth noting that we can not retrieve the number of requests for each specific replica, but rather the average number of requests per replica. This method should work, given that Kubernetes networking in most cases performs round robin that results in more or less the same amount of requests being sent to each replica.

All in all, now we know how many requests our replicas are receiving per second.

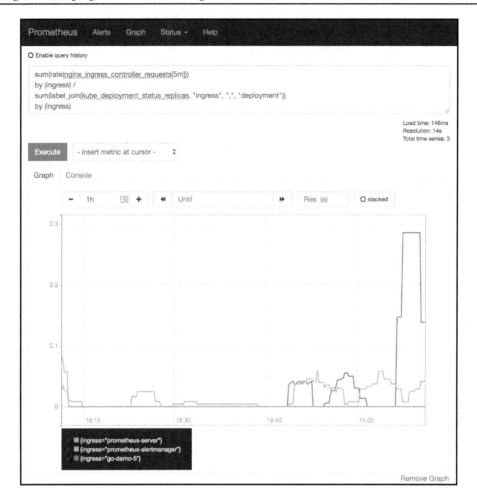

Figure 3-18: Prometheus' graph screen with the rate of requests divided by the number of Deployment replicas

Now that we learned how to write an expression to retrieve the rate of the number of requests per second per replica, we should convert it into an alert.

So, let's take a look at the difference between the old and the new definition of Prometheus' Chart values.

```
1  diff mon/prom-values-latency.yml \
2      mon/prom-values-latency2.yml
```

The output is as follows.

```
62a63,69
> - alert: TooManyRequests
>   expr: sum(rate(nginx_ingress_controller_requests[5m])) by (ingress) /
sum(label_join(kube_deployment_status_replicas, "ingress", ",",
"deployment")) by (ingress) > 0.1
>   labels:
>     severity: notify
>   annotations:
>     summary: Too many requests
>     description: There is more than average of 1 requests per second per
replica for at least one application
```

We can see that the expression is almost the same as the one we used in Prometheus' graph screen. The only difference is the threshold which we set to 0.1. As a result, that alert should notify us whenever a replica receives more than a rate of 0.1 requests per second, calculated over the period of five minutes ([5m]). As you might have guessed, 0.1 requests per second is too low of a figure to use it in production. However, it'll allow us to trigger the alert easily and see it in action.

Now, let's upgrade our Chart, and open Prometheus' alerts screen.

```
1  helm upgrade -i prometheus \
2    stable/prometheus \
3    --namespace metrics \
4    --version 7.1.3 \
5    --set server.ingress.hosts={$PROM_ADDR} \
6    --set alertmanager.ingress.hosts={$AM_ADDR} \
7    -f mon/prom-values-latency2.yml
8
9  open "http://$PROM_ADDR/alerts"
```

Please refresh the screen until the `TooManyRequests` alert appears.

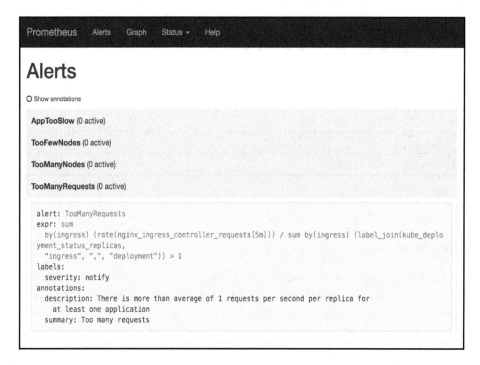

Figure 3-19: Prometheus' alerts screen

Next, we'll generate some traffic so that we can see the alert is generated and sent through Alertmanager to Slack.

```
1  for i in {1..200}; do
2      curl "http://$GD5_ADDR/demo/hello"
3  done
4
5  open "http://$PROM_ADDR/alerts"
```

We sent two hundred requests and reopened the Prometheus' alerts screen. Now we should refresh the screen until the `TooManyRequests` alert becomes red.

Once Prometheus fired the alert, it was sent to Alertmanager and, from there, forwarded to Slack. Let's confirm that.

```
1  open "https://devops20.slack.com/messages/CD8QJA8DS/"
```

We can see the `Too many requests` notification, thus proving that the flow of this alert works.

Figure 3-20: Slack with alert messages

Next, we'll jump into errors-related metrics.

# Alerting on error-related issues

We should always be aware of whether our applications or the system is producing errors. However, we cannot start panicking on the first occurrence of an error since that would generate too many notifications that we'd likely end up ignoring.

Errors happen often, and many are caused by issues that are fixed automatically or are due to circumstances that are out of our control. If we are to perform an action on every error, we'd need an army of people working 24/7 only on fixing issues that often do not need to be fixed. As an example, entering into a "panic" mode because there is a single response with code in 500 range would almost certainly produce a permanent crisis. Instead, we should monitor the rate of errors compared to the total number of requests and react only if it passes a certain threshold. After all, if an error persists, that rate will undoubtedly increase. On the other hand, if it continues being low, it means that the issue was fixed automatically by the system (for example, Kubernetes rescheduled the Pods from the failed node) or that it was an isolated case that does not repeat.

Our next mission is to retrieve requests and distinguish separate them by their statuses. If we can do that, we should be able to calculate the rate of errors.

We'll start by generating a bit of traffic.

```
1  for i in {1..100}; do
2      curl "http://$GD5_ADDR/demo/hello"
3  done
4
5  open "http://$PROM_ADDR/graph"
```

We sent a hundred requests and opened Prometheus' graph screen.

Let's see whether the `nginx_ingress_controller_requests` metric we used previously provides the statuses of the requests.

Please type the expression that follows, and press the **Execute** button.

```
1  nginx_ingress_controller_requests
```

We can see all the data recently scraped by Prometheus. If we pay closer attention to the labels, we can see that, among others, there is `status`. We can use it to calculate the percentage of those with errors (for example, 500 range) based on the total number of requests.

We already saw that we can use the `ingress` label to separate calculations per application, assuming that we are interested only in those that are public-facing.

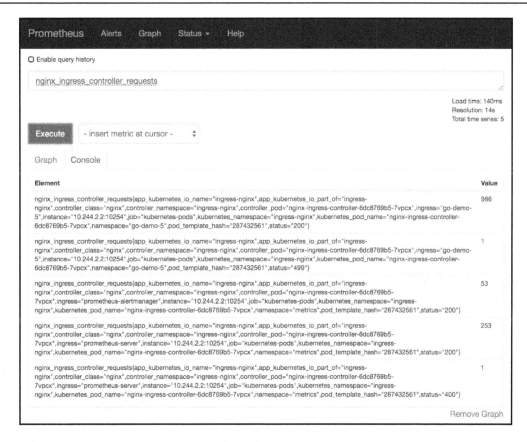

Figure 3-21: Prometheus' console view with requests entering through Ingress

The `go-demo-5` app has a special endpoint `/demo/random-error` that will generate random error responses. Approximately, one out of ten requests to that address will produce an error. We can use that to test our expressions.

```
1  for i in {1..100}; do
2    curl "http://$GD5_ADDR/demo/random-error"
3  done
```

We sent a hundred requests to the `/demo/random-error` endpoint and approximately ten percent of those responded with errors (HTTP status code `500`).

Next, we'll have to wait for a few moments for Prometheus to scrape the new batch of metrics. After that, we can open the Graph screen and try to write an expression that will retrieve the error rate of our applications.

```
1  open "http://$PROM_ADDR/graph"
```

Please type the expression that follows, and press the **Execute** button.

```
 1  sum(rate(
 2    nginx_ingress_controller_requests{
 3      status=~"5.."
 4    }[5m]
 5  ))
 6  by (ingress) /
 7  sum(rate(
 8    nginx_ingress_controller_requests[5m]
 9  ))
10  by (ingress)
```

We used `5..` RegEx to calculate the rate of the requests with errors grouped by `ingress`, and we divided the result with all the rate of all the requests. The result is grouped by `ingress`. In my case (screenshot following), the result is approximately 4 percent (`0.04`). Prometheus did not yet scrape all the metrics, and I expect that number to get closer to ten percent in the next scraping iteration.

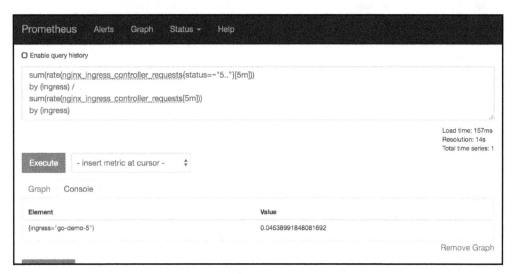

Figure 3-22: Prometheus' graph screen with the percentage with the requests with error responses

Let's compare the updated version of the Chart's values file with the one we used previously.

```
1   diff mon/prom-values-cpu-memory.yml \
2       mon/prom-values-errors.yml
```

The output is as follows.

```
127a128,136
> - name: errors
>   rules:
>   - alert: TooManyErrors
>     expr: sum(rate(nginx_ingress_controller_requests{status=~"5.."}[5m]))
by (ingress) / sum(rate(nginx_ingress_controller_requests[5m])) by
(ingress) > 0.025
>     labels:
>       severity: error
>     annotations:
>       summary: Too many errors
>       description: At least one application produced more then 5% of
error responses
```

The alert will fire if the rate of errors is over 2.5% of the total rate of requests.

Now we can upgrade our Prometheus' Chart.

```
1   helm upgrade -i prometheus \
2       stable/prometheus \
3       --namespace metrics \
4       --version 7.1.3 \
5       --set server.ingress.hosts={$PROM_ADDR} \
6       --set alertmanager.ingress.hosts={$AM_ADDR} \
7       -f mon/prom-values-errors.yml
```

There's probably no need to confirm that the alerting works. We already saw that Prometheus sends all the alerts to Alertmanager and that they are forwarded from there to Slack.

Next, we'll move to saturation metrics and alerts.

# Alerting on saturation-related issues

Saturation measures fullness of our services and the system. We should be aware if replicas of our services are processing too many requests and being forced to queue some of them. We should also monitor whether usage of our CPUs, memory, disks, and other resources reaches critical limits.

For now, we'll focus on CPU usage. We'll start by opening the Prometheus' graph screen.

```
1  open "http://$PROM_ADDR/graph"
```

Let's see if we can get the rate of used CPU by node (`instance`). We can use `node_cpu_seconds_total` metric for that. However, it is split into different modes, and we'll have to exclude a few of them to get the "real" CPU usage. Those will be `idle`, `iowait`, and any type of `guest` cycles.

Please type the expression that follows, and press the **Execute** button.

```
1  sum(rate(
2    node_cpu_seconds_total{
3      mode!="idle",
4      mode!="iowait",
5      mode!~"^(?:guest.*)$"
6    }[5m]
7  ))
8  by (instance)
```

Switch to the *Graph* view.

The output represents the actual usage of CPU in the system. In my case (screenshot following), excluding a temporary spike, all nodes are using less than a hundred CPU milliseconds.

The system is far from being under stress.

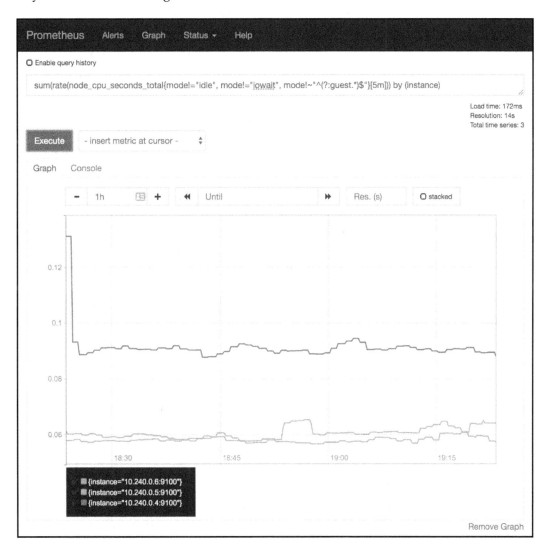

Figure 3-23: Prometheus' graph screen with the rate of used CPU grouped by node instances

As you already noticed, absolute numbers are rarely useful. We should try to discover the percentage of used CPU. We'll need to find out how much CPU our nodes have. We can do that by counting the number of metrics. Each CPU gets its own data entry, one for each mode. If we limit the result to a single mode (for example, `system`), we should be able to get the total number of CPUs.

Please type the expression that follows, and press the **Execute** button.

```
1  count (
2      node_cpu_seconds_total{
3          mode="system"
4      }
5  )
```

In my case (screenshot following), there are six cores in total. Yours is likely to be six as well if you're using GKE, EKS, or AKS from the Gists. If, on the other hand, you're running the cluster in Docker for Desktop or minikube, the result should be one node.

Now we can combine the two queries to get the percentage of used CPU

Please type the expression that follows, and press the **Execute** button.

```
1   sum(rate(
2     node_cpu_seconds_total{
3         mode!="idle",
4         mode!="iowait",
5         mode!~"^(?:guest.*)$"
6     }[5m]
7   )) /
8   count (
9     node_cpu_seconds_total{
10        mode="system"
11     }
12  )
```

We summarized the rate of used CPUs and divided it by the total number of CPUs. In my case (screenshot following), only three to four percent of CPU is currently used.

That is not a surprise since most of the system is at rest. Not much is going on in our cluster right now.

Figure 3-24: Prometheus' graph screen with the percentage of available CPU

Now that we know how to fetch the percentage of used CPU of the whole cluster, we'll move our attention to applications.

We'll try to discover how many allocatable cores we have. From application's perspective, at least when they're running in Kubernetes, allocatable CPUs show how much can be requested for Pods. Allocatable CPU is always lower than total CPU.

Please type the expression that follows, and press the **Execute** button.

```
1  kube_node_status_allocatable_cpu_cores
```

The output should be lower than the number of cores used by our VMs. The allocatable cores show the amount of CPU that can be assigned containers. To be more precise, allocatable cores are the number of CPUs assigned to nodes minus those reserved by system-level processes. In my case (screenshot following), there are almost two full allocatable CPUs.

Figure 3-25: Prometheus' graph screen with the allocatable CPU for each of the nodes in the cluster

However, in this context, we are interested in the total amount of allocatable CPUs since we are trying to discover how much is used by our Pods inside the whole cluster. So, we'll sum the allocatable cores.

Please type the expression that follows, and press the **Execute** button.

```
1  sum(
2    kube_node_status_allocatable_cpu_cores
3  )
```

In my case, the total allocatable CPUs is somewhere around 5.8 cores. For the exact number, please hover on the graph line.

Now that we know how many allocatable CPUs we have, we should try to discover how much was requested by Pods.

Please note that requested resources are not the same as used resources. We'll get to that use-case later. For now, we want to know how much we requested from the system.

Please type the expression that follows, and press the **Execute** button.

```
1  kube_pod_container_resource_requests_cpu_cores
```

We can see that requested CPU is relatively low. In my case, all the containers with requested CPU have their values below 0.15 (hundred and fifty milliseconds). Your result might differ.

Just as with allocatable CPU, we are interested in the sum of requested CPU. Later on, we'll be able to combine the two results and deduce how much is left unreserved in the cluster.

Please type the expression that follows, and press the **Execute** button.

```
1  sum(
2    kube_pod_container_resource_requests_cpu_cores
3  )
```

We summed all the CPU resource requests. As a result, in my case (screenshot following), all the requested CPUs are slightly below 1.5.

Figure 3-26: Prometheus' graph screen with the sum of the requested CPU

Now, let's combine the two expressions and see the percentage of requested CPU.

Please type the expression that follows, and press the **Execute** button.

```
1  sum(
2      kube_pod_container_resource_requests_cpu_cores
3  ) /
4  sum(
5      kube_node_status_allocatable_cpu_cores
6  )
```

In my case, the output shows that around a quarter (0.25) of all allocatable CPU is reserved. That means that we could have four times as many CPU requests before we reach the need to expand the cluster. Of course, you already know that, if present, Cluster Autoscaler will add nodes before that happens. Still, knowing that we are close to reaching CPU limits is important. Cluster Autoscaler might not be working correctly, or it might not even be active. The latter case is true for most, if not all on-prem clusters.

Let's see whether we can convert the expressions we explored into alerts.

We'll explore yet another difference between a new set of Chart values and those we used before.

```
1  diff mon/prom-values-latency2.yml \
2      mon/prom-values-cpu.yml
```

The output is as follows.

```
64c64
<    expr: sum(rate(nginx_ingress_controller_requests[5m])) by (ingress) /
sum(label_join(kube_deployment_status_replicas, "ingress", ",",
"deployment")) by (ingress) > 0.1
---
>    expr: sum(rate(nginx_ingress_controller_requests[5m])) by (ingress) /
sum(label_join(kube_deployment_status_replicas, "ingress", ",",
"deployment")) by (ingress) > 1
87a88,103
> - alert: NotEnoughCPU
>    expr: sum(rate(node_cpu_seconds_total{mode!="idle", mode!="iowait",
mode!~"^(?:guest.*)$"}[5m])) / count(node_cpu_seconds_total{mode="system"})
> 0.9
```

```
>    for: 30m
>    labels:
>      severity: notify
>    annotations:
>      summary: There's not enough CPU
>      description: CPU usage of the cluster is above 90%
> - alert: TooMuchCPURequested
>    expr: sum(kube_pod_container_resource_requests_cpu_cores) /
sum(kube_node_status_allocatable_cpu_cores) > 0.9
>    for: 30m
>    labels:
>      severity: notify
>    annotations:
>      summary: There's not enough allocatable CPU
>      description: More than 90% of allocatable CPU is requested
```

We can see from the differences that we restored the original threshold of
`TooManyRequests` back to `1` and that we added two new alerts called `NotEnoughCPU` and
`TooMuchCPURequested`.

The `NotEnoughCPU` alert will fire if more than ninety percent of CPU across the whole
cluster is used for over thirty minutes. That way we'll avoid settings alarms if there is a
temporary spike in CPU usage.

The `TooMuchCPURequested` also has the threshold of ninety percent and will be triggered
if it persists for over thirty minutes. The expression computes the total amount of requested
divided with the total among allocatable CPU.

Both alerts are reflections of the Prometheus expressions we executed short while ago, so
you should already be familiar with their purpose.

Let's upgrade Prometheus' Chart with the new values and open the alerts screen.

```
1  helm upgrade -i prometheus \
2    stable/prometheus \
3    --namespace metrics \
4    --version 7.1.3 \
5    --set server.ingress.hosts={$PROM_ADDR} \
6    --set alertmanager.ingress.hosts={$AM_ADDR} \
7    -f mon/prom-values-cpu.yml
8
9  open "http://$PROM_ADDR/alerts"
```

All that's left is to wait until the two new alerts appear. If they are not already there, please refresh your screen.

There's probably no need to see the new alerts in action. By now, you should trust the flow, and there's no reason to believe that they would not trigger.

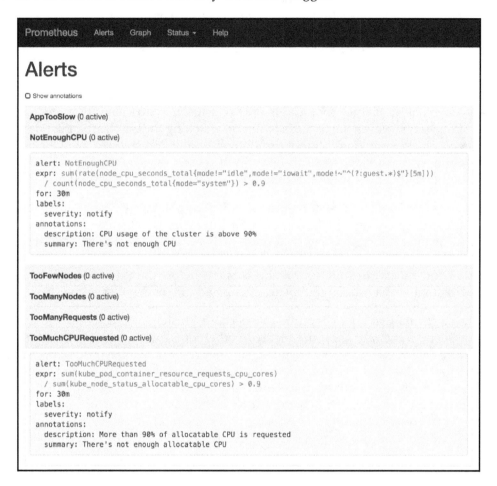

Figure 3-27: Prometheus' alerts screen

In the "real world" scenario, receiving one of the two alerts might provoke different reactions depending on the Kubernetes flavor we're using.

If we do have Cluster Autoscaler (CA), we might not need `NotEnoughCPU` and `TooMuchCPURequested` alerts. The fact that ninety percent of node CPUs is in use does not prevent the cluster from operating correctly, just as long as our CPU requests as set correctly. Similarly, having ninety percent of allocatable CPU reserved is also not an issue. If Kubernetes cannot schedule a new Pod due to all CPU being reserved, it will scale up the cluster. As a matter of fact, reaching almost full CPU usage or having nearly all allocatable CPU reserved is a good thing. That means that we are having as much CPU as we need and that we are not paying for unused resources. Still, that logic works mostly with Cloud providers and not even all of them. Today (October 2018), Cluster Autoscaler works only in AWS, GCE, and Azure.

All that does not mean that we should rely only on Cluster Autoscaler. It can malfunction, like anything else. However, since CA is based on watching for unschedulable Pods, if it does fail to work, we should detect that through observing Pod statuses, not CPU usage. Still, it might not be a bad idea to receive alerts when CPU usage is too high, but in that case, we might want to increase the threshold to a value closer to a hundred percent.

If our cluster is on-prem or, to be more precise, if it does not have Cluster Autoscaler, the alerts we explored are essential if our process for scaling up the cluster is not automated or if it's slow. The logic is simple. If we need more than a couple of minutes to add new nodes to the cluster, we cannot wait until Pods are unschedulable. That would be too late. Instead, we need to know that we are out of available capacity before the cluster becomes full (saturated) so that we have enough time to react by adding new nodes to the cluster.

Still, having a cluster that does not auto-scale because Cluster Autoscaler does not work is not an excuse good enough. There are plenty of other tools that we can use to automate our infrastructure. When we do manage to get to such a place that we can automatically add new nodes to the cluster, the destination of the alert should change. Instead of receiving notifications to Slack, we might want to send a request to a service that will execute the script that will result in a new node being added to the cluster. If our cluster is running on VMs, we can always add more through a script (or some tool).

The only real excuse to receive those notifications to Slack is if our cluster is running on bare-metal. In such a case, we cannot expect scripts to create new servers magically. For everyone else, Slack notifications when too much CPU is used or all allocated CPU is reserved should be only a temporary solution until proper automation is in place.

Now, let's try to accomplish similar goals but, this time, by measuring memory usage and reservations.

Measuring memory consumption is similar to CPU, and yet there are a few differences that we should take into account. But, before we get there, let's go back to the Prometheus' graph screen and explore our first memory-related metric.

```
1  open "http://$PROM_ADDR/graph"
```

Just as with CPU, first we need to find out how much memory each of our nodes has.

Please type the expression that follows, press the **Execute** button, and switch to the *Graph* tab.

```
1  node_memory_MemTotal_bytes
```

Your result is likely to be different than mine. In my case, each node has around 4 GB of RAM.

Knowing how much RAM each node has is of no use without knowing how much RAM is currently available. We can get that info through the `node_memory_MemAvailable_bytes` metric.

Please type the expression that follows, and press the **Execute** button.

```
1  node_memory_MemAvailable_bytes
```

We can see the available memory on each of the nodes of the cluster. In my case (screenshot following), each has around 3 GB of available RAM.

Figure 3-28: Prometheus' graph screen with available memory in each of the nodes of the cluster

Now that we know how to get total and available memory from each of the nodes, we should combine the queries to get the percentage of the used memory of the whole cluster.

Please type the expression that follows, and press the **Execute** button.

```
1  1 -
2  sum(
3    node_memory_MemAvailable_bytes
4  ) /
5  sum(
6    node_memory_MemTotal_bytes
7  )
```

Since we are searching for the percentage of used memory, and we have the metric with available memory, we started the expression with `1` – that will invert the result. The rest of the expression is a simple division of available and total memory. In my case (screenshot following), less than thirty percent of memory is used on each of the nodes.

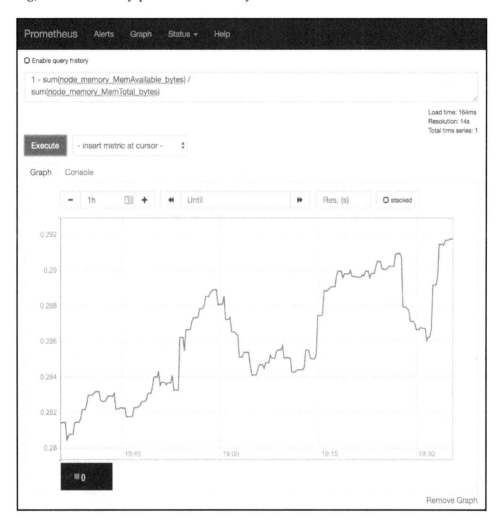

Figure 3-29: Prometheus' graph screen with the percentage of available memory

Just as with CPU, available and total memory does not paint the whole picture. While that is useful information and a base for a potential alert, we also need to know how much memory is allocatable and how much of it is in use by Pods. We can get the first figure through the `kube_node_status_allocatable_memory_bytes` metric.

Please type the expression that follows, and press the **Execute** button.

```
1  kube_node_status_allocatable_memory_bytes
```

Depending on the Kubernetes flavor and the hosting provider you're using, there might be a very small, or a big discrepancy between the total and allocatable memory. I am running the cluster in AKS, and allocatable memory is a whole GB less than total memory. While the former is around 3 GB RAM, the latter was approximately 4 GB RAM. That's a big difference. I do not have full 4 GB for my Pods, but around one quarter less than that. The rest, around 1 GB RAM, is spent on system-level services. To make things worse, that's 1 GB RAM spent on each node which, in my case, results in 3 GB less in total since my cluster has three nodes. Given such a huge difference between the total and the allocatable amount of RAM, there is a clear benefit for having less number of bigger nodes. Still, not everyone needs big nodes and reducing their number to less than three might not be a good idea if we'd like to have our nodes spread in all the zones.

Now that we know how to retrieve the amount of allocatable memory, let's see how to get the amount of requested memory for each of the applications.

Please type the expression that follows, and press the **Execute** button.

```
1  kube_pod_container_resource_requests_memory_bytes
```

We can see that Prometheus (server) has the most requested memory (500 MB), with all the others being way below. Bear in mind that we are seeing only the Pods that do have reservations. Those without are not present in the results of that query. As you already know, it is OK not to define reservations and limits only in exceptional cases like, for example, for short-lived Pods used in CI/CD processes.

Figure 3-30: Prometheus' graph screen with requested memory for each of the Pods

The previous expression returned the amount of memory used by each Pod. However, our mission is to discover how much requested memory we have in the system as a whole.

Please type the expression that follows, and press the **Execute** button.

```
1  sum(
2    kube_pod_container_resource_requests_memory_bytes
3  )
```

In my case, the total amount of requested memory is around 1.6 GB RAM.

All that's left is to divide the total requested memory with the amount of all the allocatable memory in the cluster.

Please type the expression that follows, and press the **Execute** button.

```
1  sum(
2    kube_pod_container_resource_requests_memory_bytes
3  ) /
4  sum(
5    kube_node_status_allocatable_memory_bytes
6  )
```

In my case (screenshot following), the total of the requested memory is around twenty percent (0.2) of the cluster's allocatable RAM. I am far from being in any type of danger, nor there is a need to scale up the cluster. If anything, I have too much unused memory and might want to scale down. However, we are at the moment only concerned with scaling up. Later we'll explore alerts that might result in scaling down.

Figure 3-31: Prometheus' graph screen with the percentage of the requested memory of the total allocatable memory in the cluster

Let's take a look at the differences between the old Chart's values and those we are about to use.

```
1  diff mon/prom-values-cpu.yml \
2      mon/prom-values-memory.yml
```

The output is as follows.

```
103a104,119
> - alert: NotEnoughMemory
>   expr: 1 - sum(node_memory_MemAvailable_bytes) /
sum(node_memory_MemTotal_bytes) > 0.9
>   for: 30m
>   labels:
>     severity: notify
>   annotations:
>     summary: There's not enough memory
>     description: Memory usage of the cluster is above 90%
> - alert: TooMuchMemoryRequested
>   expr: sum(kube_pod_container_resource_requests_memory_bytes) /
sum(kube_node_status_allocatable_memory_bytes) > 0.9
>   for: 30m
>   labels:
>     severity: notify
>   annotations:
>     summary: There's not enough allocatable memory
>     description: More than 90% of allocatable memory is requested
```

We added two new alerts (`NotEnoughMemory` and `TooMuchMemoryRequested`). The definitions themselves should be straightforward since we already created quite a few alerts. The expressions are the same as the ones we used in Prometheus graph screen, with the addition of the greater than ninety percent (`> 0.9`) threshold. So, we'll skip further explanation.

We'll upgrade our Prometheus Chart with the new values, and open the alerts screen to confirm that they

```
1  helm upgrade -i prometheus \
2      stable/prometheus \
3      --namespace metrics \
4      --version 7.1.3 \
5      --set server.ingress.hosts={$PROM_ADDR} \
6      --set alertmanager.ingress.hosts={$AM_ADDR} \
7      -f mon/prom-values-memory.yml
8
9  open "http://$PROM_ADDR/alerts"
```

If the alerts `NotEnoughMemory` and `TooMuchMemoryRequested` are not yet available, please wait a few moments, and refresh the screen.

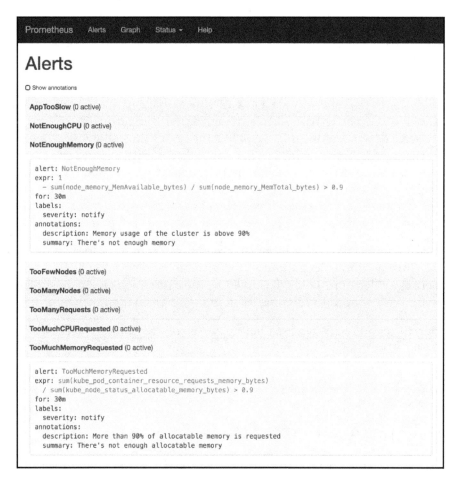

Figure 3-32: Prometheus' alerts screen

The actions based on the memory-based alerts we created so far should be similar to those we discussed with CPU. We can use them to decide whether and when to scale up our cluster, either through manual actions or through automated scripts. Just as before, if we do have our cluster hosted with one of the vendors supported by the Cluster Autoscaler (CA), those alerts should be purely informative, while on-prem or with unsupported Cloud providers, they are much more than simple notifications. They are an indication that we are about to run out of capacity, at least when memory is concerned.

The CPU and memory examples are all focused on the need to know when is the right time to scale our cluster. We might create similar alerts that would notify us when the usage of CPU or memory is too low. That would give us a clear indication that we have too many nodes in the cluster and that we might want to remove some. That, again, assumes that we do not have Cluster Autoscaler up-and-running. Still, taking only CPU or only memory into account for scaling-down is too risky and can lead to unexpected results.

Let's imagine that only twelve percent of allocatable CPU is reserved and that we have three worker nodes in the cluster. Such a low CPU usage surely does not warrant that many nodes since on average, each has a relatively small amount of reserved CPU. As a result, we can choose to scale down, and we remove one of the nodes thus allowing other clusters to reuse it. Was that a good thing to do? Well, it depends on other resources. If the percentage of memory reservations was low as well, removing a node was a good idea. On the other hand, if the reserved memory were over sixty-six percent, removal of a node would result in insufficient resources. When we removed one of the three nodes, over sixty-six percent of reserved memory across three nodes becomes over one hundred percent on two nodes.

All in all, if we are to receive notifications that our cluster is in need to scale down (and we do NOT have Cluster Autoscaler), we need to combine memory and CPU, and probably a few other metrics as alert thresholds. Fortunately, the expressions are very similar to those we used before. We just need to combine them into a single alert and change the thresholds.

As a reminder, the expressions we used before are as follows (there's no need to re-run them).

```
1   sum(rate(
2     node_cpu_seconds_total{
3       mode!="idle",
4       mode!="iowait",
5       mode!~"^(?:guest.*)$"
6     }[5m]
7   ))
8   by (instance) /
9   count(
10    node_cpu_seconds_total{
11      mode="system"
12    }
13  )
14  by (instance)
15
16  1 -
17  sum(
18    node_memory_MemAvailable_bytes
19  )
20  by (instance) /
```

```
21  sum(
22    node_memory_MemTotal_bytes
23  )
24  by (instance)
```

Now, let's compare yet another update of the Chart's values with those we're using right now.

```
1  diff mon/prom-values-memory.yml \
2      mon/prom-values-cpu-memory.yml
```

The output is as follows.

```
119a120,127
> - alert: TooMuchCPUAndMemory
>    expr: (sum(rate(node_cpu_seconds_total{mode!="idle", mode!="iowait",
mode!~"^(?:guest.*)$"}[5m])) by (instance) /
count(node_cpu_seconds_total{mode="system"}) by (instance)) < 0.5 and (1 -
sum(node_memory_MemAvailable_bytes) by (instance) /
sum(node_memory_MemTotal_bytes) by (instance)) < 0.5
>    for: 30m
>    labels:
>      severity: notify
>    annotations:
>      summary: Too much unused CPU and memory
>      description: Less than 50% of CPU and 50% of memory is used on at
least one node
```

We're adding a new alert called `TooMuchCPUAndMemory`. It is a combination of the previous two alerts. It will fire only if both CPU and memory usage are below fifty percent. That way we'll avoid sending false positives and we will not be tempted to de-scale the cluster only because one of the resource reservations (CPU or memory) is too low, while the other might be high.

All that's left, before we move into the next subject (or metric type), is to upgrade Prometheus' Chart and confirm that the new alert is indeed operational.

```
1  helm upgrade -i prometheus \
2    stable/prometheus \
3    --namespace metrics \
4    --version 7.1.3 \
5    --set server.ingress.hosts={$PROM_ADDR} \
6    --set alertmanager.ingress.hosts={$AM_ADDR} \
7    -f mon/prom-values-cpu-memory.yml
8
9  open "http://$PROM_ADDR/alerts"
```

Please refresh the alerts screen if the alert is still not present. In my case (screenshot following), the total of reserved memory and CPU is below fifty percent, and the alert is in the pending state. In your case, that might not be true, and the alert might not have reached its thresholds. Nevertheless, I'll continue explaining my case, where both CPU and memory usage is less than fifty percent of total available.

Thirty minutes later (`for: 30m`), the alert fired. It waited for a while (`30m`) to confirm that the drop in memory and CPU usage is not temporary. Given that I'm running my cluster in AKS, Cluster Autoscaler would remove one of the nodes long before thirty minutes. But, since it is configured to operate with a minimum of three nodes, CA will not perform that action. As a result, I might need to reconsider whether paying for three nodes is a worthwhile investment. If, on the other hand, my cluster would be without Cluster Autoscaler, and assuming that I do not want to waste resources while other clusters might need more, I would need to remove one of the nodes (manually or automatically). If that removal were automatic, the destination would not be Slack, but the API of the tool in charge of removing nodes.

Figure 3-33: Prometheus' alerts screen with one alert in the pending state

Now that we have a few examples of saturation, we covered each of the metrics championed by Google Site Reliability Engineers and almost any other monitoring method. Still, we're not done. There are a few other metrics and alerts I'd like to explore. They might not fall into any of the discussed categories, yet they might prove to be very useful.

# Alerting on unschedulable or failed pods

Knowing whether our applications are having trouble to respond fast to requests, whether they are being bombed with more requests than they could handle, whether they produce too many errors, and whether they are saturated, is of no use if they are not even running. Even if our alerts detect that something is wrong by notifying us that there are too many errors or that response times are slow due to an insufficient number of replicas, we should still be informed if, for example, one, or even all replicas failed to run. In the best case scenario, such a notification would provide additional info about the cause of an issue. In the much worse situation, we might find out that one of the replicas of the DB is not running. That would not necessarily slow it down nor it would produce any errors but would put us in a situation where data could not be replicated (additional replicas are not running) and we might face a total loss of its state if the last standing replica fails as well.

There are many reasons why an application would fail to run. There might not be enough unreserved resources in the cluster. Cluster Autoscaler will deal with that problem if we have it. But, there are many other potential issues. Maybe the image of the new release is not available in the registry. Or, perhaps the Pods are requesting PersistentVolumes that cannot be claimed. As you might have guessed, the list of the things that might cause our Pods to fail, be unschedulable, or in an unknown state, is almost infinite.

We cannot address all of the causes of problems with Pods individually. However, we can be notified if the phase of one or more Pods is `Failed`, `Unknown`, or `Pending`. Over time, we might extend our self-healing scripts to address some of the specific causes of those statuses. For now, our best first step is to be notified if a Pod is in one of those phases for a prolonged period of time (for example, fifteen minutes). Alerting as soon as the status of a Pod indicates a problem would be silly because that would generate too many false positives. We should get an alert and choose how to act only after waiting for a while, thus giving Kubernetes time to fix an issue. We should perform some reactive actions only if Kubernetes fails to remedy the situation.

Over time, we'll notice some patterns in the alerts we're receiving. When we do, alerts should be converted into automated responses that will remedy selected issues without our involvement. We already explored some of the low hanging fruits through HorizontalPodAutoscaler and Cluster Autoscaler. For now, we'll focus on receiving alerts for all other cases, and failed and unschedulable Pods are a few of those. Later on, we might explore how to automate responses. But, that moment is not now, so we'll move forward with yet another alert that will result in a notification to Slack.

Let's open Prometheus' graph screen.

```
1  open "http://$PROM_ADDR/graph"
```

Please type the expression that follows and click the **Execute** button.

```
1  kube_pod_status_phase
```

The output shows us each of the Pods in the cluster. If you take a closer look, you'll notice that there are five results for each Pod, one for each of the five possible phases. If you focus on the `phase` field, you'll see that there is an entry for `Failed`, `Pending`, `Running`, `Succeeded`, and `Unknown`. So, each Pod has five results, but only one has the value 1, while the values of the other four are all set to 0.

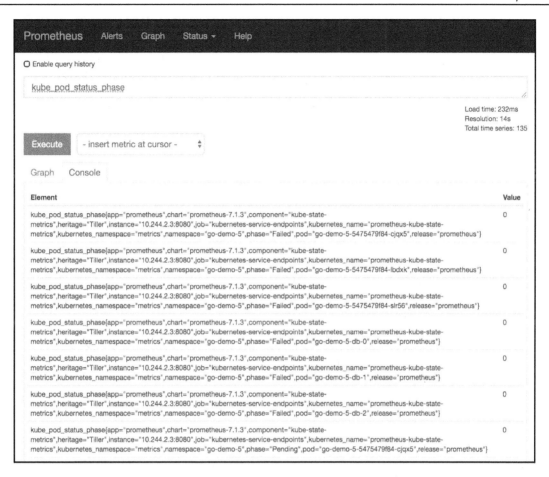

Figure 3-34: Prometheus' console view with the phases of the Pods

For now, our interest lies primarily with alerts, and they should, in most cases, be generic and not related to a specific node, an application, a replica, or some other type of resources. Only when we are alerted that there is an issue, should we start digging deeper and look for more granular data. With that in mind, we'll rewrite our expression to retrieve the number of Pods in each of the phases.

Please type the expression that follows and click the **Execute** button.

```
1  sum(
2    kube_pod_status_phase
3  )
4  by (phase)
```

The output should show that all the Pods are in the Running phase. In my case, there are twenty-seven running Pods and none in any of the other phases.

Now, we should not really care about healthy Pods. They are running, and there's nothing we should do about that. Instead, we should focus on those that are problematic. So, we might just as well rewrite the previous expression to retrieve the sum only of those that are in the Failed, Unknown, or Pending phase.

Please type the expression that follows and click the **Execute** button.

```
1  sum(
2    kube_pod_status_phase{
3      phase=~"Failed|Unknown|Pending"
4    }
5  )
6  by (phase)
```

As expected, unless you messed up something, the values of the output are all set to 0.

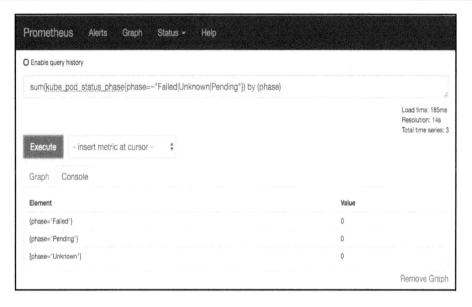

Figure 3-35: Prometheus' console view with the sum of the Pods in Failed, Unknown, or Pending phases

So far, there are no Pods we should worry about. We'll change that by creating one that will intentionally fail, by using an image that apparently does not exist.

```
1  kubectl run problem \
2      --image i-do-not-exist \
3      --restart=Never
```

As we can see from the output, the `pod/problem` was `created`. If we created it through a script (for example, CI/CD pipeline), we'd think that everything is OK. Even if we'd follow it with `kubectl rollout status`, we would only ensure that it started working, not that it continues working.

But, since we did not create that Pod through a CI/CD pipeline, but manually, we can just as well list all the Pods in the `default` Namespace.

```
1  kubectl get pods
```

The output is as follows.

```
NAME      READY STATUS       RESTARTS AGE
problem 0/1    ErrImagePull 0          27s
```

We'll imagine that we have only short-term memory and that we already forgot that the `image` is set to `i-do-not-exist`. What can be the issue? Well, the first step would be to describe the Pod.

```
1  kubectl describe pod problem
```

The output, limited to the messages of the `Events` section, is as follows.

```
...
Events:
...  Message
...  -------
...  Successfully assigned default/problem to aks-nodepool1-29770171-2
...  Back-off pulling image "i-do-not-exist"
...  Error: ImagePullBackOff
...  pulling image "i-do-not-exist"
...  Failed to pull image "i-do-not-exist": rpc error: code = Unknown desc
= Error response from daemon: repository i-do-not-exist not found: does not
exist or no pull access
 Warning  Failed    8s (x3 over 46s)   kubelet, aks-nodepool1-29770171-2
Error: ErrImagePull
```

The problem is clearly manifested through the `Back-off pulling image "i-do-not-exist"` message. Further down, we can see the message from the container server stating that `it failed to pull image "i-do-not-exist"`.

Of course, we knew in advance that will be the result, but something similar could happen without us noticing that there is an issue. The cause could be a failure to pull the image, or one of the myriads of others. Nevertheless, we are not supposed to sit in front of a terminal, listing and describing Pods and other types of resources. Instead, we should receive an alert that Kubernetes failed to run a Pod, and only after that, we should start digging for the cause of the issue. So, let's create one more alert that will notify us when Pods fail and do not recuperate.

Like many times before, we'll take a look at the differences between the old and the new definition of Prometheus' Chart values.

```
1  diff mon/prom-values-errors.yml \
2      mon/prom-values-phase.yml
```

The output is as follows.

```
136a137,146
> - name: pods
>   rules:
>   - alert: ProblematicPods
>     expr: sum(kube_pod_status_phase{phase=~"Failed|Unknown|Pending"}) by
(phase) > 0
>     for: 1m
>     labels:
>       severity: notify
>     annotations:
>       summary: At least one Pod could not run
>       description: At least one Pod is in a problematic phase
```

We defined a new group of alerts called `pod`. Inside it, we have an `alert` named `ProblematicPods` that will fire if there are one or more Pods with the `Failed`, `Unknown`, or `Pending` phase for more than one minute (`1m`). I intentionally set it to very low `for` duration so that we can test it easily. Later on, we'll switch to fifteen minutes interval that will be more than enough to allow Kubernetes to remedy the issue before we get a notification that will send us into the panic mode.

Let's update Prometheus' Chart with the updated values.

```
1  helm upgrade -i prometheus \
2      stable/prometheus \
3      --namespace metrics \
4      --version 7.1.3 \
5      --set server.ingress.hosts={$PROM_ADDR} \
6      --set alertmanager.ingress.hosts={$AM_ADDR} \
7      -f mon/prom-values-phase.yml
```

Since we did not yet fix the issue with the `problem` Pod, we should see a new notification in Slack soon. Let's confirm that.

```
1  open "https://devops20.slack.com/messages/CD8QJA8DS/"
```

If your notification did not yet arrive, please wait for a few moments.

We got the message stating that `at least one Pod could not run.`

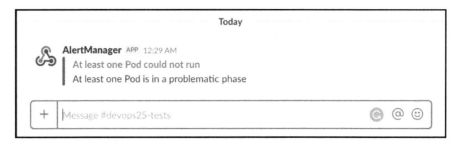

Figure 3-36: Slack with an alert message

Now that we received a notification that there is a problem with one of the Pods, we should go to Prometheus, dig through data until we find the cause of the issue, and fix it. But, since we already know what the problem is (we created it intentionally), we'll skip all that, and remove the faulty Pod, before we move onto the next subject.

```
1  kubectl delete pod problem
```

# Upgrading old Pods

Our primary goal should be to prevent issues from happening by being proactive. In cases when we cannot predict that a problem is about to materialize, we must, at least, be quick with our reactive actions that mitigate the issues after they occur. Still, there is a third category that can only loosely be characterized as being proactive. We should keep our system clean and up-to-date.

Among many things we could do to keep the system up-to-date, is to make sure that our software is relatively recent (patched, updated, and so on). A reasonable rule could be to try to renew software after ninety days, if not earlier. That does not mean that everything we run in our cluster should be newer than ninety days, but that it might be a good starting point. Further on, we might create finer policies that would allow some kinds of applications (usually third-party) to live up to, let's say, half a year without being upgraded. Others, especially software we're actively developing, will probably be upgraded much more frequently. Nevertheless, our starting point is to detect all the applications that were not upgraded in ninety days or more.

Just as in almost all other exercises in this chapter, we'll start by opening Prometheus' graph screen, and explore the metrics that might help us reach our goal.

```
1  open "http://$PROM_ADDR/graph"
```

If we inspect the available metrics, we'll see that there is `kube_pod_start_time`. Its name provides a clear indication of its purpose. It provides the Unix timestamp that represents the start time of each Pod in the form of a Gauge. Let's see it in action.

Please type the expression that follows and click the **Execute** button.

```
1   kube_pod_start_time
```

Those values alone are of no use, and there's no point in teaching you how to calculate the human date from those values. What matters, is the difference between now and those timestamps.

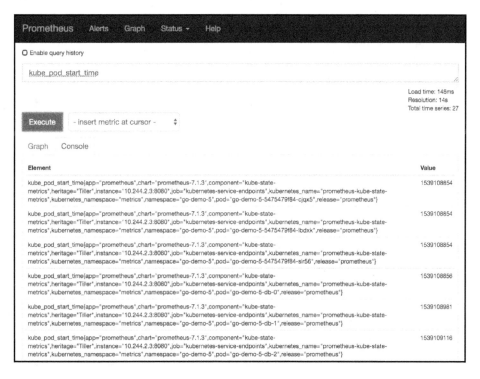

Figure 3-37: Prometheus' console view with the start time of the Pods

We can use Prometheus' `time()` function to return the number of seconds since January 1, 1970 UTC (or Unix timestamp).

Please type the expression that follows and click the **Execute** button.

```
1   time()
```

Just as with the `kube_pod_start_time`, we got a long number that represents seconds since 1970. The only noticeable difference, besides the value, is that there is only one entry, while with `kube_pod_start_time` we got a result for each Pod in the cluster.

Now, let's combine the two metrics in an attempt to retrieve the age of each of the Pods.

Please type the expression that follows and click the **Execute** button.

```
1  time() -
2  kube_pod_start_time
```

The results are this time much smaller numbers representing the seconds between now and creation of each of the Pods. In my case (screenshot following), the first Pod (one of the go-demo-5 replicas), is slightly over six thousand seconds old. That would be around a hundred minutes (6096 / 60), or less than two hours (100 min / 60 min = 1.666 h).

Figure 3-38: Prometheus' console view with the time passed since the creation of the Pods

Since there are probably no Pods older than our target of ninety days, we'll lower it temporarily to a minute (sixty seconds).

Please type the expression that follows and click the **Execute** button.

```
1  (
2    time() -
3    kube_pod_start_time{
```

```
4        namespace!="kube-system"
5    }
6  ) > 60
```

In my case, all the Pods are older than a minute (as are probably yours as well). We confirmed that it works so we can increase the threshold to ninety days. To get to ninety days, we should multiply the threshold with sixty to get minutes, with another sixty to get hours, with twenty-four to get days, and, finally, with ninety. The formula would be `60 * 60 * 24 * 90`. We could use the final value of `7776000`, but that would make the query harder to decipher. I prefer using the formula instead.

Please type the expression that follows and click the **Execute** button.

```
1  (
2    time() -
3    kube_pod_start_time{
4        namespace!="kube-system"
5    }
6  ) >
7  (60 * 60 * 24 * 90)
```

It should come as no surprise that there are (probably) no results. If you created a new cluster for this chapter, you'd need to be the slowest reader on earth if it took you ninety days to get here. This might be the longest chapter I've written so far, but it's still not worth ninety days of reading.

Now that we know which expression to use, we can add one more alert to our setup.

```
1  diff mon/prom-values-phase.yml \
2      mon/prom-values-old-pods.yml
```

The output is as follows.

```
146a147,154
> - alert: OldPods
>   expr: (time() - kube_pod_start_time{namespace!="kube-system"}) > 60
>   labels:
>     severity: notify
>     frequency: low
>   annotations:
>     summary: Old Pods
>     description: At least one Pod has not been updated to more than 90
days
```

We can see that the difference between the old and the new values is in the `OldPods` alert. It contains the same expression we used a few moments ago.

We kept the low threshold of 60 seconds so that we can see the alert in action. Later on, we'll increase that value to ninety days.

There was no need to specify `for` duration. The alert should fire the moment the age of one of the Pods reaches three months (give or take).

Let's upgrade our Prometheus' Chart with the updated values and open the Slack channel where we should see the new message.

```
1   helm upgrade -i prometheus \
2       stable/prometheus \
3       --namespace metrics \
4       --version 7.1.3 \
5       --set server.ingress.hosts={$PROM_ADDR} \
6       --set alertmanager.ingress.hosts={$AM_ADDR} \
7       -f mon/prom-values-old-pods.yml
8
9   open "https://devops20.slack.com/messages/CD8QJA8DS/"
```

All that's left is to wait for a few moments until the new message arrives. It should contain the title *Old Pods* and the text stating that *At least one Pod has not been updated to more than 90 days*.

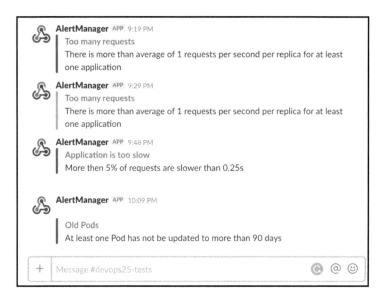

Figure 3-39: Slack with multiple fired and resolved alert messages

Such a generic alert might not work for all your use-cases. But, I'm sure that you'll be able to split it into multiple alerts based on Namespaces, names, or something similar.

Now that we have a mechanism to receive notifications when our Pods are too old and might require upgrades, we'll jump into the next topic and explore how to retrieve memory and CPU used by our containers.

# Measuring containers memory and CPU usage

If you are familiar with Kubernetes, you understand the importance of defining resource requests and limits. Since we already explored `kubectl top pods` command, you might have set the requested resources to match the current usage, and you might have defined the limits as being above the requests. That approach might work on the first day. But, with time, those numbers will change and we will not be able to get the full picture through `kubectl top pods`. We need to know how much memory and CPU containers use when on their peak loads, and how much when they are under less stress. We should observe those metrics over time, and adjust periodically.

Even if we do somehow manage to guess how much memory and CPU a container needs, those numbers might change from one release to another. Maybe we introduced a feature that requires more memory or CPU?

What we need is to observe resource usage over time and to make sure that it does not change with new releases or with increased (or decreased) number of users. For now, we'll focus on the former case and explore how to see how much memory and CPU our containers used over time.

As usual, we'll start by opening the Prometheus' graph screen.

```
1  open "http://$PROM_ADDR/graph"
```

We can retrieve container memory usage through the `container_memory_usage_bytes`.

Please type the expression that follows, press the **Execute** button, and switch to the *Graph* screen.

```
1  container_memory_usage_bytes
```

If you take a closer look at the top usage, you'll probably end up confused. It seems that some containers are using way more than the expected amount of memory.

The truth is that some of the `container_memory_usage_bytes` records contain cumulative values, and we should exclude them so that only memory usage of individual containers is retrieved. We can do that by retrieving only the records that have a value in the `container_name` field.

Please type the expression that follows, and press the **Execute** button.

```
1  container_memory_usage_bytes{
2    container_name!=""
3  }
```

Now the result makes much more sense. It reflects memory usage of the containers running inside our cluster.

We'll get to alerts based on container resources a bit later. For now, we'll imagine that we'd like to check memory usage of a specific container (for example, `prometheus-server`). Since we already know that one of the available labels is `container_name`, retrieving the data we need should be straightforward.

Please type the expression that follows, and press the **Execute** button.

```
1  container_memory_usage_bytes{
2    container_name="prometheus-server"
3  }
```

We can see the oscillations in memory usage of the container over the last hour. Normally, we'd be interested in a longer period like a day or a week. We can accomplish that by clicking **-** and **+** buttons above the graph, or by typing the value directly in the field between them (for example, `1w`). However, changing the duration might not help much since we haven't been running the cluster for too long. We might not be able to squeeze more data than a few hours unless you are a slow reader.

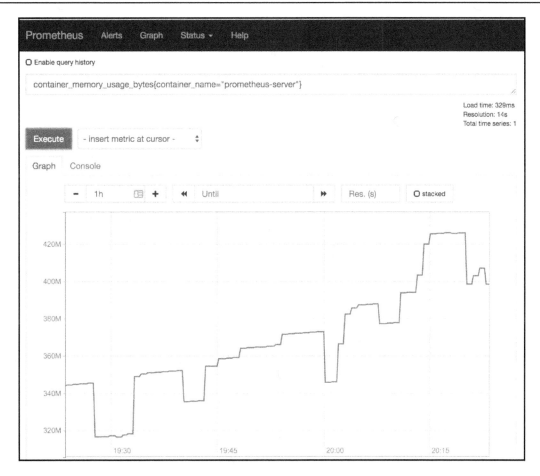

Figure 3-40: Prometheus' graph screen with container memory usage limited to prometheus-server

Similarly, we should be able to retrieve CPU usage of a container as well. In that case, the metric we're looking for could be `container_cpu_usage_seconds_total`. However, unlike `container_memory_usage_bytes` that is a gauge, `container_cpu_usage_seconds_total` is a counter, and we'll have to combine `sum` and `rate` to get the changes in values over time.

Please type the expression that follows, and press the **Execute** button.

```
1  sum(rate(
2    container_cpu_usage_seconds_total{
3      container_name="prometheus-server"
4    }[5m]
5  ))
6  by (pod_name)
```

The query shows summed CPU seconds rate over five minutes intervals. We added `by (pod_name)` to the mix so that we can distinguish different Pods and see when one was created, and the other was destroyed.

Figure 3-41: Prometheus' graph screen with the rate of container CPU usage limited to prometheus-server

If that were a "real world" situation, our next step would be to compare actual resource usage with what we defined as Prometheus `resources`. If what we defined differs considerably compared to what it actually is, we should probably update our Pod definition (the `resources` section).

The problem is that using "real" resource usage to define Kubernetes `resources` better will provide valid values only temporarily. Over time, our resource usage will change. The load might increase, new features might be more resource-hungry, and so on. No matter the reasons, the critical thing to note is that everything is dynamic and that there is no reason to think otherwise for resources. In that spirit, our next challenge is to figure out how to get a notification when the actual resource usage differs too much from what we defined in container `resources`.

# Comparing actual resource usage with defined requests

If we define container `resources` inside a Pod and without relying on actual usage, we are just guessing how much memory and CPU we expect a container to use. I'm sure that you already know why guessing, in the software industry, is a terrible idea, so I'll focus on Kubernetes aspects only.

Kubernetes treats Pods with containers that do not have specified resources as the **BestEffort Quality of Service (QoS)**. As a result, if it ever runs out of memory or CPU to serve all the Pods, those are the first to be forcefully removed to leave space for others. If such Pods are short lived as, for example, those used as one-shot agents for continuous delivery processes, BestEffort QoS is not a bad idea. But, when our applications are long-lived, BestEffort QoS should be unacceptable. That means that in most cases, we do have to define container `resources`.

If container `resources` are (almost always) a must, we need to know which values to put. I often see teams that merely guess. "It's a database; therefore it needs a lot of RAM" and "it's only an API, it shouldn't need much" are only a few of the sentences I hear a lot. Those guesstimates are often the result of not being able to measure actual usage. When something would blow up, those teams would just double the allocated memory and CPU. Problem solved!

I never understood why would anyone invent how much memory and CPU an application needs. Even without any "fancy" tools, we always had `top` command in Linux. We could know how much our application uses. Over time, better tools were developed, and all we had to do is Google "how to measure memory and CPU of my applications."

You already saw `kubectl top pods` in action when you need current data, and you are becoming familiar with the power of Prometheus to give you much more. You do not have an excuse to guesstimate.

But, why do we care about resource usage compared with requested resources? Besides the fact that might reveal a potential problem (for example, memory leak), inaccurate resource requests and limits prevent Kubernetes from doing its job efficiently. If, for example, we define memory request to 1 GB RAM, that's how much Kubernetes will remove from allocatable memory. If a node has 2 GB of allocatable RAM, only two such containers could run there, even if each uses only 50 MB RAM. Our nodes would use only a fraction of allocatable memory and, if we have Cluster Autoscaler, new nodes would be added even if the old ones still have plenty of unused memory.

Even though now we know how to get actual memory usage, it would be a waste of time to start every day by comparing YAML files with the results in Prometheus. Instead, we'll create yet another alert that will send us a notification whenever the requested memory and CPU differs too much from the actual usage. That's our next mission.

First, we'll reopen Prometheus' graph screen.

```
1 open "http://$PROM_ADDR/graph"
```

We already know how to get memory usage through `container_memory_usage_bytes`, so we'll jump straight into retrieving requested memory. If we can combine the two, we'll get the discrepancy between the requested and the actual memory usage.

The metric we're looking for is `kube_pod_container_resource_requests_memory_bytes`, so let's take it for a spin with, let's say, `prometheus-server` Pod.

Please type the expression that follows, press the **Execute** button, and switch to the *Graph* tab.

```
1 kube_pod_container_resource_requests_memory_bytes{
2   container="prometheus-server"
3 }
```

We can see from the result that we requested 500 MB RAM for the `prometheus-server` container.

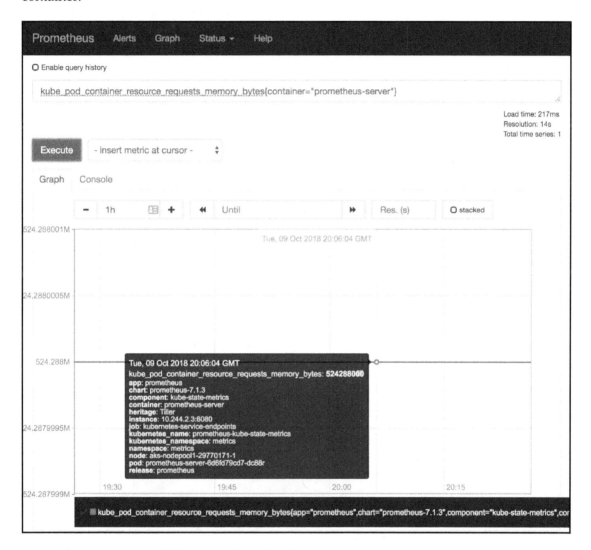

Figure 3-42: Prometheus' graph screen with container requested memory limited to prometheus-server

The problem is that the `kube_pod_container_resource_requests_memory_bytes` metric has, among others, `pod` label while, on the other hand, `container_memory_usage_bytes` uses `pod_name`. If we are to combine the two, we need to transform the label `pod` into `pod_name`. Fortunately, this is not the first time we're facing that problem, and we already know that the solution is to use the `label_join` function that will create a new label based on one or more of the existing labels.

Please type the expression that follows, and press the **Execute** button.

```
1   sum(label_join(
2     container_memory_usage_bytes{
3       container_name="prometheus-server"
4     },
5     "pod",
6     ",",
7     "pod_name"
8   ))
9   by (pod)
```

This time, not only that we added a new label to the metric, but we also grouped the results by that very same label (`by (pod)`).

Figure 3-43: Prometheus' graph screen with container memory usage limited to prometheus-server and grouped by the pod label extracted from pod_name

Now we can combine the two metrics and find out the discrepancy between the requested and the actual memory usage.

Please type the expression that follows, and press the **Execute** button.

```
 1   sum(label_join(
 2     container_memory_usage_bytes{
 3       container_name="prometheus-server"
 4     },
 5     "pod",
 6     ",",
 7     "pod_name"
 8   ))
 9   by (pod) /
10   sum(
11     kube_pod_container_resource_requests_memory_bytes{
12       container="prometheus-server"
13     }
14   )
15   by (pod)
```

In my case (screenshot following), the discrepancy was becoming gradually smaller. It started somewhere around sixty percent, and now it's approximately seventy-five percent. Such a difference is not big enough for us to take any corrective action.

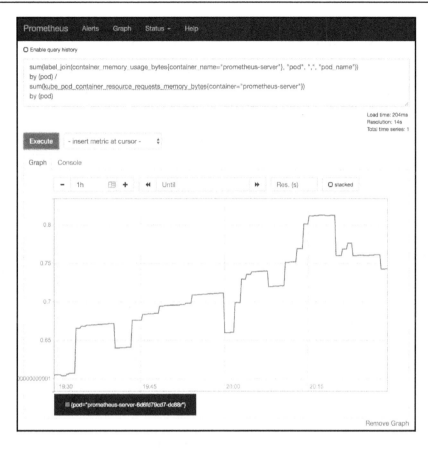

Figure 3-44: Prometheus' graph screen with the percentage of container memory usage based on requested memory

Now that we saw how to get the difference between reserved and actual memory usage for a single container, we should probably make the expression more general and get all the containers in the cluster. However, all might be a bit too much. We probably do not want to mess with the Pods running in the `kube-system` Namespace. They are likely pre-installed in the cluster, and we might want to leave them as they are, at least for now. So, we'll exclude them from the query.

Please type the expression that follows, and press the **Execute** button.

```
 1  sum(label_join(
 2    container_memory_usage_bytes{
 3      namespace!="kube-system"
 4    },
 5    "pod",
 6    ",",
 7    "pod_name"
 8  ))
 9  by (pod) /
10  sum(
11    kube_pod_container_resource_requests_memory_bytes{
12      namespace!="kube-system"
13    }
14  )
15  by (pod)
```

The result should be the list of percentages of a difference between requested and actual memory, with the Pods in the `kube-system` excluded.

In my case, there are quite a few containers that use quite a lot more memory than what we requested. The main culprit is `prometheus-alertmanager` which uses more than three times more memory than what we requested. That can be due to several reasons. Maybe we requested too little memory, or perhaps it contains containers that do not have `requests` specified. In either case, we should probably redefine requests not only for the Alertmanager but also for all the other Pods that use more than, let's say 50% more memory than requested.

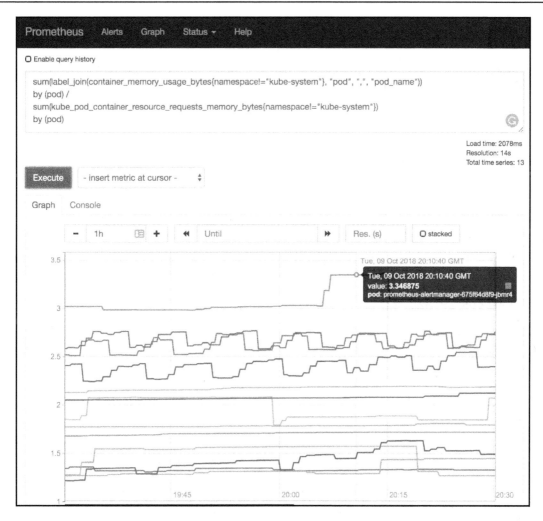

Figure 3-45: Prometheus' graph screen with the percentage of container memory usage based on requested memory and with those from the kube-system Namespace excluded

We are about to define a new alert that will deal with cases when requested memory is much more or much less than the actual usage. But, before we do that, we should discuss the conditions we should use. One alert could fire when actual memory usage is over 150% of the requested memory for over an hour. That would remove false positives caused by a temporary spike in memory usage (that's why we have limits as well). The other alert could deal with the situation when memory usage is more than 50% below the requested amount. But, in case of that alert, we might add another condition.

Some applications are too small, and we might never be able to fine-tune their requests. We can exclude those cases by adding another condition that will ignore the Pods with only 5 MB reserved RAM, or less.

Finally, this alert might not need to fire as frequently as the previous one. We should know relatively quickly if our application uses more memory than we intended to give since that can be a sign of a memory leak, significantly increased traffic, or some other, potentially dangerous situation. But, if memory uses much less than intended, the issue is not as critical. We should correct it, but there is no need to act urgently. Therefore, we'll set the duration of the latter alert to six hours.

Now that we set a few rules we should follow, we can take a look at yet another differences between the old and the new set of Chart's values.

```
1  diff mon/prom-values-old-pods.yml \
2      mon/prom-values-req-mem.yml
```

The output is as follows.

```
148c148
<    expr: (time() - kube_pod_start_time{namespace!="kube-system"}) > 60
---
>    expr: (time() - kube_pod_start_time{namespace!="kube-system"}) > (60 *
60 * 24 * 90)
154a155,172
> - alert: ReservedMemTooLow
>    expr: sum(label_join(container_memory_usage_bytes{namespace!="kube-
system", namespace!="ingress-nginx"}, "pod", ",", "pod_name")) by (pod) /
  sum(kube_pod_container_resource_requests_memory_bytes{namespace!="kube-
system"}) by (pod) > 1.5
>    for: 1m
>    labels:
>      severity: notify
>      frequency: low
>    annotations:
>      summary: Reserved memory is too low
>      description: At least one Pod uses much more memory than it reserved
> - alert: ReservedMemTooHigh
```

```
>    expr: sum(label_join(container_memory_usage_bytes{namespace!="kube-
system", namespace!="ingress-nginx"}, "pod", ",", "pod_name")) by (pod) /
sum(kube_pod_container_resource_requests_memory_bytes{namespace!="kube-
system"}) by (pod) < 0.5 and
sum(kube_pod_container_resource_requests_memory_bytes{namespace!="kube-
system"}) by (pod) > 5.25e+06
>    for: 6m
>    labels:
>      severity: notify
>      frequency: low
>    annotations:
>      summary: Reserved memory is too high
>      description: At least one Pod uses much less memory than it reserved
```

First, we set the threshold of the `OldPods` alert back to its intended value of ninety days (`60 * 60 * 24 * 90`). That way we'll stop it from firing alerts only for test purposes.

Next, we defined a new alert called `ReservedMemTooLow`. It will fire if used memory is more than `1.5` times bigger than the requested memory. The duration for the pending state of the alert is set to `1m`, only so that we can see the outcome without waiting for the full hour. Later on, we'll restore it back to `1h`.

The `ReservedMemTooHigh` alert is (partly) similar to the previous one, except that it has the condition that will cause the alert to fire if the difference between the actual and the requested memory is less than `0.5` and if that continues being the case for over `6m` (we'll change it later to `6h`). The second part of the expression is new. It requires that all the containers in a Pod have more than 5 MB of the requested memory (`5.25e+06`). Through that second statement (separated with `and`), we're saving ourselves from dealing with too small applications. If it requires less than 5 MB RAM, we should ignore it and, probably, congratulate the team behind it for making it that efficient.

Now, let's upgrade our Prometheus' Chart with the updated values and open the graph screen.

```
1  helm upgrade -i prometheus \
2    stable/prometheus \
3    --namespace metrics \
4    --version 7.1.3 \
5    --set server.ingress.hosts={$PROM_ADDR} \
6    --set alertmanager.ingress.hosts={$AM_ADDR} \
7    -f mon/prom-values-req-mem.yml
```

We won't wait until the alerts start firing. Instead, we'll try to accomplish similar objectives, but with CPU.

There's probably no need to go through the process of explaining the expressions we'll use. We'll jump straight into the CPU-based alerts by exploring the difference between the old and the new set of Chart's values.

```
1   diff mon/prom-values-req-mem.yml \
2       mon/prom-values-req-cpu.yml
```

The output is as follows.

```
157c157
<   for: 1m
---
>   for: 1h
166c166
<   for: 6m
---
>   for: 6h
172a173,190
> - alert: ReservedCPUTooLow
>   expr:
sum(label_join(rate(container_cpu_usage_seconds_total{namespace!="kube-
system", namespace!="ingress-nginx", pod_name!=""}[5m]), "pod", ",",
"pod_name")) by (pod) /
sum(kube_pod_container_resource_requests_cpu_cores{namespace!="kube-
system"}) by (pod) > 1.5
>   for: 1m
>   labels:
>     severity: notify
>     frequency: low
>   annotations:
>     summary: Reserved CPU is too low
>     description: At least one Pod uses much more CPU than it reserved
> - alert: ReservedCPUTooHigh
>   expr:
sum(label_join(rate(container_cpu_usage_seconds_total{namespace!="kube-
system", pod_name!=""}[5m]), "pod", ",", "pod_name")) by (pod) /
sum(kube_pod_container_resource_requests_cpu_cores{namespace!="kube-
system"}) by (pod) < 0.5 and
sum(kube_pod_container_resource_requests_cpu_cores{namespace!="kube-
system"}) by (pod) > 0.005
>   for: 6m
>   labels:
>     severity: notify
>     frequency: low
>   annotations:
>     summary: Reserved CPU is too high
>     description: At least one Pod uses much less CPU than it reserved
```

The first two sets of differences are defining more sensible thresholds for `ReservedMemTooLow` and `ReservedMemTooHigh` alerts we explored previously. Further down, we can see the two new alerts.

The `ReservedCPUTooLow` alert will fire if CPU usage is more than 1.5 times bigger than requested. Similarly, the `ReservedCPUTooHigh` alert will fire only if CPU usage is less than half of the requested and if we requested more than 5 CPU milliseconds. Getting notifications because 5 MB RAM is too much would be a waste of time.

Both alerts are set to fire if the issues persist for a short period (`1m` and `6m`) so that we can see them in action without having to wait for too long.

Now, let's upgrade our Prometheus' Chart with the updated values.

```
1  helm upgrade -i prometheus \
2    stable/prometheus \
3    --namespace metrics \
4    --version 7.1.3 \
5    --set server.ingress.hosts={$PROM_ADDR} \
6    --set alertmanager.ingress.hosts={$AM_ADDR} \
7    -f mon/prom-values-req-cpu.yml
```

I'll leave it to you to check whether any of the alerts fire and whether they are forwarded from Alertmanager to Slack. You should know how to do that by now.

Next, we'll move to the last alert in this chapter.

# Comparing actual resource usage with defined limits

Knowing when a container uses too much or too few resources compared to requests helps us be more precise with resource definitions and, ultimately, help Kubernetes make better decisions where to schedule our Pods. In most cases, having too big of a discrepancy between requested and actual resource usage will not result in malfunctioning. Instead, it is more likely to result in an unbalanced distribution of Pods or in having more nodes than we need. Limits, on the other hand, are a different story.

If resource usage of our containers enveloped as Pods reaches the specified `limits`, Kubernetes might kill those containers if there's not enough memory for all. It does that as a way to protect the integrity of the rest of the system. Killed Pods are not a permanent problem since Kubernetes will almost immediately reschedule them if there is enough capacity.

If we do use Cluster Autoscaling, even if there isn't enough capacity, new nodes will be added as soon as it detects that some Pods are in the pending state (unschedulable). So, the world is not likely to end if resource usage goes over the limits.

Nevertheless, killing and rescheduling Pods can result in downtime. There are, apparently, worse scenarios that might happen. But we won't go into them. Instead, we'll assume that we should be aware that a Pod is about to reach its limits and that we might want to investigate what's going on and we that might need to take some corrective measures. Maybe the latest release introduced a memory leak? Or perhaps the load increased beyond what we expected and tested and that results in increased memory usage. The cause of using memory that is close to the limit is not the focus right now. Detecting that we are reaching the limit is.

First, we'll go back to Prometheus' graph screen.

```
1  open "http://$PROM_ADDR/graph"
```

We already know that we can get actual memory usage through the `container_memory_usage_bytes` metric. Since we already explored how to get requested memory, we can guess that limits are similar. They indeed are, and they can be retrieved through the `kube_pod_container_resource_limits_memory_bytes`. Since one of the metrics is the same as before, and the other is very similar, we'll jump straight into executing the full query.

Please type the expression that follows, press the **Execute** button, and switch to the *Graph* tab.

```
1  sum(label_join(
2    container_memory_usage_bytes{
3      namespace!="kube-system"
4    },
5    "pod",
6    ",",
7    "pod_name"
8  ))
9  by (pod) /
10 sum(
11   kube_pod_container_resource_limits_memory_bytes{
12     namespace!="kube-system"
13   }
14 )
15 by (pod)
```

In my case (screenshot following), we can see that quite a few Pods use more memory than what is defined as their limits.

Fortunately, I do have spare capacity in my cluster, and there is no imminent need for Kubernetes to kill any of the Pods. Moreover, the issue might not be in Pods using more than what is set as their limits, but that not all containers in those Pods have the limits set. In either case, I should probably update the definition of those Pods/containers and make sure that their limits are above their average usage over a few days or even weeks.

Figure 3-46: Prometheus' graph screen with the percentage of container memory usage based on memory limits and with those from the kube-system Namespace excluded

Next, we'll go through the drill of exploring the difference between the old and the new version of the values.

```
1  diff mon/prom-values-req-cpu.yml \
2      mon/prom-values-limit-mem.yml
```

The output is as follows.

```
175c175
<    for: 1m
---
>    for: 1h
184c184
<    for: 6m
---
>    for: 6h
190a191,199
> - alert: MemoryAtTheLimit
>   expr: sum(label_join(container_memory_usage_bytes{namespace!="kube-
system"}, "pod", ",", "pod_name")) by (pod) /
sum(kube_pod_container_resource_limits_memory_bytes{namespace!="kube-
system"}) by (pod) > 0.8
>   for: 1h
>   labels:
>     severity: notify
>     frequency: low
>   annotations:
>     summary: Memory usage is almost at the limit
>     description: At least one Pod uses memory that is close it its limit
```

Apart from restoring sensible thresholds for the alerts we used before, we defined a new alert called `MemoryAtTheLimit`. It will fire if the actual usage is over eighty percent (`0.8`) of the limit for more than one hour (`1h`).

Next is the upgrade of our Prometheus Chart.

```
1  helm upgrade -i prometheus \
2      stable/prometheus \
3      --namespace metrics \
4      --version 7.1.3 \
5      --set server.ingress.hosts={$PROM_ADDR} \
6      --set alertmanager.ingress.hosts={$AM_ADDR} \
7      -f mon/prom-values-limit-mem.yml
```

Finally, we can open the Prometheus' alerts screen and confirm that the new alert was indeed added to the mix.

```
1  open "http://$PROM_ADDR/alerts"
```

We won't go through the drill of creating a similar alert for CPU. You should know how to do that yourself.

# What now?

We explored quite a few Prometheus metrics, expressions, and alerts. We saw how to connect Prometheus alerts with Alertmanager and, from there, to forward them to one application to another.

What we did so far is only the tip of the iceberg. If would take too much time (and space) to explore all the metrics and expressions we might use. Nevertheless, I believe that now you know some of the more useful ones and that you'll be able to extend them with those specific to you.

I urge you to send me expressions and alerts you find useful. You know where to find me (*DevOps20* (http://slack.devops20toolkit.com/) Slack, viktor@farcic email, @vfarcic on Twitter, and so on).

For now, I'll leave you to decide whether to move straight into the next chapter, to destroy the entire cluster, or only to remove the resources we installed. If you choose the latter, please use the commands that follow.

```
1   helm delete prometheus --purge
2
3   helm delete go-demo-5 --purge
4
5   kubectl delete ns go-demo-5 metrics
```

Before you leave, you might want to go over the main points of this chapter.

- Prometheus is a database (of sorts) designed to fetch (pull) and store highly dimensional time series data.
- The four key metrics everyone should utilize are latency, traffic, errors, and saturation.

# 4

# Debugging Issues Discovered Through Metrics and Alerts

*When you eliminate the impossible, whatever remains, however improbable, must be the truth.*

*- Spock*

So far, we explored how to gather metrics and how to create alerts that will notify us when there is an issue. We also learned how to query metrics and dig for information we might need when trying to find the cause of a problem. We'll expand on that and try to debug a simulated issue.

Saying that an application does not work correctly should not be enough by itself. We should be much more precise. Our goal is to be able to pinpoint not only which application is malfunctioning, but also which part of it is the culprit. We should be able to blame a specific function, a method, a request path, and so on. The more precise we are in detecting which part of an application is causing a problem, the faster we will find the cause of an issue. As a result, it should be easier and faster to fix the issue through a new release (a hotfix), scaling, or any other means at our disposal.

Let's get going. We'll need a cluster (unless you already have one) before we simulate a problem that needs to be solved.

## Creating a cluster

The `vfarcic/k8s-specs` (`https://github.com/vfarcic/k8s-specs`) repository will continue being our source of Kubernetes definitions we'll use for our examples. We'll make sure that it is up-to-date by pulling the latest version.

All the commands from this chapter are available in the `04-instrument.sh` (https://gist.github.com/vfarcic/851b37be06bb7652e55529fcb28d2c16) Gist. Just as in the previous chapter, it contains not only the commands but also Prometheus' expressions. They are all commented (with #). If you're planning to copy and paste the expressions from the Gist, please exclude the comments. Each expression has `# Prometheus expression` comment on top to help you identify it.

```
1  cd k8s-specs
2
3  git pull
```

Given that we learned how to install a fully operational Prometheus and the rest of the tools from its chart, and that we'll continue using them, I moved it to the Gists. Those that follow are copies of those we used in the previous chapter, with the addition of environment variables PROM_ADDR and AM_ADDR, and the steps for the installation of the **Prometheus Chart**. Please create a cluster that meets (or exceeds) the requirements specified in the Gists that follow, unless you already have a cluster that satisfies them.

- `gke-instrument.sh`: **GKE** with 3 n1-standard-1 worker nodes, **nginx Ingress**, **tiller**, **Prometheus** Chart, and environment variables **LB_IP**, **PROM_ADDR**, and **AM_ADDR** (https://gist.github.com/675f4b3ee2c55ee718cf132e71e04c6e).
- `eks-instrument.sh`: **EKS** with 3 t2.small worker nodes, **nginx Ingress**, **tiller**, **Metrics Server**, **Prometheus** Chart, and environment variables **LB_IP**, **PROM_ADDR**, and **AM_ADDR** (https://gist.github.com/70a14c8f15c7ffa533ea7feb75341545).
- `aks-instrument.sh`: **AKS** with 3 Standard_B2s worker nodes, **nginx Ingress**, and **tiller**, **Prometheus** Chart, and environment variables **LB_IP**, **PROM_ADDR**, and **AM_ADDR** (https://gist.github.com/65a0d5834c9e20ebf1b99225fba0d339).
- `docker-instrument.sh`: **Docker for Desktop** with **2 CPUs, 3 GB RAM, nginx Ingress, tiller, Metrics Server, Prometheus** Chart, and environment variables **LB_IP, PROM_ADDR**, and **AM_ADDR** (https://gist.github.com/1dddcae847e97219ab75f936d93451c2).
- `minikube-instrument.sh`: **minikube** with **2 CPUs, 3 GB RAM, ingress, storage-provisioner, default-storageclass**, and **metrics-server** addons enabled, **tiller, Prometheus** Chart, and environment variables **LB_IP, PROM_ADDR**, and **AM_ADDR** (https://gist.github.com/779fae2ae374cf91a5929070e47bddc8).

Now we're ready to face our first simulated issue that might require debugging.

# Facing a disaster

Let's explore one disaster scenario. Frankly, it's not going to be a real disaster, but it will require us to find a solution to an issue.

We'll start by installing the already familiar `go-demo-5` application.

```
1   GD5_ADDR=go-demo-5.$LB_IP.nip.io
2
3   helm install \
4       https://github.com/vfarcic/go-demo-5/releases/download/
    0.0.1/go-demo-5-0.0.1.tgz \
5       --name go-demo-5 \
6       --namespace go-demo-5 \
7       --set ingress.host=$GD5_ADDR
8
9   kubectl -n go-demo-5 \
10      rollout status \
11      deployment go-demo-5
```

We declared `GD5_ADDR` with the address through which we'll be able to access the application. We used it as `ingress.host` variable when we installed the `go-demo-5` Chart. To be on the safe side, we waited until the app rolled out, and all that's left, from the deployment perspective, is to confirm that it is running by sending an HTTP request.

```
1   curl http://$GD5_ADDR/demo/hello
```

The output is the developer's favorite message `hello, world!`.

Next, we'll simulate an issue by sending twenty slow requests with up to ten seconds duration. That will be our simulation of a problem that might need to be fixed.

```
1   for i in {1..20}; do
2       DELAY=$[ $RANDOM % 10000 ]
3       curl "http://$GD5_ADDR/demo/hello?delay=$DELAY"
4   done
```

Since we already have Prometheus' alerts, we should receive a notification on Slack stating that the application is too slow. However, many readers might be using the same channel for those exercises, and it might not be clear whether the message comes from us. Instead, we'll open Prometheus' alerts screen to confirm that there is a problem. In the "real" setting, you wouldn't be checking Prometheus alerts, but wait for notifications on Slack, or whichever other notifications tool you chose.

```
1   open "http://$PROM_ADDR/alerts"
```

A few moments later (don't forget to refresh the screen), the `AppTooSlow` alert should fire, letting us know that one of our applications is slow and that we should do something to remedy the problem.

True to the promise that each chapter will feature outputs and screenshots from a different Kubernetes flavor, this time it's minikube's turn.

Figure 4-1: One of Prometheus' alerts in the firing state

We'll imagine that we did not generate slow requests intentionally, so we'll try to find out what the issue is. Which application is too slow? What useful information can we pass to the team so that they can fix the problem as soon as possible?

The first logical debugging step is to execute the same expression as the one used by the alert. Please expand the `AppTooSlow` alert and click the link of the expression. You'll be redirected to the graph screen with the expression already pre-populated. Click the **Execute** button, and switch to the *Graph* tab.

We can see, from the graph, that there was a surge in the number of slow requests. The alert was fired because less than ninety-five percent of responses are within 0.25 seconds bucket. Judging from my Graph (screenshot following), zero percent of responses were inside the 0.25 seconds bucket or, in other words, all were slower than that. A moment later, that improved slightly by jumping to only six percent of fast requests.

All in all, we have a situation in which too many requests are getting slow responses, and we should fix that. The main question is how to find out what the cause of that slowness is?

Figure 4-2: The graph with the percentage of requests with fast responses

How about executing different expressions. We can, for example, output the rate of request durations for that `ingress` (application).

Please type the expression that follows, and press the **Execute** button.

```
1   sum(rate(
2       nginx_ingress_controller_request_duration_seconds_sum{
3           ingress="go-demo-5"
4       }[5m]
5   )) /
6   sum(rate(
7       nginx_ingress_controller_request_duration_seconds_count{
8           ingress="go-demo-5"
```

```
 9        }[5m]
10    ))
```

That graph shows us the history of request durations, but it does not get us any closer to revealing the cause of the issue or, to be more precise, to the part of the application that is slow. We could try using other metrics, but they are, more or less, equally generic and are probably not going to get us anywhere. We need more detailed application-specific metrics. We need data that comes from inside the `go-demo-5` app.

# Using instrumentation to provide more detailed metrics

We shouldn't just say that the `go-demo-5` application is slow. That would not provide enough information for us to quickly inspect the code in search of the exact cause of that slowness. We should be able to do better and deduce which part of the application is misbehaving. Can we pinpoint a specific path that produces slow responses? Are all methods equally slow, or the issue is limited only to one? Do we know which function produces slowness? There are many similar questions we should be able to answer in situations like that. But we can't, with the current metrics. They are too generic, and they can usually only tell us that a specific Kubernetes resource is misbehaving. The metrics we're collecting are too broad to answer application-specific questions.

The metrics we explored so far are a combination of exporters and instrumentations. Exporters are in charge of taking existing metrics and converting them into the Prometheus-friendly format. An example would be Node Exporter (`https://github.com/prometheus/node_exporter`) that is taking "standard" Linux metrics and converting them into Prometheus' time-series format. Another example is kube-state-metrics (`https://github.com/kubernetes/kube-state-metrics`) that listens to Kube API server and generates metrics with the state of the resources.

 Instrumented metrics are baked into applications. They are an integral part of the code of our apps, and they are usually exposed through the `/metrics` endpoint.

The easiest way to add metrics to your applications is through one of the Prometheus client libraries. At the time of this writing, Go (`https://github.com/prometheus/client_golang`), Java and Scala (`https://github.com/prometheus/client_java`), Python (`https://github.com/prometheus/client_python`), and Ruby (`https://github.com/prometheus/client_ruby`) libraries are officially provided.

On top of those, the community supports Bash (`https://github.com/aecolley/client_bash`), C++ (`https://github.com/jupp0r/prometheus-cpp`), Common Lisp (`https://github.com/deadtrickster/prometheus.cl`), Elixir (`https://github.com/deadtrickster/prometheus.ex`), Erlang (`https://github.com/deadtrickster/prometheus.erl`), Haskell (`https://github.com/fimad/prometheus-haskell`), Lua for Nginx (`https://github.com/knyar/nginx-lua-prometheus`), Lua for Tarantool (`https://github.com/tarantool/prometheus`), .NET / C# (`https://github.com/andrasm/prometheus-net`), Node.js (`https://github.com/siimon/prom-client`), Perl (`https://metacpan.org/pod/Net::Prometheus`), PHP (`https://github.com/Jimdo/prometheus_client_php`), and Rust (`https://github.com/pingcap/rust-prometheus`). Even if you code in a different language, you can easily provide Prometheus-friendly metrics by outputting results in a text-based exposition format (`https://prometheus.io/docs/instrumenting/exposition_formats/`).

Overhead of collecting metrics should be negligible and, since Prometheus' pulls them periodically, outputting them should have a tiny footprint as well. Even if you choose not to use Prometheus, or to switch to something else, the format is becoming the standard, and your next metrics collector tool is likely to expect the same data.

All in all, there is no excuse not to bake metrics into your applications, and, as you'll see soon, they provide invaluable information that we cannot obtain from outside.

Let's take a look at an example of the instrumented metrics in `go-demo-5`.

```
1  open "https://github.com/vfarcic/go-demo-5/blob/master/main.go"
```

 The application is written in Go. Don't worry if that's not your language of choice. We'll just take a quick look at a few examples as a way to understand the logic behind instrumentation, not the exact implementation.

The first interesting part is as follows.

```
1   ...
2   var (
3     histogram = prometheus.NewHistogramVec(prometheus.HistogramOpts{
4       Subsystem: "http_server",
5       Name:      "resp_time",
6       Help:      "Request response time",
7     }, []string{
8       "service",
9       "code",
10      "method",
11      "path",
12    })
```

```
13  )
14  ...
```

We defined a variable that contains a Prometheus Histogram Vector with a few options. The `Sybsystem` and the `Name` form the base metric `http_server_resp_time`. Since it is a histogram, the final metrics will be created by adding `_bucket`, `_sum`, and `_count` suffixes.

 Please consult *histogram* (`https://prometheus.io/docs/concepts/metric_types/#histogram`) documentation for more info about that Prometheus' metric type.

The last part is a string array (`[]string`) that defines all the labels we'd like to add to the metric. In our case, those labels are `service`, `code`, `method`, and `path`. Labels can be anything we need, just as long as they provide the sufficient information we might require when querying those metrics.

The next point of interest is the `recordMetrics` function.

```
1   ...
2   func recordMetrics(start time.Time, req *http.Request, code int) {
3     duration := time.Since(start)
4     histogram.With(
5       prometheus.Labels{
6         "service": serviceName,
7         "code":    fmt.Sprintf("%d", code),
8         "method":  req.Method,
9         "path":    req.URL.Path,
10      },
11    ).Observe(duration.Seconds())
12  }
13  ...
```

I created that as a helper function that can be called from different locations in the code. It accepts `start` time, the `Request`, and the return `code` as arguments. The function itself calculates `duration` by subtracting the current `time` with the `start` time. That `duration` is used in the `Observe` function and provides the value of the metric. There are also the labels that will help us fine-tune our expressions later on.

Finally, we'll take a look at one of the examples where the `recordMetrics` is invoked.

```
1   ...
2   func HelloServer(w http.ResponseWriter, req *http.Request) {
3     start := time.Now()
4     defer func() { recordMetrics(start, req, http.StatusOK) }()
5     ...
```

```
6  }
7  ...
```

The `HelloServer` function is the one that returns the `hello, world!` response you already saw quite a few times. The details of that function are not important. In this context, the only part that matters is the line `defer func() { recordMetrics(start, req, http.StatusOK) }()`. In Go, `defer` allows us to execute something at the end of the function where it resides. In our case, that something is the invocation of the `recordMetrics` function that will record the duration of a request. In other words, before the execution leaves the `HelloServer` function, it'll record the duration by invoking the `recordMetrics` function.

I won't go further into the code that contains instrumentation since that would assume that you are interested in intricacies behind Go and I'm trying to keep this book language-agnostic. I'll let you consult the documentation and examples from your favorite language. Instead, we'll take a look at the `go-demo-5` instrumented metrics in action.

```
1  kubectl -n metrics \
2      run -it test \
3      --image=appropriate/curl \
4      --restart=Never \
5      --rm \
6      -- go-demo-5.go-demo-5:8080/metrics
```

We created a Pod based on the `appropriate/curl` image, and we sent a request through the Service using the address `go-demo-5.go-demo-5:8080/metrics`. The first `go-demo-5` is the name of the Service, and the second is the Namespace where it resides. As a result, we got output with all the instrumented metrics available in that application. We won't go through all of them, but only those created by the `http_server_resp_time` histogram.

The relevant parts of the output are as follows.

```
...
# HELP http_server_resp_time Request response time
# TYPE http_server_resp_time histogram
http_server_resp_time_bucket{code="200",method="GET",path="/demo/hello",ser
vice="go-demo",le="0.005"} 931
http_server_resp_time_bucket{code="200",method="GET",path="/demo/hello",ser
vice="go-demo",le="0.01"} 931
http_server_resp_time_bucket{code="200",method="GET",path="/demo/hello",ser
vice="go-demo",le="0.025"} 931
http_server_resp_time_bucket{code="200",method="GET",path="/demo/hello",ser
vice="go-demo",le="0.05"} 931
http_server_resp_time_bucket{code="200",method="GET",path="/demo/hello",ser
```

```
vice="go-demo",le="0.1"} 934
http_server_resp_time_bucket{code="200",method="GET",path="/demo/hello",ser
vice="go-demo",le="0.25"} 935
http_server_resp_time_bucket{code="200",method="GET",path="/demo/hello",ser
vice="go-demo",le="0.5"} 935
http_server_resp_time_bucket{code="200",method="GET",path="/demo/hello",ser
vice="go-demo",le="1"} 936
http_server_resp_time_bucket{code="200",method="GET",path="/demo/hello",ser
vice="go-demo",le="2.5"} 936
http_server_resp_time_bucket{code="200",method="GET",path="/demo/hello",ser
vice="go-demo",le="5"} 937
http_server_resp_time_bucket{code="200",method="GET",path="/demo/hello",ser
vice="go-demo",le="10"} 942
http_server_resp_time_bucket{code="200",method="GET",path="/demo/hello",ser
vice="go-demo",le="+Inf"} 942
http_server_resp_time_sum{code="200",method="GET",path="/demo/hello",servic
e="go-demo"} 38.87928942600006
http_server_resp_time_count{code="200",method="GET",path="/demo/hello",serv
ice="go-demo"} 942
. . .
```

We can see that the Go library we used in the application code created quite a few metrics from the `http_server_resp_time` histogram. We got one for each of the twelve buckets (`http_server_resp_time_bucket`), one with the sum of the durations (`http_server_resp_time_sum`), and one with the count (`http_server_resp_time_count`). We would have much more if we made requests that would have different labels. For now, those fourteen metrics are all coming from requests that responded with the HTTP code `200`, that used `GET` method, that were sent to the `/demo/hello` path, and that are coming from the `go-demo` service (application). If we'd create requests with different methods (for example, `POST`) or to different paths, the number of metrics would increase. Similarly, if we'd implement the same instrumented metric in other applications (but with different `service` labels), we'd have metrics with the same key (`http_server_resp_time`) that would provide insights into multiple apps. That raises the question of whether we should unify metric names across all the apps, or not.

I prefer having instrumented metrics of the same type with the same name across all the applications. For example, all those that collect response times can be called `http_server_resp_time`. That simplifies querying data in Prometheus. Instead of learning about instrumented metrics from each individual application, learning those from one provides knowledge about all. On the other hand, I am in favor of giving each team full control over their applications. That includes the decisions which metrics to implement, and how to call them.

All in all, it depends on the structure and responsibilities of the teams. If a team is entirely in charge of their applications and they debug problems specific to their apps, there is no inherent need for standardization of the names of instrumented metrics. On the other hand, if monitoring is centralized and the other teams might expect help from experts in that area, creating naming conventions is a must. Otherwise, we could easily end up with thousands of metrics with different names and types, even though most of them are providing the same information.

For the rest of this chapter, I will assume that we did agree to have `http_server_resp_time` histogram in all applications, where that's applicable.

Now, let's see how we can tell Prometheus that it should pull the metrics from the `go-demo-5` application. It would be even better if we could tell Prometheus to pull data from all the apps that have instrumented metrics. Actually, now when I think about it, we did not yet discuss how did Prometheus find Node Exporter and Kube State Metrics in the previous chapter. So, let's go briefly through the discovery process.

A good starting point is the Prometheus' targets screen.

```
1  open "http://$PROM_ADDR/targets"
```

The most interesting group of targets is the `kubernetes-service-endpoints`. If we take a closer look at the labels, we'll see that each has `kubernetes_name` and that three of the targets have it set to `go-demo-5`. Prometheus somehow found that we have three replicas of the application and that metrics are available through the port `8080`. If we look further, we'll notice that `prometheus-node-exporter` is there as well, one for each node in the cluster.

The same goes for `prometheus-kube-state-metrics`. There might be others in that group.

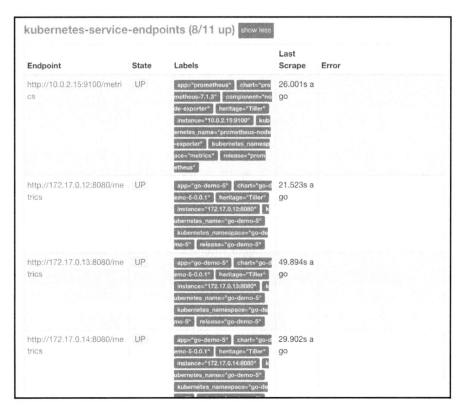

Figure 4-3: kubernetes-service-endpoints Prometheus' targets

Prometheus discovered all the targets through Kubernetes Services. It extracted the port from each of the Services, and it assumed that data is available through the `/metrics` endpoint. As a result, every application we have in the cluster, that is accessible through a Kubernetes Service, was automatically added to the `kubernetes-service-endpoints` group of Prometheus' targets. There was no need for us to fiddle with Prometheus' configuration to add `go-demo-5` to the mix. It was just discovered. Pretty neat, isn't it?

> In some cases, some of the metrics will not be accessible, and that target will be marked as red. As an example, `kube-dns` in minikube is not reachable from Prometheus. That's common, and it's not a reason to be alarmed, just as long as that's not one of the metric sources we do need.

Next, we'll take a quick look at a few expressions we can write using the instrumented metrics coming from `go-demo-5`.

```
1  open "http://$PROM_ADDR/graph"
```

Please type the expression that follows, press the **Execute** button, and switch to the *Graph* tab.

```
1  http_server_resp_time_count
```

We can see three lines that correspond to three replicas of `go-demo-5`. That should not come as a surprise since each of those is pulled from instrumented metrics coming from each of the replicas of the application. Since those metrics are counters that can only increase, the lines of the graph are continuously going up.

Figure 4-4: The graph with the http_server_resp_time_count counter

That wasn't very useful. If we were interested in the rate of the count of requests, we'd envelop the previous expression inside the `rate()` function. We'll do that later. For now, we'll write the simplest expression that will give us the average response time per request.

Please type the expression that follows, and press the **Execute** button.

```
1  http_server_resp_time_sum{
2      kubernetes_name="go-demo-5"
3  } /
4  http_server_resp_time_count{
5      kubernetes_name="go-demo-5"
6  }
```

The expression itself should be easy to understand. We are taking the sum of all the requests and dividing it with the count. Since we already discovered that the problem is somewhere inside the go-demo-5 app, we used the kubernetes_name label to limit the results. Even though that is the only application with that metric currently running in our cluster, it is a good idea to get used to the fact that there might be others at some later date when we extend instrumentation to other applications.

We can see that the average request duration increased for a while, only to drop close to the initial values a while later. That spike coincides with the twenty slow requests we sent a while ago. In my case (screenshot following), the peak is close to the average response time of 0.1 seconds, only to drop to around 0.02 seconds a while later.

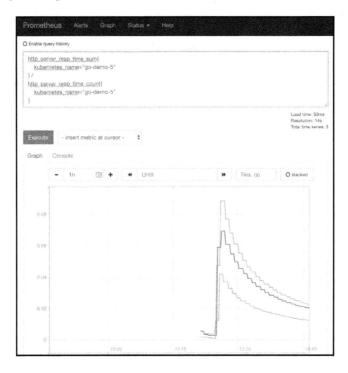

Figure 4-5: The graph with the cumulative average response time

Please note that the expression we just executed is deeply flawed. It shows the cumulative average response time, instead of displaying the `rate`. But, you already knew that. That was only a taste of the instrumented metric, not its "real" usage (that comes soon).

You might notice that even the spike is very low. It is certainly lower than what we'd expect from sending only twenty slow requests through `curl`. The reason for that lies in the fact that we were not the only ones making those requests. The `readinessProbe` and the `livenessProbe` are sending requests as well, and they are very fast. Unlike in the previous chapter when we were measuring only the requests coming through Ingress, this time we're capturing all the requests that enter the application, and that includes health-checks.

Now that we saw a few examples of the `http_server_resp_time` metric that is generated inside our `go-demo-5` application, we can use that knowledge to try to debug the simulated issue that led us towards instrumentation.

# Using internal metrics to debug potential issues

We'll re-send requests with slow responses again so that we get to the same point where we started this chapter.

```
1  for i in {1..20}; do
2      DELAY=$[ $RANDOM % 10000 ]
3      curl "http://$GD5_ADDR/demo/hello?delay=$DELAY"
4  done
5
6  open "http://$PROM_ADDR/alerts"
```

We sent twenty requests that will result in responses with random duration (up to ten seconds). Further on, we opened Prometheus' alerts screen.

A while later, the `AppTooSlow` alert should fire (remember to refresh your screen), and we have a (simulated) problem that needs to be solved. Before we start panicking and do something hasty, we'll try to find the cause of the issue.

Please click the expression of the `AppTooSlow` alert.

We are redirected to the graph screen with the pre-populated expression from the alert. Feel free to click the **Expression** button, even though it will not provide any additional info, apart from the fact that the application was fast, and then it slowed down for some inexplicable reason.

You will not be able to gather more details from that expression. You will not know whether it's slow on all methods, whether only a specific path responds slow, nor much of any other application-specific details. Simply put, the `nginx_ingress_controller_request_duration_seconds` metric is too generic. It served us well as a way to notify us that the application's response time increased, but it does not provide enough information about the cause of the issue. For that, we'll switch to the `http_server_resp_time` metric Prometheus is retrieving directly from `go-demo-5` replicas.

Please type the expression that follows, and press the **Execute** button.

```
 1   sum(rate(
 2       http_server_resp_time_bucket{
 3           le="0.1",
 4           kubernetes_name="go-demo-5"
 5       }[5m]
 6   )) /
 7   sum(rate(
 8       http_server_resp_time_count{
 9           kubernetes_name="go-demo-5"
10       }[5m]
11   ))
```

Switch to the *Graph* tab, if you're not there already.

That expression is very similar to the queries we wrote before when we were using the `nginx_ingress_controller_request_duration_seconds_sum` metric. We are dividing the rate of requests in the 0.1 seconds bucket with the rate of all the requests.

In my case (screenshot following), we can see that the percentage of fast responses dropped twice. That coincides with the simulated slow requests we sent earlier.

Figure 4-6: The graph with the percentage of fast requests measured with instrumented metrics

So far, using the instrumented metric `http_server_resp_time_count` did not provide any tangible benefit when compared with `nginx_ingress_controller_request_duration_seconds_sum`. If that would be all, we could conclude that the effort to add instrumentation was a waste. However, we did not yet include labels into our expressions.

Let's say that we'd like to group requests by the `method` and the `path`. That could give us a better idea whether slowness is global, or limited only to a specific type of requests. If it's latter, we'll know where the problem is and, hopefully, would be able to find the culprit quickly.

Please type the expression that follows, and press the **Execute** button.

```
 1  sum(rate(
 2      http_server_resp_time_bucket{
 3          le="0.1",
 4          kubernetes_name="go-demo-5"
 5      }[5m]
 6  ))
 7  by (method, path) /
 8  sum(rate(
 9      http_server_resp_time_count{
10          kubernetes_name="go-demo-5"
11      }[5m]
12  ))
13  by (method, path)
```

That expression is almost the same as the one before. The only difference is the addition of the `by (method, path)` statements. As a result, we are getting a percentage of fast responses, grouped by the `method` and the `path`.

The output does not represent a "real" world use case. Usually, we'd see many different lines, one for each method and path that was requested. But, since we only made requests to `/demo/hello` using HTTP GET, our graph is a bit boring. You'll have to imagine that there are many other lines.

By studying the graph, we discover that all but one line (we're still imagining many) are close to hundred percent of fast responses. The one with the sharp drop would be the one with the `/demo/hello` path and the `GET` method. However, if that would indeed be a real-world scenario, we would probably have too many lines in the graph, and we might not be able to distinguish them easily. Our expression could benefit with an addition of a threshold.

Please type the expression that follows, and press the **Execute** button.

```
 1  sum(rate(
 2      http_server_resp_time_bucket{
 3          le="0.1",
 4          kubernetes_name="go-demo-5"
 5      }[5m]
 6  ))
 7  by (method, path) /
```

```
 8   sum(rate(
 9       http_server_resp_time_count{
10           kubernetes_name="go-demo-5"
11       }[5m]
12   ))
13   by (method, path) < 0.99
```

The only addition is the < 0.99 threshold. As a result, our graph excludes all the results (all paths and methods) but those that are below 99 percent (0.99). We removed all the noise and focused only on the cases when more than one percent of all requests are slow (or less than 99 percent are fast). The result is now clear. The problem is in the function that handles GET requests on the path /demo/hello. We know that through the labels available below the graph.

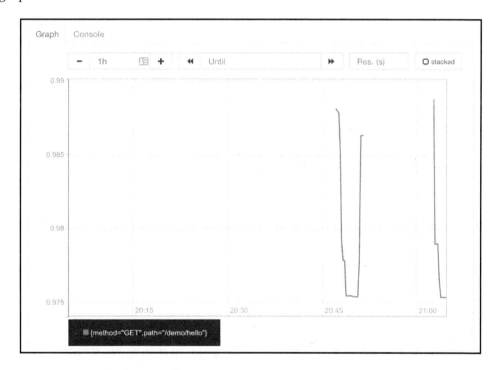

Figure 4-7: The graph with the percentage of fast requests measured with instrumented metrics limited to results below ninety-nine percent

Now that we know (almost) the exact location of the problem, all that's left is to fix the issue, push the change to our Git repository, and wait until our continuous deployment process upgrades the software with the new release.

In a relatively short period, we managed to find (debug) the issue or, to be more precise, to narrow it to a specific part of the code.

Or, maybe we discovered that the problem is not in the code, but that our application needs to scale up. In either case, without instrumented metrics, we would only know that the application is slow and that could mean that any part of the app is misbehaving. Instrumentation gave us more detailed metrics that we used to be more precise and reduce the time we'd typically require to find the issue and act accordingly.

Usually, we'd have many other instrumented metrics, and our "debugging" process would be more complicated. We'd execute other expressions and dig through different metrics. Nevertheless, the point is that we should combine generic metrics with more detailed ones coming directly from our applications. Those in the former group are often used to detect that there is an issue, while the latter type is useful when looking for the cause of the problem. Both types of metrics have their place in monitoring, alerting, and debugging our clusters and applications. With instrumented metrics, we have more application-specific details. That allows us to narrow down the locations and causes of a problem. The more confident we are about the exact cause of an issue, the better we are equipped to react.

# What now?

I don't believe that we need many other examples of instrumented metrics. They are not any different than those we are collecting through exporters. I'll leave it up to you to start instrumenting your applications. Start small, see what works well, improve and extend.

Yet another chapter is finished. Destroy your cluster and start the next one fresh, or keep it. If you choose the latter, please execute the commands that follow to remove the go-demo-5 application.

```
1  helm delete go-demo-5 --purge
2
3  kubectl delete ns go-demo-5
```

Before you leave, remember the point that follows. It summarizes instrumentation.

- Instrumented metrics are baked into applications. They are an integral part of the code of our apps, and they are usually exposed through the /metrics endpoint.

# 5

# Extending HorizontalPodAutoscaler with Custom Metrics

*Computers make excellent and efficient servants, but I have no wish to serve under them.*

*- Spock*

Adoption of **HorizontalPodAutoscaler** (**HPA**) usually goes through three phases.

The first phase is *discovery*. The first time we find out what it does, we usually end up utterly amazed. "Look at this. It scales our applications automatically. I don't need to worry about the number of replicas anymore."

The second phase is the *usage*. Once we start using HPA, we quickly realize that scaling applications based memory and CPU is not enough. Some apps do increase their memory and CPU usage with the increase in load, while many others don't. Or, to be more precise, not proportionally. HPA, for some applications, works well. For many others, it does not work at all, or it is not enough. Sooner or later, we'll need to extend HPA thresholds beyond those based on memory and CPU. This phase is characterized by *disappointment*. "It seemed like a good idea, but we cannot use it with most of our applications. We need to fall back to alerts based on metrics and manual changes to the number of replicas."

The third phase is *re-discovery*. Once we go through the HPA v2 documentation (still in beta at the time of this writing) we can see that it allows us to extend it to almost any type of metrics and expressions. We can hook HPAs to Prometheus, or nearly any other tool, though adapters. Once we master that, there is almost no limit to the conditions we can set as triggers of automatic scaling of our applications. The only restriction is our ability to transform data into Kubernetes' custom metrics.

Our next goal is to extend HorizontalPodAutoscaler definitions to include conditions based on data stored in Prometheus.

# Creating a cluster

The `vfarcic/k8s-specs` (`https://github.com/vfarcic/k8s-specs`) repository will continue to serve as our source of Kubernetes definitions. We'll make sure that it is up-to-date by pulling the latest version.

All the commands from this chapter are available in the `05-hpa-custom-metrics.sh` (`https://gist.github.com/vfarcic/cc546f81e060e4f5fc5661e4fa003af7`) Gist.

```
1   cd k8s-specs
2
3   git pull
```

The requirements are the same as those we had in the previous chapter. The only exception is **EKS**. We'll continue using the same Gists as before for all other Kuberentes flavors.

**A note to EKS users**
Even though three t2.small nodes we used so far have more than enough memory and CPU, they might not be able to host all the Pods we'll create. EKS (by default) uses AWS networking. A t2.small instance can have a maximum of three network interfaces, with four IPv4 address per each. That means that we can have up to twelve IPv4 addresses on each t2.small node. Given that each Pod needs to have its own address, that means that we can have a maximum of twelve Pods per node. In this chapter, we might need more than thirty-six Pods across the cluster. Instead of creating a cluster with more than three nodes, we'll add Cluster Autoscaler (CA) to the mix, and let the cluster expand if needed. We already explored CA in one of the previous chapters and the setup instructions are now added to the Gist `eks-hpa-custom.sh` (`https://gist.github.com/vfarcic/868bf70ac2946458f5485edea1f6fc4c`).

Please use one of the Gists that follow to create a new cluster. If you already have a cluster you'd like to use for the exercises, please use the Gists to validate that it fulfills all the requirements.

- `gke-instrument.sh`: **GKE** with 3 n1-standard-1 worker nodes, **nginx Ingress**, **tiller**, **Prometheus** Chart, and environment variables **LB_IP**, **PROM_ADDR**, and **AM_ADDR**
  (`https://gist.github.com/vfarcic/675f4b3ee2c55ee718cf132e71e04c6e`).
- `eks-hpa-custom.sh`: **EKS** with 3 t2.small worker nodes, **nginx Ingress**, **tiller**, **Metrics Server**, **Prometheus** Chart, environment variables **LB_IP**, **PROM_ADDR**, and **AM_ADDR**, and **Cluster Autoscaler**
  (`https://gist.github.com/vfarcic/868bf70ac2946458f5485edea1f6fc4c`).
- `aks-instrument.sh`: **AKS** with 3 Standard_B2s worker nodes, **nginx Ingress**, and **tiller**, **Prometheus** Chart, and environment variables **LB_IP**, **PROM_ADDR**, and **AM_ADDR**
  (`https://gist.github.com/vfarcic/65a0d5834c9e20ebf1b99225fba0d339`).
- `docker-instrument.sh`: **Docker for Desktop** with **2 CPUs**, **3 GB RAM**, **nginx Ingress, tiller, Metrics Server, Prometheus** Chart, and environment variables **LB_IP, PROM_ADDR**, and **AM_ADDR**
  (`https://gist.github.com/vfarcic/1dddcae847e97219ab75f936d93451c2`).
- `minikube-instrument.sh`: **Minikube** with **2 CPUs**, **3 GB RAM**, **ingress**, **storage-provisioner**, **default-storageclass**, and **metrics-server** addons enabled, **tiller**, **Prometheus** Chart, and environment variables **LB_IP**, **PROM_ADDR**, and **AM_ADDR**
  (`https://gist.github.com/vfarcic/779fae2ae374cf91a5929070e47bddc8`).

Now we're ready to extend our usage of HPA. But, before we do that, let's briefly explore (again) how HPA works out of the box.

# Using HorizontalPodAutoscaler without metrics adapter

If we do not create a metrics adapter, Metrics Aggregator only knows about CPU and memory usage related to containers and nodes. To make things more complicated, that information is limited only to the last few minutes. Since HPA is just concerned about Pods and containers inside them, we are limited to only two metrics. When we create an HPA, it will scale or de-scale our Pods if memory or CPU consumption of the containers that constitute those Pods is above or below predefined thresholds.

Metrics Server periodically fetches information (CPU and memory) from Kubelets running inside worker nodes.

Those metrics are passed to Metrics Aggregator which, in this scenario, does not add any additional value. From there on, HPAs periodically consult the data in the Metrics Aggregator (through its API endpoint). When there is a discrepancy between target values defined in an HPA and the actual values, an HPA will manipulate the number of replicas of a Deployment or a StatefulSet. As we already know, any change to those controllers results in rolling updates executed through creation and manipulation of ReplicaSets, which create and delete Pods, which are converted into containers by a Kubelet running on a node where a Pod is scheduled.

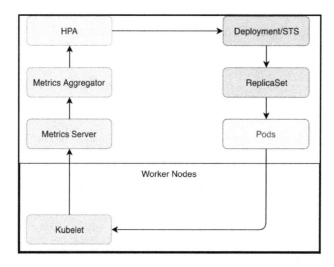

Figure 5-1: HPA with out of the box setup (arrows show the flow of data)

Functionally, the flow we just described works well. The only problem is the data available in the Metrics Aggregator. It is limited to memory and CPU. More often than not, that is not enough. So, there's no need for us to change the process, but to extend the data available to HPA. We can do that through a metrics adapter.

# Exploring Prometheus Adapter

Given that we want to extend the metrics available through the Metrics API, and that Kubernetes allows us that through it's *Custom Metrics API* (https://github.com/kubernetes/metrics/tree/master/pkg/apis/custom_metrics), one option to accomplish our goals could be to create our own adapter.

Depending on the application (DB) where we store metrics, that might be a good option. But, given that it is pointless to reinvent the wheel, our first step should be to search for a solution. If someone already created an adapter that suits our needs, it would make sense to adopt it, instead of creating a new one by ourselves. Even if we do choose something that provides only part of the features we're looking for, it's easier to build on top of it (and contribute back to the project), than to start from scratch.

Given that our metrics are stored in Prometheus, we need a metrics adapter that will be capable of fetching data from it. Since Prometheus is very popular and adopted by the community, there is already a project waiting for us to use it. It's called *Kubernetes Custom Metrics Adapter for Prometheus*. It is an implementation of the Kubernetes Custom Metrics API that uses Prometheus as the data source.

Since we adopted Helm for all our installations, we'll use it to install the adapter.

```
1   helm install \
2       stable/prometheus-adapter \
3       --name prometheus-adapter \
4       --version v0.5.0 \
5       --namespace metrics \
6       --set image.tag=v0.5.0 \
7       --set metricsRelistInterval=90s \
8       --set prometheus.url=http://prometheus-server.metrics.svc \
9       --set prometheus.port=80
10
11  kubectl -n metrics \
12      rollout status \
13      deployment prometheus-adapter
```

We installed `prometheus-adapter` Helm Chart from the `stable` repository. The resources were created in the `metrics` Namespace, and the `image.tag` is set to `v0.3.0`.

We changed `metricsRelistInterval` from the default value of `30s` to `90s`. That is the interval the adapter will use to fetch metrics from Prometheus. Since our Prometheus setup is fetching metrics from its targets every sixty seconds, we had to set the adapter's interval to a value higher than that. Otherwise, the adapter's frequency would be higher than pulling frequency of Prometheus, and we'd have iterations that would be without new data.

The last two arguments specified the URL and the port through which the adapter can access Prometheus API. In our case, the URL is set to go through Prometheus' service.

Please visit *Prometheus Adapter Chart README* (`https://github.com/helm/charts/tree/master/stable/prometheus-adapter`) for more information about all the values you can set to customize the installation.

Finally, we waited until the `prometheus-adapter` rolls out.

If everything is working as expected, we should be able to query Kubernetes' custom metrics API and retrieve some of the Prometheus data provided through the adapter.

```
1  kubectl get --raw \
2      "/apis/custom.metrics.k8s.io/v1beta1" \
3      | jq "."
```

Given the promise that each chapter will feature a different Kubernetes' flavor, and that AWS did not have its turn yet, all the outputs are taken from EKS. Depending on the platform you're using, your outputs might be slightly different.

The first entries of the output from querying Custom Metrics is as follows.

```
{
  "kind": "APIResourceList",
  "apiVersion": "v1",
  "groupVersion": "custom.metrics.k8s.io/v1beta1",
  "resources": [
    {
      "name": "namespaces/memory_max_usage_bytes",
      "singularName": "",
      "namespaced": false,
      "kind": "MetricValueList",
      "verbs": [
        "get"
      ]
    },
    {
      "name":
"jobs.batch/kube_deployment_spec_strategy_rollingupdate_max_unavailable",
      "singularName": "",
      "namespaced": true,
      "kind": "MetricValueList",
      "verbs": [
        "get"
      ]
    },
    ...
```

The list of the custom metrics available through the adapter is big, and we might be compelled to think that it contains all those stored in Prometheus. We'll find out whether that's true later. For now, we'll focus on the metrics we might need with HPA tied to `go-demo-5` Deployment. After all, providing metrics for auto-scaling is adapter's primary, if not the only function.

From now on, Metrics Aggregator contains not only the data from the metrics server but also those from the Prometheus Adapter which, in turn, is fetching metrics from Prometheus Server. We are yet to confirm whether the data we're getting through the adapter is enough and whether HPA works with custom metrics.

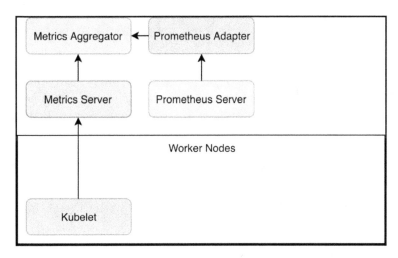

Figure 5-2: Custom metrics with Prometheus Adapter (arrows show the flow of data)

Before we go deeper into the adapter, we'll define our goals for the `go-demo-5` application.

We should be able to scale the Pods not only based on memory and CPU usage but also by the number of requests entering through Ingress or observed through instrumented metrics. There can be many other criteria we could add but, as a learning experience, those should be enough. We already know how to configure HPA to scale based on CPU and memory, so our mission is to extend it with a request counter. That way, we'll be able to set the rules that will increase the number of replicas when the application is receiving too many requests, as well as to descale it if traffic decreases.

Since we want to extend the HPA connected to `go-demo-5`, our next step is to install the application.

```
1   GD5_ADDR=go-demo-5.$LB_IP.nip.io
2
```

```
 3  helm install \
 4    https://github.com/vfarcic/go-demo-5/releases/download/
    0.0.1/go-demo-5-0.0.1.tgz \
 5      --name go-demo-5 \
 6      --namespace go-demo-5 \
 7      --set ingress.host=$GD5_ADDR
 8
 9  kubectl -n go-demo-5 \
10      rollout status \
11      deployment go-demo-5
```

We defined the address of the application, we installed the Chart, and we waited until the Deployment rolled out.

**A note to EKS users**

If you received `error: deployment "go-demo-5" exceeded its progress deadline` message, the cluster is likely auto-scaling to accommodate all the Pods and zones of the PersistentVolumes. That might take more time than the `progress deadline`. In that case, wait for a few moments and repeat the `rollout` command.

Next, we'll generate a bit of traffic by sending a hundred requests to the application through its Ingress resource.

```
1  for i in {1..100}; do
2      curl "http://$GD5_ADDR/demo/hello"
3  done
```

Now that we generated some traffic, we can try to find a metric that will help us calculate how many requests passed through Ingress. Since we already know (from the previous chapters) that `nginx_ingress_controller_requests` provides the number of requests that enter through Ingress, we should check whether it is now available as a custom metric.

```
1  kubectl get --raw \
2      "/apis/custom.metrics.k8s.io/v1beta1" \
3      | jq '.resources[]
4      | select(.name
5      | contains("nginx_ingress_controller_requests"))'
```

We sent a request to `/apis/custom.metrics.k8s.io/v1beta1`. But, as you already saw, that alone would return all the metrics, and we are interested in only one. That's why we piped the output to `jq` and used its filter to retrieve only the entries that contain `nginx_ingress_controller_requests` as the `name`.

If you received an empty output, please wait for a few moments until the adapter pulls the metrics from Prometheus (it does that every ninety seconds) and re-execute the command.

The output is as follows.

```
{
  "name": "ingresses.extensions/nginx_ingress_controller_requests",
  "singularName": "",
  "namespaced": true,
  "kind": "MetricValueList",
  "verbs": [
    "get"
  ]
}
{
  "name": "jobs.batch/nginx_ingress_controller_requests",
  "singularName": "",
  "namespaced": true,
  "kind": "MetricValueList",
  "verbs": [
    "get"
  ]
}
{
  "name": "namespaces/nginx_ingress_controller_requests",
  "singularName": "",
  "namespaced": false,
  "kind": "MetricValueList",
  "verbs": [
    "get"
  ]
}
```

We got three results. The name of each consists of the resource type and the name of the metric. We'll discard those related to `jobs.batch` and `namespaces`, and concentrate on the metric related to `ingresses.extensions` since it provides the information we need. We can see that it is `namespaced`, meaning that the metrics are, among other things, separated by namespaces of their origin. The `kind` and the `verbs` are (almost) always the same, and there's not much value going through them.

The major problem with `ingresses.extensions/nginx_ingress_controller_requests` is that it provides the number of requests for an Ingress resource. We couldn't use it in its current form as an HPA criterion. Instead, we should divide the number of requests with the number of replicas. That would give us the average number of requests per replica which should be a better HPA threshold. We'll explore how to use expressions instead of simple metrics later. Knowing the number of requests entering through Ingress is useful, but it might not be enough.

Since `go-demo-5` already provides instrumented metrics, it would be helpful to see whether we can retrieve `http_server_resp_time_count`. As a reminder, that's the same metric we used in the `Chapter 4`, *Debugging Issues Discovered Through Metrics and Alerts*.

```
1   kubectl get --raw \
2       "/apis/custom.metrics.k8s.io/v1beta1" \
3       | jq '.resources[]
4       | select(.name
5       | contains("http_server_resp_time_count"))'
```

We used `jq` to filter the result so that only `http_server_resp_time_count` is retrieved. Don't be surprised by empty output. That's normal since Prometheus Adapter is not configured to process all the metrics from Prometheus, but only those that match its own internal rules. So, this might be a good moment to take a look at the `prometheus-adapter` ConfigMap that contains its configuration.

```
1   kubectl -n metrics \
2       describe cm prometheus-adapter
```

The output is too big to be presented in a book, so we'll go only through the first rule. It is as follows.

```
...
rules:
- seriesQuery:
'{__name__=~"^container_.*",container_name!="POD",namespace!="",pod_name!="
"}'
  seriesFilters: []
  resources:
    overrides:
      namespace:
        resource: namespace
      pod_name:
        resource: pod
  name:
    matches: ^container_(.*)_seconds_total$
    as: ""
  metricsQuery:
sum(rate(<<.Series>>{<<.LabelMatchers>>,container_name!="POD"}[5m]))
    by (<<.GroupBy>>)
...
```

The first rule retrieves only the metrics with the name that starts with `container` (`__name__=~"^container_.*"`), with the label `container_name` being anything but `POD`, and with `namespace` and `pod_name` not empty.

Each rule has to specify a few resource overrides. In this case, the `namespace` label contains the `namespace` resource. Similarly, the `pod` resource is retrieved from the label `pod_name`. Further on, we can see the `name` section uses regular expressions to name the new metric. Finally, `metricsQuery` tells the adapter which Prometheus query it should execute when retrieving data.

If that setup looks confusing, you should know that you're not the only one bewildered at first sight. Prometheus Adapter, just as Prometheus Server configs are complicated to grasp at first. Nevertheless, they are very powerful allowing us to define rules for service discovery, instead of specifying individual metrics (in the case of the adapter) or targets (in the case of Prometheus Server). Soon we'll go into more details with the setup of the adapter rules. For now, the important note is that the default configuration tells the adapter to fetch all the metrics that match a few rules.

So far, we saw that `nginx_ingress_controller_requests` metric is available through the adapter, but that it is of no use since we need to divide the number of requests with the number of replicas. We also saw that the `http_server_resp_time_count` metric originating in `go-demo-5` Pods is not available. All in all, we do not have all the metrics we need, while most of the metrics currently fetched by the adapter are of no use. It is wasting time and resources with pointless queries.

Our next mission is to reconfigure the adapter so that only the metrics we need are retrieved from Prometheus. We'll try to write our own expressions that will fetch only the data we need. If we manage to do that, we should be able to create HPA as well.

# Creating HorizontalPodAutoscaler with custom metrics

As you already saw, Prometheus Adapter comes with a set of default rules that provide many metrics that we do not need, and not all those that we do. It's wasting CPU and memory by doing too much, but not enough. We'll explore how we can customize the adapter with our own rules. Our next goal is to make the adapter retrieve only the `nginx_ingress_controller_requests` metric since that's the only one we need. On top of that, it should provide that metric in two forms. First, it should retrieve the rate, grouped by the resource.

The second form should be the same as the first but divided with the number of replicas of the Deployment that hosts the Pods where Ingress forwards the resources.

That one should give us an average number of requests per replica and will be a good candidate for our first HPA definition based on custom metrics.

I already prepared a file with Chart values that might accomplish our current objectives, so let's take a look at it.

```
1  cat mon/prom-adapter-values-ing.yml
```

The output is as follows.

```
image:
  tag: v0.5.0
metricsRelistInterval: 90s
prometheus:
  url: http://prometheus-server.metrics.svc
  port: 80
rules:
  default: false
  custom:
  - seriesQuery: 'nginx_ingress_controller_requests'
    resources:
      overrides:
        namespace: {resource: "namespace"}
        ingress: {resource: "ingress"}
    name:
      as: "http_req_per_second"
    metricsQuery: 'sum(rate(<<.Series>>{<<.LabelMatchers>>}[5m])) by
(<<.GroupBy>>)'
  - seriesQuery: 'nginx_ingress_controller_requests'
    resources:
      overrides:
        namespace: {resource: "namespace"}
        ingress: {resource: "ingress"}
    name:
      as: "http_req_per_second_per_replica"
    metricsQuery: 'sum(rate(<<.Series>>{<<.LabelMatchers>>}[5m])) by
(<<.GroupBy>>) / sum(label_join(kube_deployment_status_replicas, "ingress",
",", "deployment")) by (<<.GroupBy>>)'
```

The first few entries in that definition are the same values as the ones we used previously through `--set` arguments. We'll skip those and jump into the `rules` section.

Within the `rules` section, we're setting the `default` entry to `false`. That will get rid of the default rules we explored previously, and allow us to start with a clean slate. Further on, there are two `custom` rules.

The first rule is based on the `seriesQuery` with `nginx_ingress_controller_requests` as the value. The `overrides` entry inside the `resources` section helps the adapter find out which Kubernetes resources are associated with the metric. We're setting the value of the `namespace` label to the `namespace` resource. There's a similar entry for `ingress`. In other words, we're associating Prometheus labels with Kubernetes resources `namespace` and `ingress`.

As you will see soon, the metric itself will be a part of a full query that will be treated as a single metric by HPA. Since we are creating something new, we need a name. So, we specified the `name` section with a single `as` entry set to `http_req_per_second`. That will be the reference in our HPA definitions.

You already know that `nginx_ingress_controller_requests` is not very useful by itself. When we used it in Prometheus, we had to put it inside a `rate` function, we had to `sum` everything, and we had to group the results by a resource. We're doing something similar through the `metricsQuery` entry. Think of it as an equivalent of expressions we're writing in Prometheus. The only difference is that we are using "special" syntax like `<<.Series>>`. That's adapter's templating mechanism. Instead of hard-coding the name of the metric, the labels, and the group by statements, we have `<<.Series>>`, `<<.LabelMatchers>>`, and `<<.GroupBy>>` clauses that will be populated with the correct values depending on what we put in API calls.

The second rule is almost the same as the first. The difference is in the name (now it's `http_req_per_second_per_replica`) and in the `metricsQuery`. The latter is now dividing the result with the number of replicas of the associated Deployment, just as we practiced in the `Chapter 3`, *Collecting and Querying Metrics and Sending Alerts*.

Next, we'll update the Chart with the new values.

```
1  helm upgrade prometheus-adapter \
2      stable/prometheus-adapter \
3      --version v0.5.0 \
4      --namespace metrics \
5      --values mon/prom-adapter-values-ing.yml
6
7  kubectl -n metrics \
8      rollout status \
9      deployment prometheus-adapter
```

Now that the Deployment rolled out successfully, we can double-check that the configuration stored in the ConfigMap is indeed correct.

```
1  kubectl -n metrics \
2      describe cm prometheus-adapter
```

The output, limited to the `Data` section, is as follows.

```
...
Data
====
config.yaml:
----
rules:
- metricsQuery: sum(rate(<<.Series>>{<<.LabelMatchers>>}[5m])) by
(<<.GroupBy>>)
  name:
    as: http_req_per_second
  resources:
    overrides:
      ingress:
        resource: ingress
      namespace:
        resource: namespace
  seriesQuery: nginx_ingress_controller_requests
- metricsQuery: sum(rate(<<.Series>>{<<.LabelMatchers>>}[5m])) by
(<<.GroupBy>>) /
    sum(label_join(kube_deployment_status_replicas, "ingress", ",",
"deployment"))
    by (<<.GroupBy>>)
  name:
    as: http_req_per_second_per_replica
  resources:
    overrides:
      ingress:
        resource: ingress
      namespace:
        resource: namespace
  seriesQuery: nginx_ingress_controller_requests
...
```

We can see that the default `rules` we explored earlier are now replaced with the two rules we defined in the `rules.custom` section of our Chart values file.

The fact that the configuration looks correct does not necessarily mean that the adapter now provides data as Kubernetes custom metrics. Let's check that as well.

```
1  kubectl get --raw \
2      "/apis/custom.metrics.k8s.io/v1beta1" \
3      | jq "."
```

The output is as follows.

```
{
```

```
"kind": "APIResourceList",
"apiVersion": "v1",
"groupVersion": "custom.metrics.k8s.io/v1beta1",
"resources": [
  {
    "name": "namespaces/http_req_per_second_per_replica",
    "singularName": "",
    "namespaced": false,
    "kind": "MetricValueList",
    "verbs": [
      "get"
    ]
  },
  {
    "name": "ingresses.extensions/http_req_per_second_per_replica",
    "singularName": "",
    "namespaced": true,
    "kind": "MetricValueList",
    "verbs": [
      "get"
    ]
  },
  {
    "name": "ingresses.extensions/http_req_per_second",
    "singularName": "",
    "namespaced": true,
    "kind": "MetricValueList",
    "verbs": [
      "get"
    ]
  },
  {
    "name": "namespaces/http_req_per_second",
    "singularName": "",
    "namespaced": false,
    "kind": "MetricValueList",
    "verbs": [
      "get"
    ]
  }
]
}
```

We can see that there are four metrics available, two of `http_req_per_second` and two of `http_req_per_second_per_replica`. Each of the two metrics we defined is available as both `namespaces` and `ingresses`. Right now, we do not care about `namespaces`, and we'll concentrate on `ingresses`.

I'll assume that at least five minutes (or more) passed since we sent a hundred requests. If it didn't, you are a speedy reader, and you'll have to wait for a while before we send another hundred requests. We are about to create our first HPA based on custom metrics, and I want to make sure that you see how it behaves both before and after it is activated.

Now, let's take a look at an HPA definition.

```
1  cat mon/go-demo-5-hpa-ing.yml
```

The output is as follows.

```
apiVersion: autoscaling/v2beta1
kind: HorizontalPodAutoscaler
metadata:
  name: go-demo-5
spec:
  scaleTargetRef:
    apiVersion: apps/v1
    kind: Deployment
    name: go-demo-5
  minReplicas: 3
  maxReplicas: 10
  metrics:
  - type: Object
    object:
      metricName: http_req_per_second_per_replica
      target:
        kind: Namespace
        name: go-demo-5
      targetValue: 50m
```

The first half of the definition should be familiar since it does not differ from what we used before. It will maintain between 3 and 10 replicas of the `go-demo-5` Deployment. The new stuff is in the `metrics` section.

In the past, we used `spec.metrics.type` set to `Resource`. Through that type, we defined CPU and memory targets. This time, however, our type is `Object`. It refers to a metric describing a single Kubernetes object which, in our case, happens to be a custom metric coming from Prometheus Adapter.

If we go through the *ObjectMetricSource v2beta1 autoscaling* (https://kubernetes.io/docs/reference/generated/kubernetes-api/v1.12/#objectmetricsource-v2beta1-autoscaling) documentation, we can see that the fields of the `Object` type are different than those we used before when our type was `Resources`. We set the `metricName` to the metric we defined in Prometheus Adapter (http_req_per_second_per_replica).

Remember that it is not a metric, but that we defined an expression that the adapter uses to fetch data from Prometheus and convert it into a custom metric. In this case, we are getting the number of requests entering an Ingress resource and divided by the number of replicas of a Deployment.

Finally, the `targetValue` is set to `50m` or 0.05 requests per second. I intentionally set it to a very low value so that we can easily reach the target and observe what happens.

Let's `apply` the definition.

```
1  kubectl -n go-demo-5 \
2      apply -f mon/go-demo-5-hpa-ing.yml
```

Next, we'll describe the newly created HPA, and see whether we can observe anything interesting.

```
1  kubectl -n go-demo-5 \
2      describe hpa go-demo-5
```

The output, limited to the relevant parts, is as follows.

```
...
Metrics:             ( current / target )
  "http_req_per_second_per_replica" on Namespace/go-demo-5: 0 / 50m
Min replicas:     3
Max replicas:     10
Deployment pods: 3 current / 3 desired
...
```

We can see that there is only one entry in the `Metrics` section. The HPA is using the custom metric `http_req_per_second_per_replica` based on `Namespace/go-demo-5`. At the moment, the current value is `0`, and the `target` is set to `50m` (0.05 requests per second). If, in your case, the `current` value is `unknown`, please wait for a few moments, and re-run the command.

Further down, we can see that both the `current` and the `desired` number of Deployment Pods is set to `3`.

All in all, the target is not reached (there are `0` requests) so there's no need for the HPA to do anything. It maintains the minimum number of replicas.

Let's spice it up a bit by generating some traffic.

```
1  for i in {1..100}; do
2      curl "http://$GD5_ADDR/demo/hello"
3  done
```

We sent a hundred requests to the `go-demo-5` Ingress.

Let's `describe` the HPA again, and see whether there are some changes.

```
1  kubectl -n go-demo-5 \
2      describe hpa go-demo-5
```

The output, limited to the relevant parts, is as follows.

```
...
Metrics:                                              ( current /
target )
   "http_req_per_second_per_replica" on Ingress/go-demo-5:  138m / 50m
Min replicas:                                         3
Max replicas:                                         10
Deployment pods:                                      3 current / 6
desired
...
Events:
   ... Message
   ... -------
   ... New size: 6; reason: Ingress metric http_req_per_second_per_replica
above target
```

We can see that the `current` value of the metric increased. In my case, it is `138m` (0.138 requests per second). If your output still shows `0`, you'll have to wait until the metrics are pulled by Prometheus, until the adapter fetches them, and until the HPA refreshes its status. In other words, wait for a few moments, and re-run the previous command.

Given that the `current` value is higher than the `target`, in my case, the HPA changed the `desired` number of `Deployment pods` to `6` (your number might differ depending on the value of the metric). As a result, HPA modified the Deployment by changing its number of replicas, and we should see additional Pods running. That becomes more evident through the `Events` section. There should be a new message stating `New size: 6; reason: Ingress metric http_req_per_second_per_replica above target`.

To be on the safe side, we'll list the Pods in the `go-demo-5` Namespace and confirm that the new ones are indeed running.

```
1  kubectl -n go-demo-5 get pods
```

The output is as follows.

```
NAME            READY STATUS  RESTARTS AGE
go-demo-5-db-0 2/2   Running 0        19m
go-demo-5-db-1 2/2   Running 0        19m
```

```
go-demo-5-db-2 2/2    Running 0        10m
go-demo-5-...  1/1    Running 2        19m
go-demo-5-...  1/1    Running 0        16s
go-demo-5-...  1/1    Running 2        19m
go-demo-5-...  1/1    Running 0        16s
go-demo-5-...  1/1    Running 2        19m
go-demo-5-...  1/1    Running 0        16s
```

We can see that there are now six `go-demo-5-*` Pods, with three of them much younger than the rest.

Next, we'll explore what happens when traffic drops below the HPAs `target`. We'll accomplish that by not doing anything for a while. Since we are the only ones sending requests to the application, all we have to do is to stand still for five minutes or, even better, use this time to fetch coffee.

The reason we need to wait for at least five minutes lies in the frequencies HPA uses to scale up and down. By default, an HPA will scale up every three minutes, as long as the `current` value is above the `target`. Scaling down requires five minutes. An HPA will de-scale only if the `current` value is below the target for at least three minutes since the last time it scaled up.

All in all, we need to wait for five minutes, or more, before we see the scaling effect in the opposite direction.

```
1   kubectl -n go-demo-5 \
2       describe hpa go-demo-5
```

The output, limited to the relevant parts, is as follows.

```
...
Metrics:            ( current / target )
  "http_req_per_second_per_replica" on Ingress/go-demo-5:  0 / 50m
Min replicas:    3
Max replicas:    10
Deployment pods: 3 current / 3 desired
...
Events:
... Age    ... Message
... ----   ... -------
... 10m    ... New size: 6; reason: Ingress metric
http_req_per_second_per_replica above target
... 7m10s ... New size: 9; reason: Ingress metric
http_req_per_second_per_replica above target
... 2m9s  ... New size: 3; reason: All metrics below target
```

The most interesting part of the output is the events section. We'll focus on the `Age` and `Message` fields. Remember, scale-up events are executed every three minutes if the current value is above the target, while scale-down iterations are every five minutes.

In my case, the HPA scaled the Deployment again, three minutes later. The number of replicas jumped from six to nine. Since the expression used by the adapter uses five minutes rate, some of the requests entered the second HPA iteration. Scaling up even after we stopped sending requests might not seem like a good idea (it isn't) but in the "real world" scenarios that shouldn't occur, since there's much more traffic than what we generated and we wouldn't put `50m` (0.2 requests per second) as a target.

Five minutes after the last scale-up event, the `current` value was at `0`, and the HPA scaled the Deployment down to the minimum number of replicas (`3`). There's no traffic anymore, and we're back to where we started.

We confirmed that Prometheus' metrics, fetched by Prometheus Adapter, and converted into Kuberentes' custom metrics, can be used in HPAs. So far, we used metrics pulled by Prometheus through exporters (`nginx_ingress_controller_requests`). Given that the adapter fetches metrics from Prometheus, it shouldn't matter how they got there. Nevertheless, we'll confirm that instrumented metrics can be used as well. That will give us an opportunity to cement what we learned so far and, at the same time, maybe learn a few new tricks.

```
1  cat mon/prom-adapter-values-svc.yml
```

The output is yet another set of Prometheus Adapter Chart values.

```
image:
  tag: v0.5.0
metricsRelistInterval: 90s
prometheus:
  url: http://prometheus-server.metrics.svc
  port: 80
rules:
  default: false
  custom:
  - seriesQuery:
'http_server_resp_time_count{kubernetes_namespace!="",kubernetes_name!=""}'
    resources:
      overrides:
        kubernetes_namespace: {resource: "namespace"}
        kubernetes_name: {resource: "service"}
    name:
      matches: "^(.*)server_resp_time_count"
      as: "${1}req_per_second_per_replica"
```

```
    metricsQuery: 'sum(rate(<<.Series>>{<<.LabelMatchers>>}[5m])) by
  (<<.GroupBy>>) / count(<<.Series>>{<<.LabelMatchers>>}) by (<<.GroupBy>>)'
    - seriesQuery: 'nginx_ingress_controller_requests'
      resources:
        overrides:
          namespace: {resource: "namespace"}
          ingress: {resource: "ingress"}
      name:
        as: "http_req_per_second_per_replica"
      metricsQuery: 'sum(rate(<<.Series>>{<<.LabelMatchers>>}[5m])) by
  (<<.GroupBy>>) / sum(label_join(kube_deployment_status_replicas, "ingress",
  ",", "deployment")) by (<<.GroupBy>>)'
```

This time, we're combining rules containing different metric series. The first rule is based on the `http_server_resp_time_count` instrumented metric that origins in `go-demo-5`. We used it in the `Chapter 4`, *Debugging Issues Discovered Through Metrics and Alerts* and there's nothing truly extraordinary in its definition. It follows the same logic as the rules we used before. The second rule is the copy of one of the rules we used before.

What is interesting about those rules is that there are two completely different queries producing different results. However, the name is the same (`http_req_per_second_per_replica`) in both cases.

"Wait a minute", you might say. The names are not the same. One is called `${1}req_per_second_per_replica` while the other is `http_req_per_second_per_replica`. While that is true, the final name, excluding resource type, is indeed the same. I wanted to show you that you can use regular expressions to form a name. In the first rule, the name consists of `matches` and `as` entries. The `(.*)` part of the `matches` entry becomes the first variable (there can be others) which is later on used as part of the `as` value (`${1}`). Since the metric is `http_server_resp_time_count`, it will extract `http_` from `^(.*)server_resp_time_count` which, in the next line, is used instead of `${1}`. The final result is `http_req_per_second_per_replica`, which is the same as the name of the second rule.

Now that we established that both rules will provide custom metrics with the same name, we might think that will result in a conflict. How will HPA know which metric to use, if both are called the same? Will the adapter have to discard one and keep the other? The answer lies in the `resources` sections.

A true identifier of a metric is a combination of its name and the resource it ties with. The first rule produces two custom metrics, one for Services, and the other for Namespaces. The second also generates custom metrics for Namespaces, but for Ingresses as well.

How many metrics is that in total? I'll let you think about the answer before we check the result. To do that, we'll have to `upgrade` the Chart for the new values to take effect.

```
1  helm upgrade -i prometheus-adapter \
2      stable/prometheus-adapter \
3      --version v0.5.0 \
4      --namespace metrics \
5      --values mon/prom-adapter-values-svc.yml
6
7  kubectl -n metrics \
8      rollout status \
9      deployment prometheus-adapter
```

We upgraded the Chart with the new values and waited until the Deployment rolls out.

Now we can go back to our pending question "how many custom metrics we've got?" Let's see...

```
1  kubectl get --raw \
2      "/apis/custom.metrics.k8s.io/v1beta1" \
3      | jq "."
```

The output, limited to the relevant parts, is as follows.

```
{
   ...
    {
      "name": "services/http_req_per_second_per_replica",
      ...
    },
    {
      "name": "namespaces/http_req_per_second_per_replica",
      ...
    },
    {
      "name": "ingresses.extensions/http_req_per_second_per_replica",
      ...
```

Now we have three custom metrics, not four. I already explained that the unique identifier is the name of the metric combined with the Kubernetes resource it's tied to. All the metrics are called `http_req_per_second_per_replica`. But, since both rules override two resources, and `namespace` is set in both, one had to be discarded. We don't know which one was removed and which stayed. Or, maybe, they were merged. It does not matter since we shouldn't override the same resource with the metrics with the same name. There was no practical reason for me to include `namespace` in adapter's rule, other than to show you that there can be multiple overrides, and what happens when they are the same.

Other than that silly reason, you can mentally ignore the
`namespaces/http_req_per_second_per_replica` metric.

We used two different Prometheus' expressions to create two different custom metrics, with
the same name but related to other resources. One (based on
`nginx_ingress_controller_requests` expression) comes from Ingress resources, while
the other (based on `http_server_resp_time_count`) comes from Services. Even though
the latter originates in `go-demo-5` Pods, Prometheus discovered it through Services (as
discussed in the previous chapter).

We can use the `/apis/custom.metrics.k8s.io` endpoint not only to discover which
custom metrics we have but also to inspect details, including values. For example, we can
retrieve `services/http_req_per_second_per_replica` metric through the command
that follows.

```
1  kubectl get --raw \
2      "/apis/custom.metrics.k8s.io/v1beta1/namespaces/go-demo5
   /services/*/http_req_per_second_per_replica" \
3          | jq .
```

The output is as follows.

```
{
  "kind": "MetricValueList",
  "apiVersion": "custom.metrics.k8s.io/v1beta1",
  "metadata": {
    "selfLink": "/apis/custom.metrics.k8s.io/v1beta1/namespaces/go-
demo-5/services/%2A/http_req_per_second_per_replica"
  },
  "items": [
    {
      "describedObject": {
        "kind": "Service",
        "namespace": "go-demo-5",
        "name": "go-demo-5",
        "apiVersion": "/v1"
      },
      "metricName": "http_req_per_second_per_replica",
      "timestamp": "2018-10-27T23:49:58Z",
      "value": "1130m"
    }
  ]
}
```

The `describedObject` section shows us the details of the items. Right now, we have only
one Service with that metric.

We can see that the Service resides in the `go-demo-5` Namespace, that its name is `go-demo-5`, and that it is using `v1` API version.

Further down, we can see the current value of the metric. In my case, it is `1130m`, or slightly above one request per second. Since nobody is sending requests to the `go-demo-5` Service, that value is as expected, considering that a health check is executed once a second.

Next, we'll explore updated HPA definition that will use the Service-based metric.

```
1  cat mon/go-demo-5-hpa-svc.yml
```

The output is as follows.

```
apiVersion: autoscaling/v2beta1
kind: HorizontalPodAutoscaler
metadata:
  name: go-demo-5
spec:
  scaleTargetRef:
    apiVersion: apps/v1
    kind: Deployment
    name: go-demo-5
  minReplicas: 3
  maxReplicas: 10
  metrics:
  - type: Object
    object:
      metricName: http_req_per_second_per_replica
      target:
        kind: Service
        name: go-demo-5
      targetValue: 1500m
```

When compared with the previous definition, the only change is in the `target` and `targetValue` fields. Remember, the full identifier is a combination of the `metricName` and `target`. Therefore, this time we changed the `kind` to `Service`. We also had to change the `targetValue` since our application is receiving not only external requests through Ingress but also internal ones. They could be originating in other applications that might communicate with `go-demo-5` or, as in our case, in Kubernetes' health checks. Since their frequency is one second, we set the `targetValue` to `1500m`, or 1.5 requests per second. That way, scaling will not be triggered if we do not send any requests to the application. Normally, you'd set a much bigger value. But, for now, we're only trying to observe how it behaves before and after scaling.

Next, we'll apply the changes to the HPA, and describe it.

```
1  kubectl -n go-demo-5 \
2      apply -f mon/go-demo-5-hpa-svc.yml
3
4  kubectl -n go-demo-5 \
5      describe hpa go-demo-5
```

The output of the latter command, limited to the relevant parts, is as follows.

```
...
Metrics:                                              ( current /
target )
  "http_req_per_second_per_replica" on Service/go-demo-5: 1100m / 1500m
...
Deployment pods:                                   3 current / 3
desired
...
Events:
  Type     Reason              Age    From                  Message
  ----     ------              ----   ----                  -------
  Normal   SuccessfulRescale   12m    horizontal-pod-autoscaler  New size: 6;
reason: Ingress metric http_req_per_second_per_replica above target
  Normal   SuccessfulRescale   9m20s  horizontal-pod-autoscaler  New size: 9;
reason: Ingress metric http_req_per_second_per_replica above target
  Normal   SuccessfulRescale   4m20s  horizontal-pod-autoscaler  New size: 3;
reason: All metrics below target
```

For now, there's no reason for the HPA to scale up the Deployment. The current value is below the threshold. In my case, it's 1100m.

Now we can test whether autoscaling based on custom metrics originating from instrumentation works as expected. Sending requests through Ingress might be slow, especially if our cluster runs in Cloud. The round-trip from out laptop all the way to the service might be too slow. So, we'll send requests from inside the cluster, by spinning up a Pod and executing a request loop from inside it.

```
1  kubectl -n go-demo-5 \
2      run -it test \
3      --image=debian \
4      --restart=Never \
5      --rm \
6      -- bash
```

Normally, I prefer `alpine` images since they are much small and efficient. However, `for` loops do not work from `alpine` (or I don't know how to write them), so we switched to `debian` instead. It doesn't have `curl` though, so we'll have to install it.

```
1  apt update
2
3  apt install -y curl
```

Now we can send requests that will generate enough traffic for HPA to trigger the scale-up process.

```
1  for i in {1..500}; do
2      curl "http://go-demo-5:8080/demo/hello"
3  done
4
5  exit
```

We sent five-hundred requests to `/demo/hello` endpoint, and we exited the container. Since we used the `--rm` argument when we created the Pod, it will be removed automatically from the system, so we do not need to execute any cleanup operation.

Let's `describe` the HPA and see what happened.

```
1  kubectl -n go-demo-5 \
2      describe hpa go-demo-5
```

The output, limited to the relevant parts, is as follows.

```
...
Reference:                                              Deployment/go-
demo-5
Metrics:                                                ( current /
target )
  "http_req_per_second_per_replica" on Service/go-demo-5: 1794m / 1500m
Min replicas:                                           3
Max replicas:                                           10
Deployment pods:                                        3 current / 4
desired
...
Events:
... Message
... -------
... New size: 6; reason: Ingress metric http_req_per_second_per_replica
above target
... New size: 9; reason: Ingress metric http_req_per_second_per_replica
above target
... New size: 3; reason: All metrics below target
```

```
... New size: 4; reason: Service metric http_req_per_second_per_replica
above target
```

HPA detected that the `current` value is above the target (in my case it's `1794m`) and changed the desired number of replicas from `3` to `4`. We can observe that from the last event as well. If, in your case, the `desired` number of replicas is still `3`, please wait for a few moments for the next iteration of HPA evaluations, and repeat the `describe` command.

If we need an additional confirmation that scaling indeed worked as expected, we can retrieve the Pods in the `go-demo-5` Namespace.

```
1   kubectl -n go-demo-5 get pods
```

The output is as follows.

```
NAME              READY STATUS  RESTARTS AGE
go-demo-5-db-0 2/2    Running 0        33m
go-demo-5-db-1 2/2    Running 0        32m
go-demo-5-db-2 2/2    Running 0        32m
go-demo-5-...  1/1    Running 2        33m
go-demo-5-...  1/1    Running 0        53s
go-demo-5-...  1/1    Running 2        33m
go-demo-5-...  1/1    Running 2        33m
```

There's probably no need to confirm that the HPA will soon scale down the `go-demo-5` Deployment after we stopped sending requests. Instead, we'll jump into the next topic.

# Combining Metric Server data with custom metrics

So far, the few HPA examples used a single custom metric to decide whether to scale the Deployment. You already know from the `Chapter 1`, *Autoscaling Deployments and StatefulSets Based on Resource Usage*, that we can combine multiple metrics in an HPA. However, all the examples in that chapter used data from the Metrics Server. We learned that in many cases memory and CPU metrics from the Metrics Server are not enough, so we introduced Prometheus Adapter that feeds custom metrics to the Metrics Aggregator. We successfully configured an HPA to use those custom metrics. Still, more often than not, we'll need a combination of both types of metrics in our HPA definitions. While memory and CPU metrics are not enough by themselves, they are still essential. Can we combine both?

Let's take a look at yet another HPA definition.

```
1   cat mon/go-demo-5-hpa.yml
```

The output, limited to the relevant parts, is as follows.

```
...
  metrics:
  - type: Resource
    resource:
      name: cpu
      targetAverageUtilization: 80
  - type: Resource
    resource:
      name: memory
      targetAverageUtilization: 80
  - type: Object
    object:
      metricName: http_req_per_second_per_replica
      target:
        kind: Service
        name: go-demo-5
      targetValue: 1500m
```

This time, HPA has three entries in the `metrics` section. The first two are the "standard" `cpu` and `memory` entries based on `Resource` type. The last entry is one of the `Object` types we used earlier. With those combined, we're telling HPA to scale up if any of the three criteria are met. Similarly, it will scale down as well but for that to happen all three criteria need to be below the targets.

Let's `apply` the definition.

```
1   kubectl -n go-demo-5 \
2       apply -f mon/go-demo-5-hpa.yml
```

Next, we'll describe the HPA. But, before we do that, we'll have to wait for a bit until the updated HPA goes through its next iteration.

```
1   kubectl -n go-demo-5 \
2       describe hpa go-demo-5
```

The output, limited to the relevant parts, is as follows.

```
...
Metrics:                                              ( current /
target )
  resource memory on pods  (as a percentage of request):   110%
(5768533333m) / 80%
```

```
   "http_req_per_second_per_replica" on Service/go-demo-5: 825m / 1500m
   resource cpu on pods   (as a percentage of request):      20% (1m) / 80%
...
Deployment pods:                                          5 current / 5
desired
...
Events:
... Message
... -------
... New size: 6; reason: Ingress metric http_req_per_second_per_replica
above target
... New size: 9; reason: Ingress metric http_req_per_second_per_replica
above target
... New size: 4; reason: Service metric http_req_per_second_per_replica
above target
... New size: 3; reason: All metrics below target
... New size: 5; reason: memory resource utilization (percentage of
request) above target
```

We can see that the memory-based metric is above the threshold from the start. In my case, it is 110%, while the target is 80%. As a result, HPA scaled up the Deployment. In my case, it set the new size to 5 replicas.

There's no need to confirm that the new Pods are running. By now, we should trust HPA to do the right thing. Instead, we'll comment briefly on the whole flow.

# The complete HorizontalPodAutoscaler flow of events

Metrics Server is fetching memory and CPU data from Kubelets running on the worker nodes. In parallel, Prometheus Adapter is fetching data from Prometheus Server which, as you already know, pulls data from different sources. Data from both Metrics Server and Prometheus Adapter is combined in Metrics Aggregator.

> HPA is periodically evaluating metrics defined as scaling criteria. It's fetching data from Metrics Aggregator, and it does not really care whether they're coming from Metrics Server, Prometheus Adapter, or any other tool we could have used.

Once scaling criteria is met, HPA manipulates Deployments and StatefulSets by changing their number of replicas.

As a result, rolling updates are performed by creating and updating ReplicaSets which, in turn, create or remove Pods.

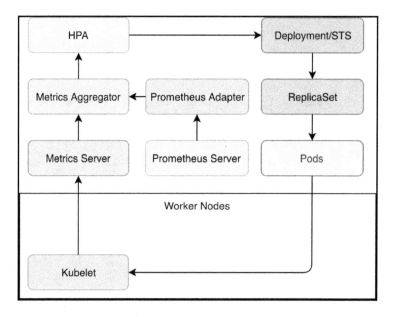

Figure 5-3: HPA using a combination of metrics from Metrics Server and those provided by Prometheus Adapter (arrows show the flow of data)

# Reaching nirvana

Now that we know how to add almost any metric to HPAs, they are much more useful than what it seemed in the Chapter 1, *Autoscaling Deployments and StatefulSets Based on Resource Usage*. Initially, HPAs weren't very practical since memory and CPU are, in many cases, insufficient for making decisions on whether to scale our Pods. We had to learn how to collect metrics (we used Prometheus Server for that), and how to instrument our applications to gain more detailed visibility. Custom Metrics was the missing piece of the puzzle. If we extend the "standard" metrics (CPU and memory) with the additional metrics we need (for example, Prometheus Adapter), we gain a potent process that will keep the number of replicas of our applications in sync with internal and external demands. Assuming that our applications are scalable, we can guarantee that they will (almost) always be as performant as needed. There is no need for manual interventions any more, at least when scaling is in question. HPA with "standard" and custom metrics will guarantee that the number of Pods meets the demand, and Cluster Autoscaler (when applicable) will ensure that we have the sufficient capacity to run those Pods.

Our system is one step closer to being self-sufficient. It will self-adapt to changed conditions, and we (humans) can turn our attention towards more creative and less repetitive tasks than those required to maintain the system in the state that meets the demand. We are one step closer to nirvana.

# What now?

Please note that we used `autoscaling/v2beta1` version of HorizontalPodAutoscaler. At the time of this writing (November 2018), only `v1` is stable and production-ready. However, `v1` is so limited (it can use only CPU metrics) that it's almost useless. Kubernetes community worked on new (v2) HPA for a while and, in my experience, it works reasonably well. The main problem is not stability but potential changes in the API that might not be backward compatible. A short while ago, `autoscaling/v2beta2` was released, and it uses a different API. I did not include it in the book because (at the time of this writing) most Kubernetes clusters do not yet support it. If you're running Kubernetes 1.11+, you might want to switch to `v2beta2`. If you do so, remember that you'll need to make a few changes to the HPA definitions we explored. The logic is still the same, and it behaves in the same way. The only visible difference is in the API.

 Please consult *HorizontalPodAutoscaler v2beta2 autoscaling* (`https://kubernetes.io/docs/reference/generated/kubernetes-api/v1.12/#horizontalpodautoscaler-v2beta2-autoscaling`) for the changes from `v2beta1` we used to `v2beta2` available in Kubernetes 1.11+.

That's it. Destroy the cluster if its dedicated to this book, or keep it if it's not or if you're planning to jump to the next chapter right away. If you're keeping it, please delete the `go-demo-5` resources by executing the commands that follow.

```
1  helm delete go-demo-5 --purge
2
3  kubectl delete ns go-demo-5
```

Before you leave, you might want to go over the main points of this chapter.

- HPA is periodically evaluating metrics defined as scaling criteria.
- HPA fetching data from Metrics Aggregator, and it does not really care whether they're coming from Metrics Server, Prometheus Adapter, or any other tool we could have used.

# Visualizing Metrics and Alerts

6

*It is curious how often you humans manage to obtain that which you do not want.*

*- Spock*

**Dashboards are useless! They are a waste of time. Get Netflix if you want to watch something. It's cheaper than any other option.**

I repeated those words on many public occasions. I think that companies exaggerate the need for dashboards. They spend a lot of effort creating a bunch of graphs and put a lot of people in charge of staring at them. As if that's going to help anyone. The main advantage of dashboards is that they are colorful and full of lines, boxes, and labels. Those properties are always an easy sell to decision makers like CTOs and heads of departments. When a software vendor comes to a meeting with decision makers with authority to write checks, he knows that there is no sale without "pretty colors". It does not matter what that software does, but how it looks like. That's why every software company focuses on dashboards.

Think about it. What good is a dashboard for? Are we going to look at graphs until a bar reaches a red line indicating that a critical threshold is reached? If that's the case, why not create an alert that will trigger under the same conditions and stop wasting time staring at screens and waiting until something happens. Instead, we can be doing something more useful (like staring Netflix).

Is our "panic criteria" more complex than what can be expressed through alerts? I do think that it is more complex. However, that complexity cannot be reflected through pre-defined graphs. Sure, unexpected things happen, and we need to dig through data. However, the word "unexpected" defies what dashboards provide. They are all about the expected outcomes. Otherwise, how are we going to define a graph without knowing what to expect? "It can be anything" cannot be translated to a graph. Dashboards with graphs are our ways to assume what might go wrong and put those assumptions on a screen or, more often than not, on a lot of screens.

However, unexpected can only be explored by querying metrics and going deeper and deeper until we find the cause of an issue. That's investigative work that does not translate well to dashboards. We use Prometheus queries for that.

And yet, here I am dedicating a chapter to dashboards.

I do admit that dashboards are not (fully) useless. They are useful, sometimes. What I truly wanted to convey is that their usefulness is exaggerated and that we might require to construct and use dashboards differently than what many are used to.

But, I'm jumping ahead of myself. We'll discuss the details of dashboards a bit later. For now, we need to create a cluster that will allow us to experiment and take this conversation to a more practical level.

# Creating a cluster

The `vfarcic/k8s-specs` (`https://github.com/vfarcic/k8s-specs`) repository will continue to serve as our source of Kubernetes definitions. We'll make sure that it is up-to-date by pulling the latest version.

 All the commands from this chapter are available in the `06-grafana.sh` (`https://gist.github.com/vfarcic/b94b3b220aab815946d34af1655733c b`) Gist.

```
1  cd k8s-specs
2
3  git pull
```

The requirements are the same as those we had in the previous chapter. For your convenience, the Gists are available here as well. Feel free to use them to create a new cluster, or to validate that the one you're planning to use meets the requirements.

- `gke-instrument.sh`: **GKE** with 3 n1-standard-1 worker nodes, **nginx Ingress**, **tiller**, **Prometheus** Chart, and environment variables **LB_IP**, **PROM_ADDR**, and **AM_ADDR**
  (`https://gist.github.com/vfarcic/675f4b3ee2c55ee718cf132e71e04c6e`).
- `eks-hpa-custom.sh`: **EKS** with 3 t2.small worker nodes, **nginx Ingress**, **tiller**, **Metrics Server**, **Prometheus** Chart, environment variables **LB_IP**, **PROM_ADDR**, and **AM_ADDR**, and **Cluster Autoscaler**
  (`https://gist.github.com/vfarcic/868bf70ac2946458f5485edea1f6fc4c`).

- `aks-instrument.sh`: **AKS** with 3 Standard_B2s worker nodes, **nginx Ingress**, and **tiller**, **Prometheus** Chart, and environment variables **LB_IP**, **PROM_ADDR**, and **AM_ADDR**
  (`https://gist.github.com/vfarcic/65a0d5834c9e20ebf1b99225fba0d339`).
- `docker-instrument.sh`: **Docker for Desktop** with **2 CPUs**, **3 GB RAM**, **nginx Ingress**, **tiller**, **Metrics Server**, **Prometheus** Chart, and environment variables **LB_IP**, **PROM_ADDR**, and **AM_ADDR**
  (`https://gist.github.com/vfarcic/1dddcae847e97219ab75f936d93451c2`).
- `minikube-instrument.sh`: **minikube** with **2 CPUs**, **3 GB RAM**, **ingress**, **storage-provisioner**, **default-storageclass**, and **metrics-server** addons enabled, **tiller**, **Prometheus** Chart, and environment variables **LB_IP**, **PROM_ADDR**, and **AM_ADDR**
  (`https://gist.github.com/vfarcic/779fae2ae374cf91a5929070e47bddc8`).

# Which tools should we use for dashboards?

It doesn't take more than a few minutes with Prometheus to discover that it is not designed to serve as a dashboard. Sure, you can create graphs in Prometheus but they are not permanent, nor do they offer much in terms of presenting data. Prometheus' graphs are designed to be used as a way to visualize ad-hoc queries. And that's what we need most of the time. When we receive a notification from an alert that there is a problem, we usually start our search for the culprit by executing the query of the alert and, from there on, we go deeper into data depending on the results. That is, if the alert does not reveal the problem immediately, in which case there is no need to receive notifications since those types of apparent issues can usually be fixed automatically.

But, as I already mentioned, Prometheus' does not have dashboarding features, so we'll have to look for a different tool.

These days, the choice of a dashboard is easy. *Grafana* (`https://grafana.com/`) is the undisputed ruler in the area. Other solutions are too old to bother with, or they do not support Prometheus. That is not to say that Grafana is the best tool on the market. But the price is right (it's free), and it works with many different data sources. We could, for example, argue that *Kibana* (`https://www.elastic.co/products/kibana`) is just as good as Grafana, or even better. But, it is limited to data from ElasticSearch. While Grafana can also use data from ElasticSearch, it supports many others. Some might say that *DataDog* (`https://www.datadoghq.com/`) is a better choice. Still, it suffers from the same problem as Kibana. It is tied to a specific source of metrics.

There is no flexibility and no option to combine data from other data sources. More importantly, neither of the two supports Prometheus.

I'll save you from further comparison with other tools. You can try them yourself. For now, you'll need to trust me that Grafana is good, if not the best choice. If we do not agree on that point, it will be pointless for you to read the rest of this chapter.

Now that I enforced Grafana as the choice, we'll move on and install it.

# Installing and setting up Grafana

You probably know what's coming next. We Google "Grafana Helm" and hope that the community already created a Chart we can use. I'll save you from the search by revealing that there is Grafana in Helm's *stable* channel. All we have to do is inspect the values and choose which ones we'll use.

```
1   helm inspect values stable/grafana
```

I won't go through all the values we could use. I assume that, by now, you are a Helm ninja and that you can explore them yourself. Instead, we'll use the values I already defined.

```
1   cat mon/grafana-values-bare.yml
```

The output is as follows.

```
ingress:
  enabled: true
persistence:
  enabled: true
  accessModes:
  - ReadWriteOnce
  size: 1Gi
resources:
  limits:
    cpu: 20m
    memory: 50Mi
  requests:
    cpu: 5m
    memory: 25Mi
```

There's nothing special about those values. We enabled Ingress, we set `persistence`, and we defined the `resources`. As the name of the file indicates, it's a very bare setup without anything fluffy.

All that's left is to install the Chart.

```
 1  GRAFANA_ADDR="grafana.$LB_IP.nip.io"
 2
 3  helm install stable/grafana \
 4      --name grafana \
 5      --namespace metrics \
 6      --version 1.17.5 \
 7      --set ingress.hosts="{$GRAFANA_ADDR}" \
 8      --values mon/grafana-values-bare.yml
 9
10  kubectl -n metrics \
11      rollout status deployment grafana
```

Now we can open Grafana in your favorite browser.

```
 1  open "http://$GRAFANA_ADDR"
```

You are presented with the login screen. Just as with many other Helm Charts, the installation comes with the `admin` user and the password stored as a Secret.

```
 1  kubectl -n metrics \
 2      get secret grafana \
 3      -o jsonpath="{.data.admin-password}" \
 4      | base64 --decode; echo
```

Please go back to the Grafana login screen, type `admin` as the **username**, and paste the output of the previous command as the **password**.

Grafana does not collect metrics. Instead, it uses other sources of data, so our first action is to set Prometheus as the data source.

Please click the **Add data source** icon.

Type `Prometheus` as the **Name** and choose it as the **Type** as well. We'll let Grafana connect to it through the Kubernetes Service `prometheus-server`. Since both are in the same Namespace, the **URL** should be set to `http://prometheus-server`. All that's left is to **Save & Test**.

The outputs and screenshots in this chapter are taken from Docker for Desktop. There might be slight differences between what you see here and what you can observe on your screen.

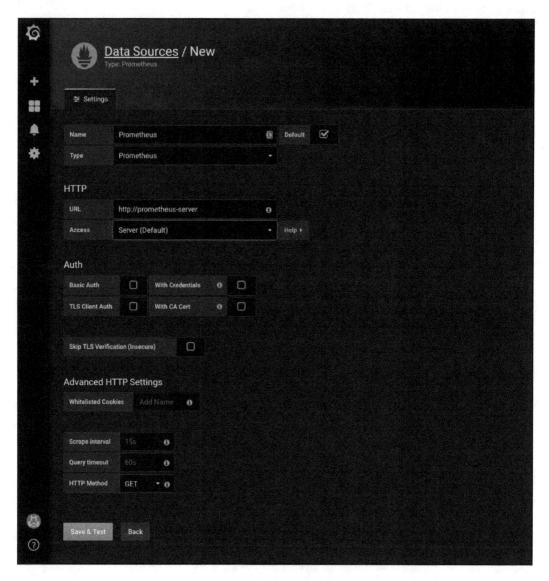

Figure 6-1: Grafana's new data source screen

We'll have more screenshots in this chapter than usual. I believe that they will help you replicate the steps we'll discuss.

# Importing and customizing pre-made dashboards

Data sources are useless by themselves. We need to visualize them somehow. We could do that by creating our own dashboard, but that might not be the best (and easiest) introduction to Grafana. Instead, we'll import one of the existing community-maintained dashboards. We just need to choose one that suits our needs.

```
1  open "https://grafana.com/dashboards"
```

Feel free to spend a bit of time exploring the available dashboards.

I think that *Kubernetes cluster monitoring* (https://grafana.com/dashboards/3119) dashboard is a good starting point. Let's import it.

Please click the + icon from the left-hand menu, followed with the **Import** link, and you'll be presented with a screen that allows us to import one of the Grafana.com dashboards, or to paste JSON that defines it.

We'll go with the former option.

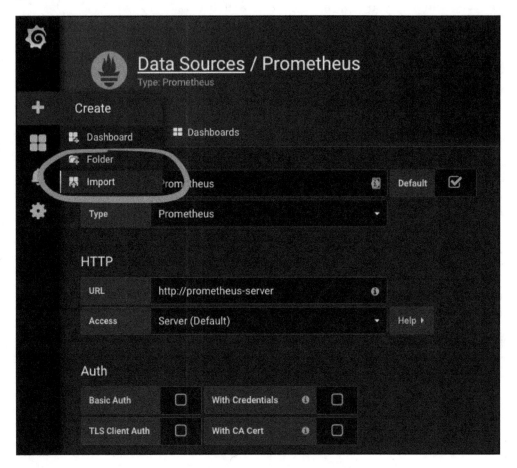

Figure 6-2: Grafana's import dashboard option

Please type `3119` into the *Grafana.com Dashboard* field, and click the **Load** button. You'll be presented with a few fields. The only important one, in this case, is the *prometheus* drop-down list. We must use it to set the data source. The choice is easy since we defined only one. Select **Prometheus**, and click the **Import** button.

What you see in front of you is a dashboard with some of the essential Kubernetes metrics.

Figure 6-3: Kubernetes cluster monitoring dashboard

However, some of the graphs might not work. Does that mean that we imported a wrong dashboard? A simple answer is quite the opposite. Of all the available dashboards, this one probably has the most graphs working. At least, if we count only those that are, more or less, useful. Such an outcome is common. Those dashboards are maintained by the community, but most of them are made for personal use. They are configured to work in specific clusters and to use particular metrics. You won't be able to find many dashboards that work without any changes and that, at the same time, show the things you truly need. Instead, I consider those dashboards a good starting point.

I import them only to get a base that I can modify to serve my specific needs. That's what we're going to do next, at least partially.

For now, we'll focus only on the changes aimed at making it fully operational. We'll make some of the graphs that are currently without data operational, and we'll remove those that are of no use to us.

If we take a closer look at the *Total usage* row, we'll see that *Cluster filesystem usage* is *N/A*. There's probably something wrong with the metrics it's using. Let's take a closer look.

 In some clusters (for example, EKS) the hard-coded file system in this dashboard is the correct one. If that's the case (if *Cluster filesystem usage* is not *N/A*) you do not have to make any changes. However, I suggest you still go through the exercise while imagining that your cluster uses a different file system. That way you'll learn a few tips that you could apply to other dashboards.

Please press the arrow next to the *Cluster filesystem usage* title, and click the **Edit** link.

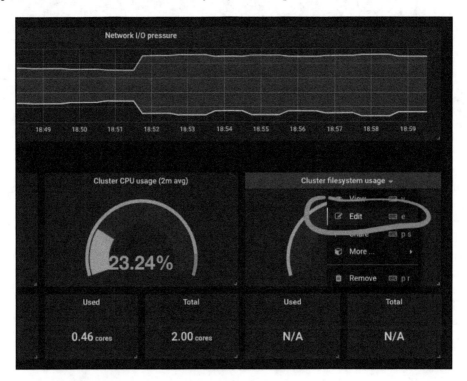

Figure 6-4: Grafana's option to edit a panel

The query used by that graph (formatted for readability) is as follows.

```
 1   sum (
 2       container_fs_usage_bytes{
 3           device=~"^/dev/xvda.$",
 4           id="/",
 5           kubernetes_io_hostname=~"^$Node$"
 6       }
 7   ) /
 8   sum (
 9       container_fs_limit_bytes{
10           device=~"^/dev/xvda.$",
11           id="/",
12           kubernetes_io_hostname=~"^$Node$"
13       }
14   ) * 100
```

We won't go into the details of that query. You should be familiar with Prometheus expressions by now. Instead, we'll focus on the likely cause of the issue. We probably do not have filesystem device called /dev/xvda (unless you're using EKS or, in some cases, GKE). If that's the problem, we can fix the Graph by simply changing the value to whatever our device is. But, before we go down that road, we might explore Grafana variables. After all, changing one hard-coded value with another will do us no good if we do not even know what our device is.

We could go to Prometheus and retrieve the list of all the devices, or we can let Grafana do that for us. We'll choose the latter.

Take a closer look at the kubernetes_io_hostname. It's set to ^$Node$. That is an example of using Grafana variables. We'll explore them next, in an attempt to replace the hard-coded device.

Please click the **Back to dashboard** button located in the top-right corner of the screen.

Click the *Settings* icon located in the top of the screen. You'll be presented with all the dashboard-wide configurations we can change. Feel free to explore the options in the left-hand menu.

Since we are interested in creating a new variable that will dynamically populate the device label of the query, our next action is to click the **Variables** link in the *Settings* section, followed with the **+ New** button.

Please type device as the variable **Name** and IO Device as the **Label**. We will retrieve the values from Prometheus (the data source), so we'll leave the **Type** to **Query**.

Next, we need to specify the **Data source**. Select **$datasource**. That tells Grafana that we want to query data from whichever data source we selected when we imported the dashboard.

So far, everything was probably self-explanatory. What comes next isn't. We need to consult the documentation and learn how to write Grafana queries used as variable values.

```
1  open
   "http://docs.grafana.org/features/datasources/prometheus/#query-variable"
```

Let this be an exercise. Find out, through the documentation, how to write a query that retrieves all distinct values of the label `device` available in the `container_fs_usage_bytes` metric.

Grafana supports only four types of variable queries so I suppose that you did not have a hard time finding out that the expression we should add to the **Query** field is `label_values(container_fs_usage_bytes, device)`.

With the query in place, all that's left is to click the **Add** button.

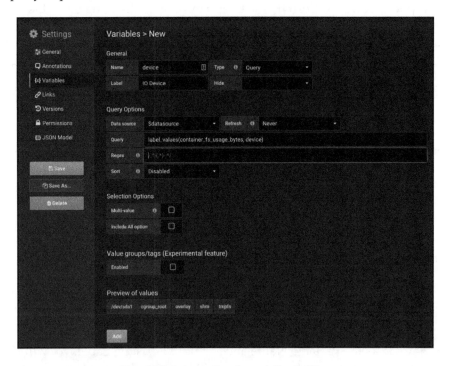

Figure 6-5: Grafana's screen for creating new dashboard variables

Now we should go *Back to dashboard* and confirm that the new variable is available.

You should see a new drop-down list with the label *IO Device* at the top-left section of the screen. If you expand it, you'll see all the devices used in our cluster. Make sure that the correct device is selected. That is likely `/dev/sda1` or `/dev/xvda1`.

Next, we need to change the graph to use the variable we just created.

Please click the arrow next to the *Cluster filesystem usage* graph, and select **edit**. The metric (query) contains two hard-coded `^/dev/xvda.$` values. Change them to `$device`, and click the **Back to dashboard** button located in the top-right corner of the screen.

That's it. The graph now works correctly by showing us the percentage of cluster file system usage (`/dev/sda1`).

However, the *Used* and *Total* numbers below it are still *N/A*. I believe you know what to do to fix them. Edit those graphs and replace `^/dev/xvda.$` with `$device`.

There are still two issues to solve with that dashboard. Or, to be more precise, two graphs are useless to us. The purpose of the *System services CPU usage* and *System services memory usage* graphs should be deducible from their titles. Yet, most Kubernetes clusters do not provide access to system-level services (for example, GKE). Even if they do, our Prometheus is not configured to fetch the data. If you don't believe me, copy the query of one of those graphs and execute it in Prometheus. As it is now, those graphs are only wasting space, so we'll remove them.

Please click the *trash* icon next to the title of the *System services CPU usage* row. Click **Yes** to remove both the row and the panel. Repeat the same actions for the *System services memory usage* row.

Now we're done with making changes to the dashboard. It is fully operational, and we should persist the changes by clicking the *Save dashboard* icon in the top-right corner of the screen, or by pressing **CTRL+S**.

We won't go into all the Grafana options and the actions we can do. I'm sure that you can figure them out yourself. It is a very intuitive application. Instead, we'll try to create our own dashboard. Or, at least, explore a few things that will allow you to continue on your own.

# Creating custom dashboards

It would be great if all our needs could be covered by existing dashboards. But, that is probably not the case. Each organization is "special", and our needs have to be reflected in our dashboards. Sometimes we can get away with dashboards made by others, and sometimes we need to change them. In other cases, we need to create our own dashboards. That's what we'll explore next.

Please click the + icon in the left-hand menu and choose to `Create Dashboard`. You'll be presented with the choice of a few types of panels. Select `Graph`.

Before we define our first graph, we'll change a few dashboard settings. Please click the *Settings* icon in the top-right part of the screen.

Inside the *General* section, type the **Name** of the dashboard. If you are not inspired today, you can call it `My Dashboard`. Set the **Tags** to `Prometheus` and `Kubernetes`. You'll have to press the enter key after typing each tag. Finally, change the **Timezone** to **Local browser time**.

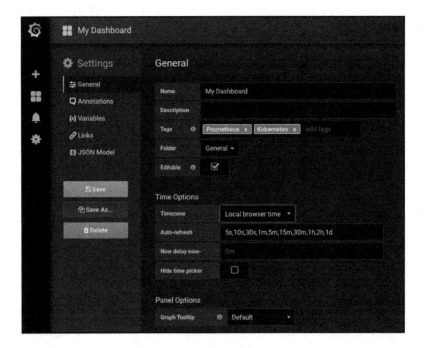

Figure 6-6: Grafana's dashboard general settings screen

That was the boring part. Now let's switch to something more interesting. We are about to convert one of the alerts we created in Prometheus into a graph. We'll use the one that tells us the percentage of actual vs. reserved CPU. For that, we'll need a few variables. To be more precise, we don't really need them since we could hard-code the values. But, that would cause problems later on if we decide to change them. It is much easier to modify variables than to change the queries.

Specifically, we'll need variables that will tell us what is the minimum CPU so that we can ignore the thresholds for the applications that are set to use very low reservations. Also, we'll define variables that will act as lower and upper boundaries. Our goal is to be notified if reserved CPU is too low or too high when compared with the actual usage, just as we did with Prometheus alerts.

Please select the **Variables** section from the left-hand menu, and click the **Add Variable** button.

You already saw the screen with Grafana variables when we created a new one for the dashboard we imported. This time, however, we'll use slightly different settings.

Type minCpu as the **Name** and choose **Constant** as the **Type**. Unlike the device variable we created earlier, this time we do not need Grafana to query the values. By using that type, we are going to define a constant value. Please set the **Value** *to* 0.005 (five CPU milliseconds). Finally, we do not need to see that variable in the dashboard, since the value is not likely to change often. If we do need to change it in the future, we can always come back to this screen and update it. Therefore, change the **Hide** value to **Variable**.

All that's left is to click the **Add** button, twice.

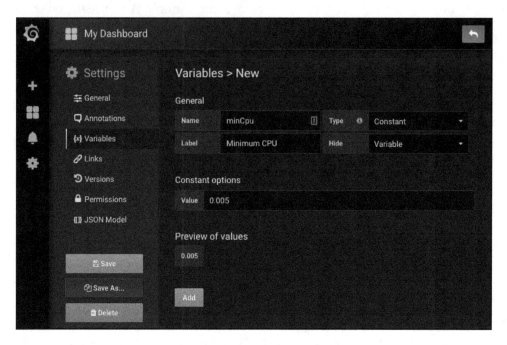

Figure 6-7: Grafana's dashboard new variable screen

We need two more variables. There's probably no need to repeat the same instructions, so please use the following information to create them.

```
 1  Name:  cpuReqPercentMin
 2  Type:  Constant
 3  Label: Min % of requested CPU
 4  Hide:  Variable
 5  Value: 50
 6
 7  Name:  cpuReqPercentMax
 8  Type:  Constant
 9  Label: Max % of requested CPU
10  Hide:  Variable
11  Value: 150
```

Now we can go back and define our graph. Please click the *Back to dashboard* icon from the top-right part of the screen.

You already know how to edit a panel. Click on the arrow next to *Panel Title,* and select **Edit**.

We'll start with the *General* section. Please select it.

Next, write % of actual vs reserved CPU as the **Title** and the text that follows as the **Description**.

```
1  The percentage of actual CPU usage compared to reserved. The
   calculation excludes Pods with reserved CPU equal to or smaller than
   $minCpu. Those with less than $minCpu of requested CPU are ignored.
```

Please note the usage of $minCpu variable in the description. When we go back to the dashboard, it will expand to its value.

Next, please switch to the *Metrics* tab. That's where the real action is happening.

We can define multiple queries but, for our use case, one should be enough. Please type the query that follows in the field to the right of *A*.

For your convenience, the query is available in the grafana-actual-vs-reserved-cpu
(https://gist.github.com/vfarcic/1b027a1e2b2415e1d156687c1cf14012) Gist.

```
1   sum(label_join(
2       rate(
3           container_cpu_usage_seconds_total{
4               namespace!="kube-system",
5               pod_name!=""
6           }[5m]
7       ),
8       "pod",
9       ",",
10      "pod_name"
11  )) by (pod) /
12  sum(
13      kube_pod_container_resource_requests_cpu_cores{
14          namespace!="kube-system",
15          namespace!="ingress-nginx"
16      }
17  ) by (pod) and
18  sum(
19      kube_pod_container_resource_requests_cpu_cores{
20          namespace!="kube-system",
21          namespace!="ingress-nginx"
22      }
23  ) by (pod) > $minCpu
```

That query is almost the same as one of those we used in the `Chapter 3`, *Collecting and Querying Metrics and Sending Alerts*. The only difference is the usage of the `$minCpu` variable.

A few moments after entering the query, we should see the graph come alive. There is probably only one Pod included since many of our applications are defined to use five CPU milliseconds (the value of `$minCpu`), or less.

Figure 6-8: Grafana's panel based on a graph

Next, we'll adjust the units on the left side of the graph. Please click the **Axes** tab.

Expand the *Left Y Unit*, select **none**, followed with **percent (0.0-1.0)**. Since we're not using the *Right Y* axis, please uncheck the *Show* checkbox.

The next section in line is *Legend*. Please select it.

Check the *Options As Table, Options To the right*, and *Values > Current* checkboxes. The changes are applied to the graph immediately, and you should not have trouble deducing what each of those does.

There's only one more thing missing. We should define upper and lower thresholds that will provide a clear indication that the results are outside expected boundaries.

Please click the **Alert** tab.

Click the **Create Alert** button and change the **IS ABOVE** condition to **IS OUTSIDE RANGE**. Set the values of the next two fields to 0,5 and 1,5. That should notify is if the actual CPU usage is below 50% or above 150% when compared to the reserved value.

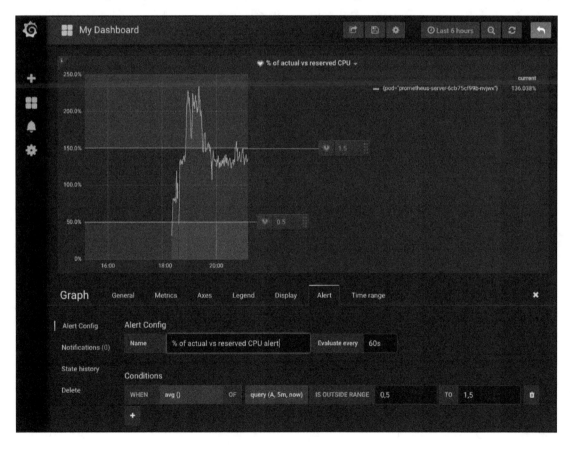

Figure 6-9: Grafana's graph with alerts

We're done with the graph, so please go *Back to dashboard* and enjoy "pretty colors". You might want to drag the bottom-right corner of the graph to adjust its size.

We can see the difference between the requested and the actual CPU usage. We also have the thresholds (marked in red) that will tell us whether the usage goes outside the established boundaries.

Now comes the big question. Is such a graph useful? The answer depends on what we're going to use it for.

If the goal is to stare at it waiting for one of the Pods to start using too much or too little CPU, I can only say that you're wasting your talent that can be used on more productive tasks. After all, we already have a similar alert in Prometheus that will send us a Slack notification when the criteria are met. It is more advanced than what we have in that graph because it will notify us only if the CPU usage spikes for a given period, thus avoiding temporary issues that might be resolved a few seconds or a few minutes later. We should discard those cases as false alarms.

Another usage of that graph could be more passive. We could ignore it (close Grafana) and come back to it only if the above mentioned Prometheus alert is fired. That might make more sense. Even though we could run a similar query in Prometheus and get the same results, having a predefined graph could save us from writing such a query. You can think of it as a way to have a query registry with corresponding graphical representations. That is something that does make more sense. Instead of staring at the dashboard (choose Netflix instead), we can come back to it in time of need. While in some situations that might be a reasonable strategy, it will work only in very simple cases. When there is an issue, and a single pre-defined graph solves the problem or, to be more precise, provides a clear indication of the cause of the issue, graphs do provide significant value. However, more often than not, finding the cause of a problem is not that simple and we'll have to turn to Prometheus to start digging deeper into metrics.

 Looking at dashboards with graphs is a waste of time. Visiting dashboards after receiving a notification about an issue makes a bit more sense. Still, all but trivial problems require deeper digging through Prometheus metrics.

Never the less, the graph we just made might prove itself useful, so we'll keep it. What we might want to do, in such a case, is to change the link of the Prometheus alert (the one we're currently receiving in Slack) so that it takes us directly to the Graph (not the dashboard). We can get that link by clicking the arrow next to the panel name, and choosing the **View** option.

I believe that we can make our dashboard more useful if we change the type of panels from graphs to something less colorful, with fewer lines, fewer axes, and without other pretty things.

# Creating semaphore dashboards

If I'm claiming that the value dashboards bring to the table is lower than we think, you might be asking yourself the same question from the beginning of this chapter. Why are we talking about dashboards? Well, I already changed my statement from "dashboards are useless" to "there is some value in dashboards". They can serve as a registry for queries. Through dashboards, we do not need to memorize expressions that we would need to write in Prometheus. They might be a good starting point of our search for the cause of an issue before we jump into Prometheus for some deeper digging into metrics. But, there is another reason I am including dashboards into the solution.

I love big displays. It's very satisfying to enter into a room with large screens showing stuff that seem to be important. There is usually a room where operators sit surrounded with monitors on all four walls. That's usually an impressive sight. However, there is a problem with many such situations. A bunch of monitors displaying a lot of graphs might not amount to much more than a pretty sight. After the initial few days, nobody will stare at graphs. If that's not true, you can just as well fire that person knowing that he was faking his work.

Let me repeat it one more time.

 Dashboards are not designed for us to stare at them, especially not when they are on big screens where everyone can see them.

So, if it's a good idea to have big screens, but graphs are not a good candidate to decorate them, what should we do instead? The answer lies in semaphores. They are similar to alerts, and they should provide a clear indication of the status of the system. If everything on the screen is green, there is no reason for us to do anything. One of them turning red is a cue that we should do something to correct the problem. Therefore, it is imperative that we try to avoid false positives. If something turns red, and that does not require any action, we are likely to start ignoring it in the future. When that happens, we are risking the situation in which when we ignore a real issue, thinking that it is just another false positive. Hence, every appearance of an alarm should be followed by an action.

That can be either a fix that will correct the system or a change in the conditions that turned one of the semaphores red. In either case, we should not ignore it.

The main problem with semaphores is that they are not as appealing to CTOs and other decision makers. They are not colorful, nor do they show a lot of boxes, lines, and numbers. People often confuse usefulness with how pleasing something is to look at. Never the less, we are not building something that should be sold to CTOs, but something that can be helpful in our day-to-day work.

 Semaphores are much more useful than graphs as a way to see the status of the system, even though they do not look as colorful and eye-pleasing as graphs.

Let's create our first semaphore.

Please click the *Add panel* icon from the top-right part of the screen, and select **Singlestat**. Click the arrow icon next to the *Panel Title*, and select **Edit**.

For the most part, creating a single stat (a semaphore) is not much different from creating a graph. The significant difference is in the metric (query) that should produce a single value. We'll get there soon. For now, we'll change some general info of the panel.

Please select the **General** tab.

Type `Pods with <$cpuReqPercentMin%||>$cpuReqPercentMax% actual compared to reserved CPU` as the **Title** and the text that follows as the **Description**.

> 1  The number of Pods with less than $cpuReqPercentMin% or more than
>    $cpuReqPercentMax% actual compared to reserved CPU

This single stat will use a similar query as the graph we made earlier. However, while the graph is displaying current usage compared to reserved CPU, this panel is supposed to show how many Pods have actual CPU usage outside of the boundaries based on reserved CPU. That is reflected in the title and the description we just entered. As you can see, this time we're relying on more variables to formulate our intentions.

Now, let's turn our attention to the query. Please click the **Metrics** tab and type the expression that follows into the field next to *A*.

 For your convenience, the query is available in the `grafana-single-stat-actual-vs-reserved-cpu` (`https://gist.github.com/vfarcic/078674efd3b379c211c4da2c9844f5bd`) Gist.

```
 1   sum(
 2       (
 3           sum(
 4               label_join(
 5                   rate(container_cpu_usage_seconds_total{
 6                       namespace!="kube-system",
 7                       pod_name!=""}[5m]),
 8                       "pod",
 9                       ",",
10                       "pod_name"
11               )
12           ) by (pod) /
13           sum(
14               kube_pod_container_resource_requests_cpu_cores{
15                   namespace!="kube-system",
16                   namespace!="ingress-nginx"
17               }
18           ) by (pod) and
19           sum(
20               kube_pod_container_resource_requests_cpu_cores{
21                   namespace!="kube-system",
22                   namespace!="ingress-nginx"
23               }
24           ) by (pod) > $minCpu
25       ) < bool ($cpuReqPercentMin / 100)
26   ) +
27   sum(
28       (
29           sum(
30               label_join(
31                   rate(
32                       container_cpu_usage_seconds_total{
33                           namespace!="kube-system",
34                           pod_name!=""
35                       }[5m]
36                   ),
37                   "pod",
38                   ",",
39                   "pod_name"
40               )
41           ) by (pod) /
42           sum(
43               kube_pod_container_resource_requests_cpu_cores{
44                   namespace!="kube-system",
45                   namespace!="ingress-nginx"
46               }
47           ) by (pod) and
48           sum(
```

```
49                   kube_pod_container_resource_requests_cpu_cores{
50                       namespace!="kube-system",
51                       namespace!="ingress-nginx"
52                   }
53              ) by (pod) > $minCpu
54          ) > bool ($cpuReqPercentMax / 100)
55      )
```

That query is similar to one of those we used as the Prometheus alert. To be more precise, it is a combination of the two Prometheus alerts. The first half returns the number of Pods with more than $minCpu (5 CPU milliseconds) of reserved CPU and with actual CPU usage lower than $cpuReqPercentMin (50%). The second half is almost the same as the first, except that it returns Pods with CPU usage higher than $cpuReqPercentMax (150%).

Since our goal is to return a single stat which, in this case, is the number of Pods, you might be surprised that we used sum instead of count. Counting Pods would indeed make more sense, except that would return N/A if there are no results. To avoid that, we're using a trick with bool. By putting it in front of an expression, it returns 1 if there is a match, and 0 if there isn't. That way, if none of the Pods match the conditions, we won't get an empty result, but 0, which is a better representation of the number of problematic Pods.

All in all, we are retrieving a sum of all the Pods with the actual CPU below $cpuReqPercentMin (50%) of the reserved CPU, plus the sum of all the Pods with the actual CPU above $cpuReqPercentMax (150%) of the reserved CPU. In both cases, only the Pods with more than $minCpu (five CPU milliseconds) are included. The query itself is not the simplest one we could write but, considering that we already spent a lot of time with Prometheus queries, I thought that I should not "insult" you with something trivial.

Next, please click the **Options** tab. That is where we'll define the conditions that should trigger the change of colors.

We do NOT want average value over the specified period, but the current number of problematic Pods. We'll accomplish that by changing the value of the **Stat** drop-down list to **Current**.

We want this panel to be very visible, so we'll change the **Stat Font size** to 200%. I'd prefer even bigger font, but Grafana does not allow us to go higher than that.

Next, we want to change the background color of the panel, so please check the **Coloring Background** checkbox.

We could use up to three colors, but I believe that we need only two. Either one or more of the Pods meet the conditions, or none of them do.

We should be notified as soon as the query returns 1, or a higher number. Please type 1 as the **Coloring Thresholds**. If we had more, we'd separate them with commas.

Finally, since we have only two conditions, green and red, we'll need to change the second color from orange to red. Please click the *red* icon in **Coloring Colors**, and replace the value with the word *red*. The third color is not used, so we'll leave it intact.

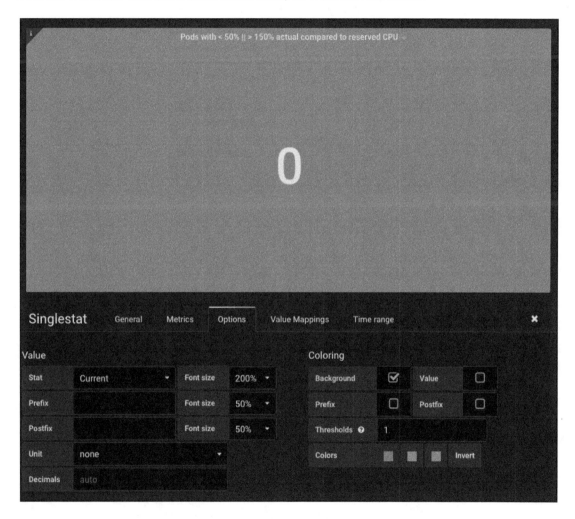

Figure 6-10: Grafana's single stat panel

We're finished with our panel, so go *Back to dashboard*.

Before we proceed, please click the *Save Dashboard* icon, followed with the **Save** button.

So far, we created a dashboard with a graph and a single stat (semaphore). The former shows the deviation of CPU usage compared to reserved CPU over time. It has alerts (red areas) that tell us whether one of the vectors is outside predefined boundaries. The single stat (semaphore) shows a single number with green or red background depending on whether that number reached a threshold which, in our case, is set to 1.

We just started, and we need many other panels before this dashboard becomes useful. I'll save you from repetitive instructions for defining the others. I feel that you got a grip on how Grafana works. You should, at least, have the base knowledge that you can expand on your own.

We'll fast forward. We'll import a dashboard I prepared and discuss the design choices.

# A better dashboard for big screens

We explored how to create a dashboard with a graph and a single stat (semaphore). Both are based on similar queries, and the significant difference is in the way they display the results. We'll assume that the primary purpose of the dashboard we started building is to be available on a big screen, visible to many, and not as something we keep open on our laptops. At least, not continuously.

What should be the primary purpose of such a dashboard? Before I answer that question, we'll import a dashboard I created for this chapter.

Please click the + button from the left-hand menu and select **Import**. Type 9132 as the *Grafana.com Dashboard* and press the **Load** button. Select a *Prometheus data source*. Feel free to change any of the values to suit your needs. Never the less, you might want to postpone that until you get more familiar with the dashboard.

In any case, click the **Import** button once you're finished.

Figure 6-11: Grafana dashboard based on semaphores

You are likely to see one or more red semaphores. That's normal since some of the resources in our cluster are not configured properly. For example, Prometheus is likely to have less memory requested than it needs. That's OK because it allows us to see the dashboard in action. The definitions used in the Gists are not supposed to be production-ready, and you already know that you have to adjust their resources, and likely a few other things.

You'll notice that the dashboard we imported consists only of semaphores. At least, on the first look. Even though they might not be as appealing as graphs and other types of panels, they are much more effective as indicators of the health of our system. We do not need to look at that dashboard. It's enough if it's displayed on a big screen, while we work on something else. If one of the boxes turns red, we'll notice that. It will be a call to action. Or, to be more precise, we'll need to do something if a red box continues being red for longer, thus excluding the possibility that it's a false positive that will be resolved by itself after a few moments.

You can think of this dashboard as a supplement to Prometheus alerts. It does not replace them, since there are some subtle, yet significant differences we'll discuss later.

I won't describe each of the panels since they are a reflection of the Prometheus alerts we created earlier. You should be familiar with them by now. If in doubt, please click on the **i** icon in the top-left corner of a panel. If the description is not enough, enter the panel's edit mode and check the query and the coloring options.

Please note that the dashboard might not be the perfect fit as-is. You might need to change some of the variable values or the coloring thresholds. For example, the threshold of the *Nodes* panel is set to 4, 5. Judging by the colors, we can see that it'll turn orange (warning) if the number of nodes jumps to four, and red (panic) if it goes to five. Your values are likely to be different. Ideally, we should use variables instead of hard-coded thresholds, but that is currently not possible with Grafana. Variables are not supported everywhere. You, as a supporter of open source projects, should make a PR. Please let me know if you do.

Does all that mean that all our dashboards should be green and red boxes with a single number inside them? I do believe that semaphores should be the "default" display. When they are green, there's no need for anything else. If that's not the case, we should extend the number of semaphores, instead of cluttering our monitors with random graphs. However, that begs the question. What should we do when some of the boxes turn red or even orange?

Below the boxes, you'll find the *Graph* row with additional panels. They are not visible by default for a reason.

There is no justification for seeing them under normal circumstances. But, if one of the semaphores does raise an alert, we can expand *Graphs* and see more details about the issue.

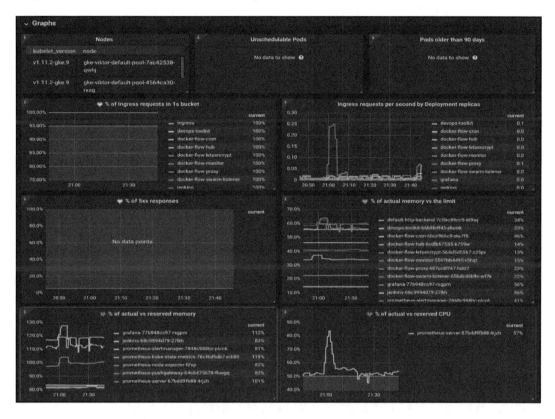

Figure 6-12: Grafana dashboard based on tables and graphs

The panels inside the *Graphs* row are a reflection of the panels (semaphores) in the *Alerts* row. Each graph shows more detailed data related to the single stat from the same location (but a different row). That way, we do not need to waste our time trying to figure out which graph corresponds to the "red box".

Instead, we can jump straight into the corresponding graph. If the semaphore on in the second row on the right turns red, look at the graphs in the second row on the right. If multiple boxes turn red, we can take a quick look at related graphs and try to find the relation (if there is any). More often than not, we'll have to switch from Grafana to Prometheus and dig deeper into metrics.

Dashboards like the one in front of you should give us a quick head start towards the resolution of an issue. The semaphores on the top provide alerting mechanism that should lead to the graphs below that should give a quick indication of the possible causes of the problem. From there on, if the cause is an obvious one, we can move to Prometheus and start debugging (if that's the right word).

 Dashboards with semaphores should be displayed on big screens around the office. They should provide an indication of a problem. Corresponding graphs (and other panels) provide a first look at the issue. Prometheus serves as the debugging tool we use to dig into metrics until we find the culprit.

We explored a few things that provide similar functionality. Still, it might not be clear what the difference between Prometheus alerts, semaphores, graph alerts, and Grafana notifications is? Why didn't we create any Grafana notification? We'll explore those and a few other questions next.

# Prometheus alerts vs. Grafana notifications vs. semaphores vs. graph alerts

The title might be confusing by itself, so let us briefly describe each of the elements mentioned in it.

Prometheus alerts and Grafana notifications serve the same purpose, even though we did not explore the latter. I'll let you learn how Grafana notifications work on your own. Who knows? After the discussion that follows you might not even want to spend time with them.

Grafana notifications can be forwarded to different recipients in a similar manner as how Prometheus' alerts are forwarded with Alertmanager. However, there are a few things that make Grafana notifications less appealing.

If we can accomplish the same result with Prometheus alerts as with Grafana alerts, there is a clear advantage with the former. If an alert is fired from Prometheus, that means that the rules that caused the alert to fire are also defined in Prometheus.

As a result, evaluations are happening at the data source, and we are avoiding unnecessary latency between Grafana and Prometheus. The closer we are to the data source, the better. In case of alerts/notifications, closer means inside Prometheus.

Another advantage for defining alerts in Prometheus is the fact that it allows us to do more. For example, there is no equivalent to Prometheus' `for` statement in Grafana. We cannot define a notification that will fire only if the conditions persist for a while. We'd need to resort to non-trivial additions to the queries to accomplish the same. Alertmanager, on the other hand, provides more sophisticated ways to filter the alerts, to group them, and to forward only those that match certain criteria. There are many other advantages to defining alerts in Prometheus and Alertmanager instead of notifications in Grafana. But, we won't go into all of them. I'll leave it to you to find all the differences unless you are already convinced to ditch Grafana notifications in favor of Prometheus alerts and Alertmanager.

There is one important reason why you shouldn't dismiss Grafana notifications completely. The data source you're using might not have alerting/notifications mechanism, or it might be part of enterprise license you do not possess. Since Grafana supports many different data sources, with Prometheus being only one of them, Grafana notifications allow us to use any of those data sources, or even to combine them.

 Stick with Prometheus for alerts/notifications based on metrics stored there. For other data sources, Grafana alerts might be a better or even the only option.

Now that we briefly explored the differences between Prometheus alerts and Grafana notifications, we'll move into semaphores.

Semaphores (Grafana dashboards based on single stat panels) do not replace Prometheus alerts. First of all, it is hard, or even impossible, to create semaphores that turn red only if a value reaches a threshold for some time (for example, like the `for` statement in Prometheus alerts). That means that a semaphore might turn red, only to go back to green a few moments later. That is not a cause for action since the problem was resolved automatically short while later. If we would jump every time something turns red in Grafana, we'd be in excellent physical shape, but we wouldn't do much useful work.

Semaphores are an indication of a possible problem that might not require any intervention. While such false positives should be avoided, it's almost impossible to get rid of them altogether. That means that we should stare at the screen to see whether a red box continues being red for at least a few minutes before we act. The primary purpose of semaphores is not to provide a notification to a person or a team that should fix the issue. Notifications to Slack, email, and other destinations do that. Semaphores provide awareness of the state of the system.

Finally, we explored alerts defined on graphs. Those are the red lines and zones in the graphs. They are not good indicators that there is something wrong. They are not that easy to spot so they cannot raise awareness, and they definitely do not replace notifications. Instead, they help us after we discover that there is an issue. If a notification or a semaphore alerts us that there is a problem that might need to be fixed, graph alerts help us identify the culprit. Which Pod is in the red zone? Which ingress received more requests than expected? Those are only a few questions that we can answer through graph alerts.

# What now?

Grafana is relatively simple to use and intuitive. If you know how to write queries for the data source hooked to Grafana (for example, Prometheus), you already learned the most challenging part. The rest is mostly about checking boxes, choosing panel types, and arranging things on the screen. The main difficulty is to avoid being carried away by creating a bunch of flashy dashboards that do not provide much value. A common mistake is to create a graph for everything we can imagine. That only reduces the value of those that are truly important. Less is often more.

That's it. Destroy the cluster if its dedicated to this book, or keep it if it's not or if you're planning to jump to the next chapter right away. If you're keeping it, please delete the `grafana` Chart by executing the command that follows. If we need it in one of the next chapters, I'll make sure that it's included in the Gists.

```
1  helm delete grafana --purge
```

Before you leave, you might want to go over the main points of this chapter.

- Looking at dashboards with graphs is a waste of time. Visiting dashboards after receiving a notification about an issue makes a bit more sense. Still, all but trivial problems require deeper digging through Prometheus metrics.
- Dashboards are not designed for us to stare at them, especially not when they are on big screens where everyone can see them.
- Semaphores are much more useful than graphs as a way to see the status of the system, even though they do not look as colorful and eye-pleasing as graphs.
- Dashboards with semaphores should be displayed on big screens around the office. They should provide an indication of a problem. Corresponding graphs (and other panels) provide a first look at the issue. Prometheus serves as the debugging tool we use to dig into metrics until we find the culprit.
- Stick with Prometheus for alerts/notifications based on metrics stored there. For other data sources, Grafana alerts might be a better or even the only option.

# 7

# Collecting and Querying Logs

*In critical moments, men sometimes see exactly what they wish to see.*

*- Spock*

So far, our primary focus was on metrics. We used them in different forms and for different purposes. In some cases, we used metrics to scale Pods and nodes. In others, metrics were used to create alerts that would notify us when there is an issue that cannot be fixed automatically. We also created a few dashboards.

However, metrics are often not enough. That is especially true when dealing with issues that require manual interventions. When metrics alone are insufficient, we usually need to consult logs hoping that they will reveal the cause of the problem.

Logging is often misunderstood or, to be more precise, mixed with metrics. For many, the line between logs and metrics is blurred. Some are extracting metrics from logs. Others are treating metrics and logs as the same source of information. Both approaches are wrong. Metrics and logs are separate entities, they serve different purposes, and there is a clear distinction between them. We store them separately, and we use them to solve different types of issues. We'll park that and a few other discussions. Instead of going into details based on theory, we'll explore them through hands-on examples. For that, we need a cluster.

## Creating a cluster

You know the drill. We'll move into the directory with the `vfarcic/k8s-specs` (`https://github.com/vfarcic/k8s-specs`) repository, we'll pull the latest version of the code just in case I pushed something recently, and we'll create a new cluster unless you already have one at hand.

All the commands from this chapter are available in the `07-logging.sh` (https://gist.github.com/vfarcic/74774240545e638b6cf0e01460894f34) Gist.

```
1  cd k8s-specs
2
3  git pull
```

This time, the requirements for the cluster changed. We need much more memory than before. The main culprit is ElasticSearch which is very resource hungry.

If you're using **Docker for Desktop** or **minikube**, you'll need to increase the memory dedicated to the cluster to **10 GB**. If that's too much for your laptop, you might choose to read the *Exploring Centralized Logging Through Elasticsearch, Fluentd, and Kibana* without running the examples or you might have to switch to one of the Cloud providers (AWS, GCP, or Azure).

In the case of **EKS** and **AKS**, we'll need bigger nodes. For EKS we'll use **t2.large** and for AKS **Standard_B2ms**. Both are based on **2 CPUs** and **8 GB RAM**.

**GKE** requirements are the same as before.

On top of new requirements, it should be noted that we do NOT need Prometheus in this chapter, so I removed it from the Gists.

Feel free to use one of the Gists that follow to create a new cluster, or to validate that the one you're planning to use meets the requirements.

- `gke-monitor.sh`: **GKE** with 3 n1-standard-1 worker nodes, **nginx Ingress**, **tiller**, and cluster IP stored in environment variable **LB_IP** (https://gist.github.com/vfarcic/10e14bfbec466347d70d11a78fe7eec4).
- `eks-logging.sh`: **EKS** with 3 t2.large worker nodes, **nginx Ingress, tiller, Metrics Server, Cluster Autoscaler**, and cluster IP stored in environment variable **LB_IP** (https://gist.github.com/vfarcic/a783351fc9a3637a291346dd4bc346e7).
- `aks-logging.sh`: **AKS** with 3 Standard_B2ms worker nodes, **nginx Ingress**, and **tiller**, and cluster IP stored in environment variable **LB_IP** (https://gist.github.com/vfarcic/c4a63b92c03a0a1c721cb63b07d2ddfc).
- `docker-logging.sh`: **Docker for Desktop** with **2 CPUs** and **10 GB RAM**, **nginx Ingress, tiller, Metrics Server**, and cluster IP stored in environment variable **LB_IP** (https://gist.github.com/vfarcic/17d4f11ec53eed74e4b5e73debb4a590).

- `minikube-logging.sh`: **minikube** with **2 CPUs** and **10 GB RAM**, **ingress**, **storage-provisioner**, **default-storageclass**, and **metrics-server** addons enabled, **tiller**, and cluster IP stored in environment variable **LB_IP** (`https://gist.github.com/vfarcic/9f72c8451e1cca71758c70195c1c9f07`).

Now that we have a working cluster, we'll explore how to use logs through `kubectl`. That will provide a base for more comprehensive solutions that follow.

# Exploring logs through kubectl

The first contact most people have with logs in Kubernetes is through `kubectl`. It is almost unavoidable not to use it.

As we're learning how to tame the Kubernetes beast, we are bound to check logs when we get stuck. In Kubernetes, the term "logs" is reserved for the output produced by our and third-party applications running inside a cluster. However, those exclude the events generated by different Kubernetes resources. Even though many would call them logs as well, Kubernetes separates them from logs and calls them events. I'm sure that you already know how to retrieve logs from the applications and how to see Kubernetes events. Nevertheless, we'll explore them briefly here as well since that will add relevance to the discussion we'll have later on. I promise to keep it short, and you are free to skip this section if a brief overview of logging and events baked into Kubernetes is too basic for you.

We'll install the already familiar `go-demo-5` application. It should generate enough logs for us to explore them. Since it consists of a few resources, we are bound to create some Kubernetes events as well.

Off we go.

```
 1  GD5_ADDR=go-demo-5.$LB_IP.nip.io
 2
 3  echo $GD5_ADDR
 4
 5  helm upgrade -i go-demo-5 \
 6      https://github.com/vfarcic/go-demo-5/releases/download/
    0.0.1/go-demo-5-0.0.1.tgz \
 7      --namespace go-demo-5 \
 8      --set ingress.host=$GD5_ADDR
 9
10  kubectl -n go-demo-5 \
11    rollout status deployment go-demo-5
12
13  curl "http://$GD5_ADDR/demo/hello"
```

We rolled out `go-demo-5` and sent a `curl` request to confirm that it is indeed working.

 The outputs and screenshots in this chapter are taken from minikube, except inside the sections dedicated to exclusively GKE, EKS, and AKS. There might be slight differences between what you see here and what you can observe on your screen.

To see "logs" generated by Kubernetes and limited to a specific resource, we need to retrieve the events.

```
1  kubectl -n go-demo-5 \
2    describe sts go-demo-5-db
```

The output, limited to the messages in the `Events` section, is as follows.

```
...
Events:
... Message
... -------
... create Claim go-demo-5-db-go-demo-5-db-0 Pod go-demo-5-db-0 in
StatefulSet go-demo-5-db success
... create Pod go-demo-5-db-0 in StatefulSet go-demo-5-db successful
... create Claim go-demo-5-db-go-demo-5-db-1 Pod go-demo-5-db-1 in
StatefulSet go-demo-5-db success
... create Pod go-demo-5-db-1 in StatefulSet go-demo-5-db successful
... create Claim go-demo-5-db-go-demo-5-db-2 Pod go-demo-5-db-2 in
StatefulSet go-demo-5-db success
... create Pod go-demo-5-db-2 in StatefulSet go-demo-5-db successful
```

The events you see in front of you are, in a way, Kubernetes logs generated by, in this case, the `go-demo-5-db` StatefulSet.

While those events are useful, they are often insufficient. More often than not, we do not know in advance where the problem is. If one of our Pods misbehaves, the cause might be in that Pod, but it might also be in the ReplicaSet that created it, or it might be in the Deployment that created the ReplicaSet, or maybe the node got detached from the cluster, or it might be something completely different.

 For any but the smallest systems, going from one resource to another and from one node to another to find the cause of an issue is anything but practical, reliable, and fast.

Simply put, looking at events by describing a resource is not the way to go and we need to find an alternative.

But, before we do that, let's see what happens with logs from applications.

We deployed a few replicas of the go-demo-5 API and a few replicas of the MongoDB. How can we explore their logs if we suspect that there is a problem with one of them? We can execute kubectl logs command like the one that follows.

```
1  kubectl -n go-demo-5 \
2      logs go-demo-5-db-0 -c db
```

The output shows the logs of the db container inside the go-demo-5-db-0 Pod.

While the previous output is limited to a single container and a single Pod, we can use labels to retrieve logs from multiple Pods.

```
1  kubectl -n go-demo-5 \
2      logs -l app=go-demo-5
```

This time, the output comes from all the Pods with the label app set to go-demo-5. We broadened our results, and that is often all we need. If we know that there is something wrong with, let's say, go-demo-5 Pods, we need to figure out whether the issue is present in multiple Pods or it is limited to a single one. While the previous command allowed us to broaden our search, if there were something suspicious in those logs, we would not know where that comes from. Retrieving logs from multiple Pods does not get us any closer to knowing which Pods are misbehaving.

Using labels is still very limiting. They are by no means a substitute for more complex querying. We might need to filter the results based on timestamps, nodes, keywords, and so on. While we could accomplish some of those things with additional kubectl logs arguments and creative usage of grep, sed, and other Linux commands, this approach to retrieving, filtering, and outputting logs is far from optimum.

 More often than not, kubectl logs command does not provide us with enough options to perform anything but simplest retrieval of logs.

We need a few things to improve our debugging capabilities. We need a potent query language that will allow us to filter log entries, we need sufficient information about the origin of those logs, we need queries to be fast, and we need access to logs created in any part of the cluster. We'll try to accomplish that, and a few other things, by setting up a centralized logging solution.

# Choosing a centralized logging solution

The first thing we need to do is to find a place where we'll store logs. Given that we want to have the ability to filter log entries, storing them in files should be discarded from the start. What we need is a database, of sorts. It is more important that it is fast than transactional, so we are most likely looking into a solution that is an in-memory database. But, before we take a look at the choices, we should discuss the location of our database. Should we run it inside our cluster, or should we use a service? Instead of making that decision right away, we'll explore both options, before we make a choice.

There are two major groups of logging-as-a-service types. If we are running our cluster with one of the Cloud providers, an obvious choice might be to use a logging solution they provide. EKS has AWS CloudWatch, GKE has GCP Stackdriver, and AKS has Azure Log Analytics. If you choose to use one of the Cloud vendors, that might make a lot of sense. Why bother with setting up your own solution of looking for a third-party service, if everything is already set up and waiting for you? We'll explore them soon.

Since my mission is to provide instructions that work for (almost) anyone, we'll also explore one of the logging-as-a-service solutions found outside hosting vendors. But, which one should we select? There are too many solutions in the market. We could, for example, choose *Splunk* (https://www.splunk.com/) or *DataDog* (https://www.datadoghq.com/). Both are excellent choices, and both are much more than only logging solutions. We can use them to collect metrics (like with Prometheus). They provide dashboards (like Grafana), and a few other things. Later on, we'll discuss whether we should combine logs and metrics in a single tool. For now, our focus is only on logging, and that's the main reason we'll skip Splunk, DataDog, and similar comprehensive tools that offer much more than what we need. That does not mean that you should discard them, but rather that this chapter tries to maintain the focus on logging.

There are many logging services available, with *Scalyr* (https://www.scalyr.com/pricing), *logdna* (https://logdna.com/), *sumo logic* (https://www.sumologic.com/) being only a few. We won't go through all of them since would take much more time and space than I feel is useful. Given that most services are very similar when logging is involved, I'll skip a detailed comparison and jump straight into *Papertrail* (https://papertrailapp.com/), my favorite logging service. Please bear in mind that we'll use it only as an example. I will assume that you'll check at least a few others and make your own choice based on your needs.

Logging-as-a-service might not be a good fit for all. Some might prefer a self-hosted solution, while others might not even be allowed to send data outside their clusters. In those cases, a self-hosted logging solution is likely the only choice.

Even if you are not restrained to your own cluster, there might be other reasons to keep it inside, latency being only one of many. We'll explore a self-hosted solution as well, so let us pick one. Which one will it be?

Given that we need a place to store our logs, we might look into traditional databases. However, most of them would not fit our needs. Transactional databases like MySQL require fixed schemas so we can discard them immediately. NoSQL is a better fit so we might choose something like MongoDB. But, that would be a poor choice since we require the ability to perform very fast free-text searches. For that we probably need an in-memory database. MongoDB is not one of those. We could use Splunk Enterprise, but this book is dedicated to free (mostly open source) solutions. The only exception we made so far is with Cloud providers, and I intend to keep it that way.

The few requirements we mentioned (fast, free-text, in-memory, and a free solution) limit our potential candidates to only a few. *Solr* (`http://lucene.apache.org/solr/`) is one of those, but its usage has been dropping, and it is rarely used today (for a good reason). The solution that sticks from a tiny crowd is *Elasticsearch* (`https://www.elastic.co/products/elasticsearch`). If you have a preference for a different on-prem solution, consider the examples we'll go through as a set of practices that you should be able to apply to other centralized logging solutions.

All in all, we'll explore an example of independent logging-as-a-service offering (Papertrail), we'll explore the solutions provided with Cloud hosting vendors (AWS CloudWatch, GCP Stackdriver, and Azure Log Analytics), and we'll try to set up ElasticSearch with a few friends. Those should provide enough examples for you to choose which type of a solution fits your use case the best.

But, before we explore the tools where we will store logs, we need to figure out how to collect them and ship them to their final destination.

# Exploring logs collection and shipping

For a long time now, there are two major contestants for the "logs collection and shipping" throne. Those are *Logstash* (`https://www.elastic.co/products/logstash`) and *Fluentd* (`https://www.fluentd.org/`). Both are open source, and both are widely accepted and actively maintained. While both have their pros and cons, Fluentd turned up to have an edge with cloud-native distributed systems. It consumes fewer resources and, more importantly, it is not tied to a single destination (Elasticsearch). While Logstash can push logs to many different targets, it is primarily designed to work with Elasticsearch. For that reason, other logging solutions adopted Fluentd.

As of today, no matter which logging product you embrace, the chances are that it will support Fluentd. The culmination of that adoption can be seen by Fluentd's entry into the list of *Cloud Native Computing Foundation* (https://www.cncf.io/) projects. Even Elasticsearch users are adopting Fluentd over Logstash. What was previously commonly referred to as **ELK** (**Elasticsearch, Logstash, Kibana**) stack, is now called **EFK** (**Elasticsearch, Fluentd, Kibana**).

We'll follow the trend and adopt Fluentd as the solution for collecting and shipping logs, no matter whether the destination is Papertrail, Elasticsearch, or something else.

We'll install Fluentd soon. But, since Papertrail is our first target, we need to create and set up an account. For now, remember that we need to collect logs from all the nodes of the cluster and, as you already know, Kubernetes' DaemonSet will ensure that a Fluentd Pod will run in each of our servers.

# Exploring centralized logging through Papertrail

The first centralized logging solution we'll explore is *Papertrail* (https://papertrailapp.com/). We'll use it as a representative of a logging-as-a-service solution that can save us from installing and, more importantly, maintaining a self-hosted alternative.

Papertrail features live trailing, filtering by timestamps, powerful search queries, pretty colors, and quite a few other things that might (or might not) be essential when skimming through logs produced inside our clusters.

The first thing we need to do is to register or, if this is not the first time you tried Papertrail, to log in.

```
1  open "https://papertrailapp.com/"
```

Please follow the instructions to register or to log in if you already have a user in their system.

You will be glad to find out that Papertrail provides a free plan that allows storage of 50 MB of logs searchable for one day, as well as a full year of downloadable archives. That should be more than enough for running the examples we are about to explore. If you have a relatively small cluster, that should keep you going indefinitely. Their prices are reasonable, even if your cluster is bigger and you have more monthly logs than 50 MB.

Arguably, they are so cheap that we can say that it provides a better return on investment than if we'd run an alternative solution inside our own cluster. After all, nothing is free. Even self-hosted solutions based on open source create costs in maintenance time as well as in compute power.

For now, what matters is that the examples we'll run with Papertrail will be well within their free plan.

If you have a small operation, Papertrail will work well. But, if you're having many applications and a bigger cluster, you might be wondering whether Papertrail scales to suit your needs. Worry not. One of their customers is GitHub, and they are likely bigger than you are. Papertrail can handle (almost) any load. Whether it is a good solution for you is yet to be discovered. Read on.

Let's go to the start screen unless you are already there.

```
1  open "https://papertrailapp.com/start"
```

If you were redirected to the welcome screen, you are not authenticated (your session might have expired). Login and repeat the previous command to get to the start screen.

Click the **Add systems** button.

If you read the instructions, you'll probably think that the setup is relatively easy. It is. However, Kubernetes is not available as one of the options. If you change the value of the *from* drop-down list to *something else...*, you'll see a fairly big list of log sources that can be plugged into Papertrail. Still, there is no sign of Kubernetes. The closest one on that list is *Docker*. Even that one will not do. Don't worry. I prepared instructions for you or, to be more precise, I extracted them from the documentation buried in Papertrail's site.

Please note the `Your logs will go to logsN.papertrailapp.com:NNNNN and appear in Events` message at the top of the screen. We'll need that address soon, so we better store the values in environment variables.

```
1  PT_HOST=[...]
2
3  PT_PORT=[...]
```

Please replace the first `[...]` with the host. It should be something like `logsN.papertrailapp.com`, where `N` is the number assigned to you by Papertrail. The second `[...]` should be replaced with the port from the before mentioned message.

Now that we have the host and the port stored in environment variables, we can explore the mechanism we'll use to collect and ship the logs to Papertrail.

Since I already claimed that most vendors adopted Fluentd for collecting and shipping logs to their solutions, it should come as no surprise that Papertrail recommends it as well. Folks from SolarWinds (Papertrail's parent company) created an image with customized Fluentd that we can use. In turn, I created a YAML file with all the resources we'll need to run their image.

```
1   cat logging/fluentd-papertrail.yml
```

As you can see, the YAML defines a DaemonSet with ServiceAccount, SolarWind's Fluentd, and a ConfigMap that uses a few environment variables to specify the host and the port where logs should be shipped.

We'll have to change the `logsN.papertrailapp.com` and `NNNNN` entries in that YAML before we apply it. Also, I prefer running all logs-related resources in `logging` Namespace, so we'll need to change that as well.

```
1   cat logging/fluentd-papertrail.yml \
2       | sed -e \
3       "s@logsN.papertrailapp.com@$PT_HOST@g" \
4       | sed -e \
5       "s@NNNNN@$PT_PORT@g" \
6       | kubectl apply -f - --record
7
8   kubectl -n logging \
9       rollout status ds fluentd-papertrail
```

Now that we're running Fluentd in our cluster and that it is configured to forward logs to our Papertrail account, we should turn back to its UI.

Please switch back to Papertrail console in your browser. You should see a green box stating that logs were received. Click the **Events** link.

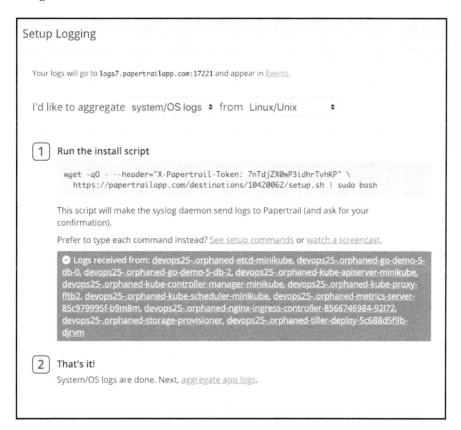

Figure 7-1: Papertrail's Setup Logging screen

Next, we'll produce a few logs and explore how they appear in Papertrail.

```
1  cat logging/logger.yml
2  apiVersion: v1
3  kind: Pod
4  metadata:
5    name: random-logger
6  spec:
7    containers:
8    - name: random-logger
9      image: chentex/random-logger
```

That Pod uses `chentex/random-logger` image that has a single purpose. It periodically outputs random log entries.

Let's create `random-logger`.

```
1  kubectl create -f logging/logger.yml
```

Please wait for a minute or two to accumulate a few logs entries.

```
1  kubectl logs random-logger
```

The output should be similar to the one that follows.

```
. . .
2018-12-06T17:21:15+0000 ERROR something happened in this execution.
2018-12-06T17:21:20+0000 DEBUG first loop completed.
2018-12-06T17:21:24+0000 ERROR something happened in this execution.
2018-12-06T17:21:27+0000 ERROR something happened in this execution.
2018-12-06T17:21:29+0000 WARN variable not in use.
2018-12-06T17:21:31+0000 ERROR something happened in this execution.
2018-12-06T17:21:33+0000 DEBUG first loop completed.
2018-12-06T17:21:35+0000 WARN variable not in use.
2018-12-06T17:21:40+0000 WARN variable not in use.
2018-12-06T17:21:43+0000 INFO takes the value and converts it to string.
2018-12-06T17:21:44+0000 INFO takes the value and converts it to string.
2018-12-06T17:21:47+0000 DEBUG first loop completed.
```

As you can see, the container is outputting random entries, some of them as `ERROR`, and others as `DEBUG`, `WARN`, and `INFO`. Messages are random as well. After all, that is not a real application, but a simple image that produces log entries we can use to explore our logging solution.

Please go back to Papertrail UI. You should notice that all the logs from our system are available. Some are coming from Kubernetes, while others are from system-level services.

Those from `go-demo-5` are also there, together with the `random-logger` we just installed. We'll focus on the latter.

Let's imagine that we found out through alerts that there is an issue and that we limited the scope to the `random-logger` application. Alerts helped us detect the problem and we narrowed it down to a single application by digging through metrics. We still need to consult logs to find the cause. Given what we know (or invented), the logical next step would be to retrieve only the log entries related to the `random-logger`.

Please type `random-logger` in the **Search** field at the bottom of the screen, and press the enter key.

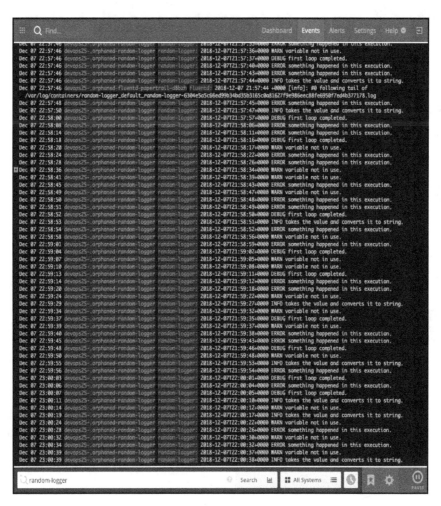

Figure 7-2: Papertrail's Events screen

From now on, we'll see only log entries that contain the word `random-logger`. That does not necessarily mean that only the log entries from that application are displayed. Instead, any mention of that word is shown on the screen. What we did was to instruct Papertrail to perform a free-text search inside all the log entries and retrieve only those that contain the beforementioned word.

While free-text search across all the records is probably the most commonly used query, there are a few other ways we could filter logs. We won't go through all of them. Instead, click the **Search tips** button in the right-hand side of the **Search** field and explore the syntax yourself. If those few examples are not enough, click the **Full Syntax Guide** link.

Figure 7-3: Papertrail's Syntax & Examples screen

There's probably no need to explore Papertrail in more detail. It is intuitive, easy to use, and well-documented service. I'm sure you'll figure out the details if you choose to use it. For now, we'll remove the DaemonSet and the ConfigMap before we move into exploring alternatives.

```
1  kubectl delete \
2    -f logging/fluentd-papertrail.yml
```

Next, we'll explore logging solutions available in Cloud providers. Feel free to jump directly to *GCP Stackdriver*, *AWS CloudWatch*, or *Azure Log Analytics*. If you do not use any of the three providers, you can skip them altogether and go directly to the *Exploring centralized logging through Elasticsearch, Fluentd, and Kibana* sub-chapter.

# Combining GCP Stackdriver with a GKE cluster

If you're using GKE cluster, logging is already set up, even though you might not know about it. By default, every GKE cluster comes by default with a Fluentd DaemonSet that is configured to forward logs to GCP Stackdriver. It is running in the `kube-system` Namespace.

Let's describe GKE's Fluentd DaemonSet and see whether there is any useful information we might find.

```
1   kubectl -n kube-system \
2     describe ds -l k8s-app=fluentd-gcp
```

The output, limited to the relevant parts, is as follows.

```
...
Pod Template:
  Labels:      k8s-app=fluentd-gcp
               kubernetes.io/cluster-service=true
               version=v3.1.0
...
  Containers:
   fluentd-gcp:
    Image: gcr.io/stackdriver-agents/stackdriver-logging-
agent:0.3-1.5.34-1-k8s-1
    ...
```

We can see that, among others, the DaemonSet's Pod Template has the label `k8s-app=fluentd-gcp`. We'll need it soon. Also, we can see that one of the containers is based on the `stackdriver-logging-agent` image. Just as Papertrail extended Fluentd, Google did the same.

Now that we know that Stackdriver-specific Fluentd is running in our cluster as a DaemonSet, the logical conclusion would be that there is already a UI we can use to explore the logs.

UI is indeed available but, before we see it in action, we'll output the logs of the Fluentd containers and verify that everything is working as expected.

```
1  kubectl -n kube-system \
2    logs -l k8s-app=fluentd-gcp \
3    -c fluentd-gcp
```

Unless you already enabled Stackdriver Logging API, the output should contain at least one message similar to the one that follows.

```
. . .
18-12-12 21:36:41 +0000 [warn]: Dropping 1 log message(s)
error="7:Stackdriver Logging API has not been used in project 152824630010
before or it is disabled. Enable it by visiting
https://console.developers.google.com/apis/api/logging.googleapis.com/overv
iew?project=152824630010 then retry. If you enabled this API recently, wait
a few minutes for the action to propagate to our systems and retry."
error_code="7"
```

Fortunately, the warning already tells us not only what the issue is, but also what to do. Open the link from the log entry in your favorite browser, and click the **ENABLE** button.

Now that we enabled Stackdriver Logging API, Fluentd will be able to ship log entries there. All we have to do is wait for a minute or two until the action propagates.

Let's see the Stackdriver UI.

```
1  open "https://console.cloud.google.com/logs/viewer"
```

Please type random-logger in the **Filter by label or text search** field and select **GKE Container** from the drop-down list.

The output should display all the logs that contain `random-logger` text.

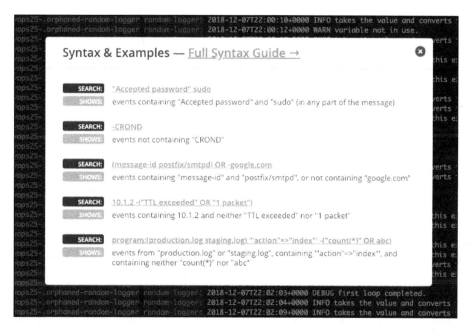

Figure 7-4: GCP Stackdriver logs screen

We won't go into details how to use Stackdriver. It is easy and, hopefully, intuitive. So, I'll leave it to you to explore it in more detail. What matters is that it is very similar to what we experienced with Papertrail. Most of the differences are cosmetic.

If you are using GCP, Stackdriver is ready and waiting for you. As such, it probably makes sense to use it over any other third-party solution. Stackdriver contains not only the logs coming from the cluster but also logs of all GCP services (for example, load balancers). That is probably the significant difference between the two solutions. It is a massive bonus in favor of Stackdriver. Still, check the pricing before making a decision.

# Combining AWS CloudWatch with an EKS cluster

Unlike GKE that has a logging solution baked into a cluster, EKS requires us to set up a solution. It does provide CloudWatch service, but we need to ensure that the logs are shipped there from our cluster.

Just as before, we'll use Fluentd to collect logs and ship them to CloudWatch. Or, to be more precise, we'll use a Fluentd tag built specifically for CloudWatch. As you probably already know, we'll also need an IAM policy that will allow Fluentd to communicate with CloudWatch.

All in all, the setup we are about to make will be very similar to the one we did with Papertrail, except that we'll store the logs in CloudWatch, and that we'll have to put some effort into creating AWS permissions.

Before we proceed, I'll assume that you still have the environment variables `AWS_ACCESS_KEY_ID`, `AWS_SECRET_ACCESS_KEY`, and `AWS_DEFAULT_REGION` used in the `eks-logging.sh` (`https://gist.github.com/vfarcic/a783351fc9a3637a291346dd4bc346e7`) Gist. If you don't, please create them.

Off we go.

We need to create a new AWS **Identity and Access Management (IAM)** (`https://aws.amazon.com/iam/`) policy. For that, we need to find out the IAM role, and for that we need the IAM profile. If you're confused with that, it might help to know that you're not the only one. AWS permissions are anything but straightforward. Nevertheless, that's not the subject of this chapter (nor the book), so I will assume at least a basic understanding of how IAM works.

If we reverse engineer the route to creating an IAM policy, the first thing we need is the profile.

```
1  PROFILE=$(aws iam \
```

```
2      list-instance-profiles \
3      | jq -r \
4      ".InstanceProfiles[]\
5      .InstanceProfileName" \
6      | grep eksctl-$NAME-nodegroup-0)
7
8   echo $PROFILE
```

The output should be similar to the one that follows.

```
eksctl-devops25-nodegroup-0-NodeInstanceProfile-SBTFOBLRAKJF
```

Now that we know the profile, we can use it to retrieve the role.

```
1   ROLE=$(aws iam get-instance-profile \
2     --instance-profile-name $PROFILE \
3     | jq -r ".InstanceProfile.Roles[] \
4     | .RoleName")
5
6   echo $ROLE
```

With the role at hand, we can finally create the policy. I already created one we can use, so let's take a quick look at it.

```
1   cat logging/eks-logs-policy.json
```

The output is as follows.

```
{
  "Version": "2012-10-17",
  "Statement": [
    {
      "Action": [
        "logs:DescribeLogGroups",
        "logs:DescribeLogStreams",
        "logs:CreateLogGroup",
        "logs:CreateLogStream",
        "logs:PutLogEvents"
      ],
      "Resource": "*",
      "Effect": "Allow"
    }
  ]
}
```

As you can see, there's nothing special about that policy. It defines permissions required for interaction with `logs` (CloudWatch) from inside our cluster.

So, let's move on and create it.

```
1  aws iam put-role-policy \
2    --role-name $ROLE \
3    --policy-name eks-logs \
4    --policy-document file://logging/eks-logs-policy.json
```

Finally, to be on the safe side, we'll retrieve the eks-logs policy and confirm that it was indeed created correctly.

```
1  aws iam get-role-policy \
2    --role-name $ROLE \
3    --policy-name eks-logs
```

The PolicyDocument section of the output should be the same as the JSON file we used to create the policy.

Now that we have the policy in place, we can turn our attention to Fluentd.

Unfortunately, at this moment (December 2018), there is no CloudWatch-friendly Fluentd Helm Chart. So, we'll fall back to good old YAML. I prepared one, so let's take a quick look at it.

```
1  cat logging/fluentd-eks.yml
```

I won't go into the details of the YAML. You should be able to understand what it does by exploring it on your own. The key resources are the fluentd-cloudwatch ConfigMap that contains the configuration and the DaemonSet with the same name that will run Fluentd Pod in each node of your cluster. The only difficulty you might have with that YAML is to understand the Fluentd configuration, especially if that is the first time you're working with it. Nevertheless, we won't go into details, and I'll let you explore Fluentd's documentation on your own. Instead, we'll apply that YAML hoping that everything works as expected.

```
1  kubectl apply \
2    -f logging/fluentd-eks.yml
```

Before we move into Cloudwatch UI, we'll retrieve Fluentd Pods and confirm that there is one in each node of the cluster.

```
1  kubectl -n logging get pods
```

In my case, the output shows three fluentd-cloudwatch Pods matching the number of nodes in my EKS cluster.

```
NAME                         READY   STATUS    RESTARTS   AGE
fluentd-cloudwatch-7dp5b     1/1     Running   0          19s
fluentd-cloudwatch-zq98z     1/1     Running   0          19s
```

```
fluentd-cloudwatch-zrrk7   1/1      Running   0           19s
```

Now that everything seems to be working inside our cluster, the time has come to move into CloudWatch UI.

```
1  open "https://$AWS_DEFAULT_REGION.console.aws.amazon.com/
    cloudwatch/home?#logStream:group=/eks/$NAME/containers"
```

Please type `random-logger` in the **Log Stream Name Prefix** field and press the enter key. As a result, only one stream should be available. Click it.

Once inside the `random-logger` screen, you should see all the logs generated by that Pod. I'll leave it to you to explore the available options (there aren't many).

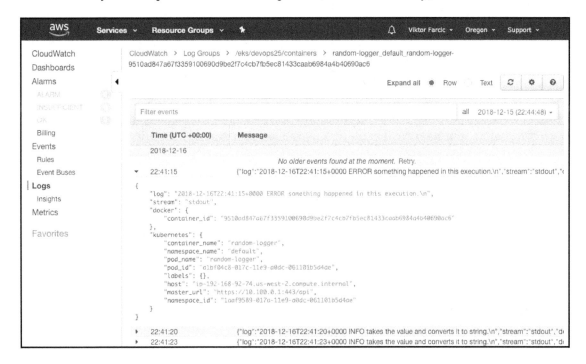

Figure 7-5: AWS CloudWatch events screen

Once you're done exploring CloudWatch, we'll proceed by deleting the Fluentd resources as well as the policy and the log group. We still have more logging solutions to explore. If you choose to use CloudWatch with Fluentd, you should be able to replicate the same installation steps in your "real" cluster.

```
1  kubectl delete \
2    -f logging/fluentd-eks.yml
```

```
 3
 4  aws iam delete-role-policy \
 5      --role-name $ROLE \
 6      --policy-name eks-logs
 7
 8  aws logs delete-log-group \
 9    --log-group-name \
10    "/eks/devops25/containers"
```

# Combining Azure Log Analytics with an AKS cluster

Just like GKE (and unlike EKS), AKS comes with an integrated logging solution. All we have to do is enable one of the AKS addons. To be more precise, we'll enable the `monitoring` addon. As the name indicates, the addon does not fulfill only the needs to collect logs, but it also handles metrics. However, we are interested just in logs. I believe that nothing beats Prometheus for metrics, especially since it integrates with HorizontalPodAutoscaler. Still, you should explore AKS metrics as well and reach your own conclusion. For now, we'll explore only the logging part of the addon.

```
1  az aks enable-addons \
2    -a monitoring \
3    -n devops25-cluster \
4    -g devops25-group
```

The output is a rather big JSON with all the information about the newly enabled `monitoring` addon. There's nothing exciting in it.

It's important to note that we could have enabled the addon when we created the cluster by adding `-a monitoring` argument to the `az aks create` command.

If you're curious what we got, we can list the Deployments in the `kube-system` Namespace.

```
1  kubectl -n kube-system get deployments
```

The output is as follows.

```
NAME                    DESIRED CURRENT UP-TO-DATE AVAILABLE AGE
heapster                1       1       1          1         1m
kube-dns-v20            2       2       2          2         1h
kubernetes-dashboard    1       1       1          1         1h
metrics-server          1       1       1          1         1h
```

```
omsagent-rs       1       1       1       1       1m
tiller-deploy     1       1       1       1       59m
tunnelfront       1       1       1       1       1h
```

The new addition is the `omsagent-rs` Deployment that will ship the logs (and metrics) to Azure Log Analytics. If you `describe` it, you'll see that it is based on `microsoft/oms` image. That makes it the first and the only time we switched from Fluentd to a different log shipping solution. We'll use it simply because Azure recommends it.

Next, we need to wait for a few minutes until the logs are propagated to Log Analytics. This is the perfect moment for you to take a short break. Go fetch a cup of coffee.

Let's open Azure portal and see Log Analytics in action.

```
1   open "https://portal.azure.com"
```

Please click the **All services** item from the left-hand menu, type `log analytics` in the **Filter** field, and click the **Log Analytics** item.

Figure 7-6: Azure portal All services screen with log analytics filter

Unless you are already using Log Analytics, there should be only one active workspace. If that's the case, click it. Otherwise, if there are multiple workspaces, choose the one with the ID that matches the *id* entry of the `az aks enable-addons` output.

Click the menu item **Logs** in the *General* section.

Next, we'll try to limit the output entries only to those that contain `random-logger`. Please type the query that follows in the **Type your query here...** field.

```
1  ContainerLog | where Name contains "random-logger"
```

Click the **Run** button, and you'll be presented with all the `random-logger` entries.

By default, all the fields are shown in the table, and many of them are either not used, or not very useful. The extra columns probably distract us from absorbing the logs, so we'll change the output.

It's easier to specify which columns we need, than which ones we don't. Please expand the **Columns** list, and click the **SELECT NONE** button. Next, select **LogEntry**, **Name**, and **TimeGenerated** fields and, once you're finished, contract the **Columns** list.

What you see in front of you are logs limited to `random-logger` and presented only through the three columns we selected.

Figure 7-7: Azure Log Analytics screen with filtered entries

I'll let you explore Log Analytics features on your own. Even though Azure portal's UI is not as intuitive as it could be, I'm sure you'll manage to get your way around it. If you choose to adopt AKS integration with Log Analytics, you should probably explore *Log Analytics query language* (https://docs.microsoft.com/en-us/azure/azure-monitor/log-query/query-language) documentation that will help you write more complex queries than the one we used.

Given that there is at least one more solution we should explore before we choose the one that fits your needs the best, we'll disable the addon. Later on, if you do like Log Analytics more than the alternatives, all you'll have to do is to enable it again.

```
1  az aks disable-addons \
2    -a monitoring \
3    -n devops25-cluster \
4    -g devops25-group
```

# Exploring centralized logging through Elasticsearch, Fluentd, and Kibana

Elasticsearch is probably the most commonly used in-memory database. At least, if we narrow the scope to self-hosted databases. It is designed for many other scenarios, and it can be used to store (almost) any type of data. As such, it is almost perfect for storing logs which could come in many different formats. Given its flexibility, some use it for metrics as well and, as such, Elasticsearch competes with Prometheus. We'll leave metrics aside, for now, and focus only on logs.

The **EFK** (**Elasticsearch**, **Fluentd**, and **Kibana**) stack consists of three components. Data is stored in Elasticsearch, logs are collected, transformed, and pushed to the DB by Fluentd, and Kibana is used as UI through which we can explore data stored in Elasticsearch. If you are used to ELK (Logstash instead of Fluentd), the setup that follows should be familiar.

The first components we'll install is Elasticsearch. Without it, Fluentd would not have a destination to ship logs, and Kibana would not have a source of data.

As you might have guessed, we'll continue using Helm and, fortunately, *Elasticsearch Chart* (https://github.com/helm/charts/tree/master/stable/elasticsearch) is already available in the stable channel. I'm confident that you know how to find the chart and explore all the values you can use. So, we'll jump straight into the values I prepared. They are the bare minimum and contain only the resources.

```
1  cat logging/es-values.yml
```

The output is as follows.

```
client:
  resources:
    limits:
      cpu: 1
      memory: 1500Mi
    requests:
      cpu: 25m
      memory: 750Mi
master:
  resources:
    limits:
      cpu: 1
      memory: 1500Mi
    requests:
      cpu: 25m
      memory: 750Mi
data:
  resources:
    limits:
      cpu: 1
      memory: 3Gi
    requests:
      cpu: 100m
      memory: 1500Mi
```

As you can see, there are three sections (client, master, and data) that correspond with ElasticSearch components that will be installed. All we're doing is setting up resource requests and limits, and leaving the rest to the Chart's default values.

Before we proceed, please note that you should NOT use those values in production. You should know by now that they differ from one case to another and that you should adjust resources depending on the actual usage that you can retrieve from tools like kubectl top, Prometheus, and others.

Let's install Elasticsearch.

```
1  helm upgrade -i elasticsearch \
2      stable/elasticsearch \
3      --version 1.14.1 \
4      --namespace logging \
5      --values logging/es-values.yml
6
7  kubectl -n logging \
8    rollout status \
9    deployment elasticsearch-client
```

It might take a while until all the resources are created. On top of that, if you're using GKE, new nodes might need to be created to accommodate requested resources. Be patient.

Now that Elasticsearch is rolled out, we can turn our attention to the second component in the EFK stack. We'll install Fluentd. Just as Elasticsearch, Fluentd is also available in Helm's stable channel.

```
1   helm upgrade -i fluentd \
2       stable/fluentd-elasticsearch \
3       --version 1.4.0 \
4       --namespace logging \
5       --values logging/fluentd-values.yml
6
7   kubectl -n logging \
8       rollout status \
9       ds fluentd-fluentd-elasticsearch
```

There's no much to say about Fluentd. It is running as DaemonSet and, as the name of the chart suggests, it is already preconfigured to work with Elasticsearch. I did not even bother showing you the contents of the values file `logging/fluentd-values.yml` since it contains only the resources.

To be on the safe side, we'll check Fluentd's logs to confirm that it managed to connect to Elasticsearch.

```
1   kubectl -n logging logs \
2       -l app=fluentd-fluentd-elasticsearch
```

The output, limited to the messages, is as follows.

```
... Connection opened to Elasticsearch cluster => {:host=>"elasticsearch-
client", :port=>9200, :scheme=>"http"}
... Detected ES 6.x: ES 7.x will only accept `_doc` in type_name.
```

### A note to Docker for Desktop users

You will likely see much more than the few log entries presented above. There will be a lot of warnings due to the differences in Docker for Desktop API when compared to other Kubernetes flavors. Feel free to ignore those warnings since they do not affect the examples we are about to explore and you are not going to use Docker for Desktop in production but only for practice and local development.

That was simple and beautiful. The only thing left is to install the K from EFK.

Let's take a look at the values file we'll use for the Kibana chart.

```
1   cat logging/kibana-values.yml
```

The output is as follows.

```
ingress:
  enabled: true
  hosts:
  - acme.com
env:
  ELASTICSEARCH_URL: http://elasticsearch-client:9200
resources:
  limits:
    cpu: 50m
    memory: 300Mi
  requests:
    cpu: 5m
    memory: 150Mi
```

Again, this is a relatively straightforward set of values. This time, we are specifying not only the resources but also the Ingress host, as well as the environment variable ELASTICSEARCH_URL that'll tell Kibana where to find Elasticsearch. As you might have guessed, I did not know in advance what will be your host, so we'll need to overwrite hosts at runtime. But, before we do that, we need to define it.

```
1   KIBANA_ADDR=kibana.$LB_IP.nip.io
```

Off we go towards installing the last component in the EFK stack.

```
1   helm upgrade -i kibana \
2       stable/kibana \
3       --version 0.20.0 \
4       --namespace logging \
5       --set ingress.hosts="{$KIBANA_ADDR}" \
6   --values logging/kibana-values.yml
7
8   kubectl -n logging \
9       rollout status \
10      deployment kibana
```

Now we can finally open Kibana and confirm that all three EFK components indeed work together and that they are fulfilling our centralized logging objectives.

```
1   open "http://$KIBANA_ADDR"
```

If you do not see Kibana just yet, wait for a few moments and refresh the screen.

You should see the *Welcome* screen. Ignore the offer to try their sample data by clicking the link to **Explore on my own**. You'll be presented with the screen that allows you to add data.

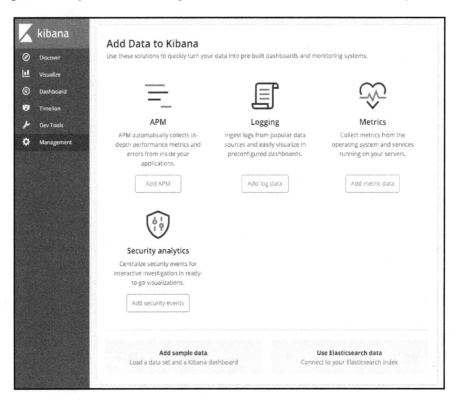

Figure 7-8: Kibana's home screen

The first thing we need to do is create a new Elasticsearch index that will match the one created by Fluentd. The version we're running is already pushing data to Elasticsearch, and it's doing that by using LogStash indexing pattern as a way to simplify things since that's what Kibana expects to see.

Click the **Management** item from the left-hand menu, followed with the **Index Patterns** link.

All the logs Fluentd is sending to Elasticsearch are indexes with the *logstash* prefix followed with the date. Since we want Kibana to retrieve all the logs, type `logstash-*` into the **Index pattern** field, and click the **> Next step** button.

Next, we need to specify which field contains timestamps. It is an easy choice. Select **@timestamp** from the **Time Filter field name**, and click the **Create index pattern** button.

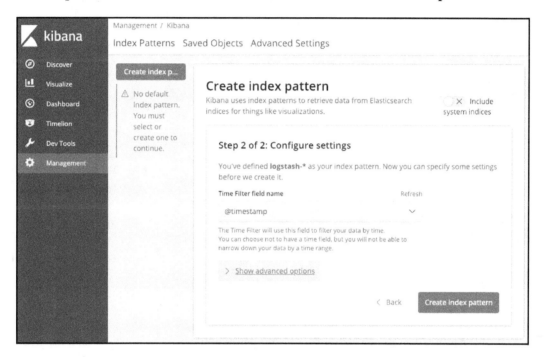

Figure 7-9: Kibana's Create index pattern screen

That's it. All we have to do now is wait for a few moments until the index is created, and explore the logs collected from across the whole cluster.

Please click the **Discover** item from the left-hand menu.

What you see in front of you are all the logs generated in the last fifteen minutes (can be extended to any period). The list of fields is available on the left-hand side.

There is a silly (and useless) graph on the top and the logs themselves are in the main body of the screen.

Figure 7-10: Kibana's Discover screen

Just as with Papertrail, we won't go into all the options available in Kibana. I trust you can figure them out yourself. We'll just go through a few basic operations in case this is your first contact with Kibana.

Our scenario is the same as before. We'll try to find all the log entries generated from the random-logger application.

Please type kubernetes.pod_name: "random-logger" into the **Search** field and click the **Refresh** (or **Update**) button located on the right.

More often than not, we want to customize the fields presented by default. For example, it would be more useful to see the log entry only, instead of the full source.

Click the **Add** button next to the **log** field, and it will replace the default _source_ column.

If you'd like to see an entry with all the fields, please expand one by clicking the arrow on the left side of the row.

Figure 7-11: Kibana's Discover screen with filtered entries

I'll leave you to explore the rest of Kibana on your own. But, before you do that, there's a word of warning. Do not get fooled by all the flashy options. If all we're having are logs, there's probably no point creating visualizations, dashboards, timelines, and other nice looking, but useless things we can do with logs. Those might be useful with metrics, but we do not have any. For now, they are in Prometheus. Later on, we'll discuss the option of pushing metrics to Elasticsearch instead of pulling them from Prometheus.

Now, take your time and see what else you can do in Kibana, at least within the *Discover* screen.

We're done with the EFK stack and, given that we did not yet make a decision which solution to use, we'll purge it from the system. Later on, if you do choose EFK, you should not have any trouble creating it in your "real" cluster.

```
1  helm delete kibana --purge
2
3  helm delete fluentd --purge
4
5  helm delete elasticsearch --purge
6
7  kubectl -n logging \
8      delete pvc \
9      -l release=elasticsearch,component=data
```

```
10
11  kubectl -n logging \
12      delete pvc \
13      -l release=elasticsearch,component=master
```

# Switching to Elasticsearch for storing metrics

Now that we had Elasticsearch running in our cluster and knowing that it can handle almost any data type, a logical question could be whether we can use it to store our metrics besides logs. If you explore *elastic.co* (`https://www.elastic.co/`), you'll see that metrics are indeed something they advertise. If it could replace Prometheus, it would undoubtedly be beneficial to have a single tool that can handle not only logs but also metrics. On top of that, we could ditch Grafana and keep Kibana as a single UI for both data types.

Nevertheless, I would strongly advise against using Elasticsearch for metrics. It is a general-purpose free-text no-SQL database. That means that it can handle almost any data but, at the same time, it does not excel at any specific format. Prometheus, on the other hand, is designed to store time-series data which are the preferred way of exposing metrics. As such, it is more limited in what it does. But, it handles metrics much better than Elasticsearch. I believe that using the right tool for the job is better than having a single tool that does too many things, and if you believe the same, Prometheus is a much better choice for metrics.

When compared to Elasticsearch, and focused only on metrics, Prometheus' requires much fewer resources (as you already noticed), it is faster, and it has a much better query language. That shouldn't come as a surprise given that both tools are great, but only Prometheus is designed to work exclusively with metrics. The increased cost of maintaining an additional tool is well paid off by having a better (and more focused) solution.

Did I mention that notifications generated through Prometheus and Alertmanager and better than those through Elasticsearch?

There's one more important thing to note. Prometheus integration with Kubernetes is way better than what Elasticsearch offers. That is not a surprise since Prometheus is based on the same cloud-native principles as Kubernetes and both belong to *Cloud Native Computing Foundation* (`https://www.cncf.io/`). Elasticsearch, on the other hand, comes from a more traditional background.

Elasticsearch is excellent, but it does too much. Its lack of focus makes it inferior to Prometheus for storing and querying metrics, as well as sending alerts based on such data.

If replacing Prometheus with Elasticsearch is not a good idea, can we invert the question? Can we use Prometheus for logs? The answer is a definite no. As already stated, Prometheus is focused only on metrics. If you do adopt it, you need a different tool for storing logs. That can be Elasticsearch, Papertrail, or any other solution that fits your needs.

How about Kibana? Can we ditch it in favor of Grafana? The answer is yes, but don't do that. While we could create a table in Grafana and attach it to Elasticsearch as a data source, its capability to display and filter logs is inferior. On the other hand, Grafana is much more flexible than Kibana for displaying graphs based on metrics. So, the answer is similar to the Elasticsearch vs. Prometheus dilemma. Keep Grafana for metrics and use Kibana for logs, if you chose to store them in Elasticsearch.

Should you add Elasticsearch as yet another data source in Grafana? If you took previous recommendations, the answer is most likely no. There is not much value in presenting logs as graphs. Even the pre-defined graph available in Kibana's *Explore* section is, in my opinion, a waste of space. There is no point in showing how many logs entries we have in total, nor even how many are error entries. We use metrics for that.

 Logs themselves are too expensive to parse, and most of the time they do not provide enough data to act as metrics.

We saw several tools in action, but we did not yet discuss what we truly need from a centralized logging solution. We'll explore that in more detail next.

# What should we expect from centralized logging?

We explored several products that can be used to centralize logging. As you saw, all are very similar, and we can assume that most of the other solutions follow the same principles. We need to collect logs across the cluster. We used Fluentd for that, which is the most widely accepted solution that you will likely use no matter which database receives those logs (Azure being an exception).

Log entries collected with Fluentd are shipped to a database which, in our case, is Papertrail, Elasticsearch, or one of the solutions provided by hosting vendors. Finally, all solutions offer a UI that allows us to explore the logs.

I usually provide a single solution for a problem but, in this case, there are quite a few candidates for your need for centralized logging. Which one should you choose? Will it be Papertrail, Elasticsearch-Fluentd-Kibana stack (EFK), AWS CloudWatch, GCP Stackdriver, Azure Log Analytics, or something else?

When possible and practical, I prefer a centralized logging solution provided as a service, instead of running it inside my clusters. Many things are easier when others are making sure that everything works. If we use Helm to install EFK, it might seem like an easy setup. However, maintenance is far from trivial. Elasticsearch requires a lot of resources. For smaller clusters, compute required to run Elasticsearch alone is likely higher than the price of Papertrail or similar solutions. If I can get a service managed by others for the same price as running the alternative inside my own cluster, service wins most of the time. But, there are a few exceptions.

I do not want to lock my business into a service provider. Or, to be more precise, I think it's crucial that core components are controlled by me, while as much of the rest is given to others. A good example is VMs. I do not honestly care who creates them, as long as the price is competitive and the service is reliable. I can easily move my VMs from on-prem to AWS, and from there to, let's say, Azure. I can even go back to on-prem. There's not much logic in the creation and maintenance of VMs. Or, at least, there shouldn't be.

What I genuinely care are my applications. As long as they are running, they are fault-tolerant, they are highly available, and their maintenance is not costly, it does not matter where they run. But, I need to make sure that the system is done in a way that allows me to switch from one provider to another, without spending months in refactoring. That's one of the big reasons why Kubernetes is so widely adopted. It abstracts everything below it, thus allowing us to run our applications in (almost) any Kubernetes cluster. I believe the same can be applied to logs. We need to be clear what we expect, and any solution that meets our requirements is as good as any other. So, what do we need from a logging solution?

 We need logs centralized in a single location so that we can explore logs from any part of the system.

 We need a query language that will allow us to filter the results.

We need the solution to be fast.

All of the solutions we explored meets those requirements. Papertrail, EFK, AWS CloudWatch, GCP Stackdriver, and Azure Log Analytics all fulfill those requirements. Kibana might be a bit prettier, and Elasticsearch's query language might be a bit richer than those provided by the other solutions. The importance of prettiness is up to you to establish. As for Elasticsearch' query language being more powerful... It does not really matter. Most of the time, we need simple operations with logs. Find me all the entries that have specific keywords. Return all logs from that application. Limit the result to the last thirty minutes.

 When possible and practical, logging-as-a-service provided by a third party like Papertrail, AWS, GCP, or Azure is a better option than to host it inside our clusters.

With a service, we accomplish the same goals, while getting rid of one of the things we need to worry about. The reasoning behind that statement is similar to the logic that makes me believe that managed Kubernetes services (for example, EKS, AKS, GKE) are a better choice than Kubernetes maintained by us. Nevertheless, there might be many reasons why using a third-party something-as-a-service solution is not possible. Regulations might not allow us to go outside the internal network. Latency might be too big. Decision makers are stubborn. No matter the reasons, when we can not use something-as-a-service, we have to host that something ourselves. In such a case, EFK is likely the best solution, excluding enterprise offerings that are out of the scope of this book.

If EFK is likely one of the best solutions for self-hosted centralized logging, which one should be our choice when we can use logging-as-a-service? Is Papertrail a good choice?

If our cluster is running inside one of the Cloud providers, there is likely already a good solution offered by it. For example, EKS has AWS CloudWatch, GKE has GCP Stackdriver, and AKS has Azure Log Analytics. Using one of those makes perfect sense. It's already there, it is likely already integrated with the cluster you are running, and all you have to do is say yes. When a cluster is running with one of the Cloud providers, the only reason to choose some other solution could be the price.

Use a service provided by your Cloud provider, unless it is more expensive than alternatives. If your cluster is on-prem, use a third-party service like Papertrail, unless there are rules that prevent you from sending logs outside your internal network. If everything else fails, use EFK.

At this point, you might be wondering why do I suggest to use a service for logs, while I proposed that our metrics should be hosted inside our clusters. Isn't that contradictory? Following that logic, shouldn't we use metrics-as-a-service as well?

Our system does not need to interact with our logs storage. The system needs to ship logs, but it does not need to retrieve them. As an example, there is no need for HorizontalPodAutoscaler to hook into Elasticsearch and use logs to decide whether to scale the number of Pods. If the system does not need logs to make decisions, can we say the same for humans? What do we need logs for? We need logs for debugging. We need them to find the cause of a problem. What we do NOT need are alerts based on logs. Logs do not help us discover that there is an issue, but to find the cause of a problem detected through alerts based on metrics.

Wait a minute! Shouldn't we create an alert when the number of log entries with the word *ERROR* goes over a certain threshold? The answer is no. We can (and should) accomplish the same objective through metrics. We already explored how to fetch errors from exporters as well as through instrumentation.

What happens when we detect that there is an issue through a metrics-based notification? Is that the moment we should start exploring logs? Most of the time, the first steps towards finding the cause of a problem does not lie in exploring logs, but in querying metrics. Is the application down? Does it have a memory leak? Is there a problem with networking? Is there a high number of error responses? Those and countless other questions are answered through metrics. Sometimes metrics reveal the cause of the problem, and in other cases, they help us narrow it down to a specific part of the system. Logs are becoming useful only in the latter case.

We should start exploring logs only when metrics reveal the culprit, but not the cause of the issue.

If we do have comprehensive metrics, and they do reveal most (if not all) of the information we need to solve an issue, we do not need much from a logging solution. We need logs to be centralized so that we can find them all in one place, we need to be able to filter them by application or a specific replica, we need to be able to narrow the scope to a particular time frame, and we need to be able to search for specific keywords.

That's all we need. As it happens, almost all solutions offer those features. As such, the choice should be based on simplicity and the cost of ownership.

Whatever you choose, do not fall into the trap of getting impressed with shiny features that you are not going to use. I prefer solutions that are simple to use and manage. Papertrail fulfills all the requirements, and its cheap. It's the perfect choice for both on-prem and Cloud clusters. The same can be said for CloudWatch (AWS), Stackdriver (GCP), and Log Analytics (Azure). Even though I have a slight preference towards Papertrail, those three do, more or less, the same job, and they are already part of the offer.

If you are not allowed to store your data outside your cluster, or you have some other impediment towards one of those solutions, EFK is a good choice. Just be aware that it'll eat your resources for breakfast, and still complain that it's hungry. Elasticsearch alone requires a few GB of RAM as a minimum, and you will likely need much more. That, of course, is not that important if you're already using Elasticsearch for other purposes. If that's the case, EFK is a no-brainer. It's already there, so use it.

# What now?

You know what to do. Destroy the cluster if you created it specifically for this chapter.

Before you leave, you might want to go over the main points of this chapter.

- For any but the smallest systems, going from one resource to another and from one node to another to find the cause of an issue is anything but practical, reliable, and fast.
- More often than not, `kubectl logs` command does not provide us with enough options to perform anything but simplest retrieval of logs.
- Elasticsearch is excellent, but it does too much. Its lack of focus makes it inferior to Prometheus for storing and querying metrics, as well as sending alerts based on such data.
- Logs themselves are too expensive to parse, and most of the time they do not provide enough data to act as metrics.
- We need logs centralized in a single location so that we can explore logs from any part of the system.
- We need a query language that will allow us to filter the results.
- We need the solution to be fast.

- Use a service provided by your Cloud provider, unless it is more expensive than alternatives. If your cluster is on-prem, use a third-party service like Papertrail, unless there are rules that prevent you from sending logs outside your internal network. If everything else fails, use EFK.
- We should start exploring logs only when metrics reveal the culprit, but not the cause of the issue.

# What Did We Do?

We explored quite a few topics that are beyond "normal" Kubernetes usage. We learned how to scale Pods using HorizontalPodAutoscaler. We saw that scaling Pods does not provide enough benefits if we cannot scale cluster nodes as well. We explored how to do just that using Cluster Autoscaler. Unfortunately, it is currently available only for AWS, GKE, and AKS.

While scaling Pods and nodes is essential, we had to gather metrics as well. They give us insights into the behavior of our clusters and applications running inside it. For that, we adopted Prometheus. More importantly, we saw how we can leverage Alertmanager to create notifications that will alert us when there is an issue, instead of staring at a screen waiting for a graph to reach a "red line".

We learned that gathering metrics from exporters might not be enough, so we instrumented our applications as a way of providing lower level metrics that give us deep insights into the state of our applications.

We also explored HorizontalPodAutoscaler's ability to use custom metrics. We hooked it into Prometheus thus extending scaling thresholds to almost any formula we could imagine.

Given that we collect metrics in Prometheus and that it doesn't provide dashboarding functionality, we connected it to Grafana. During the process, we explored ways that dashboards can be made more useful than traditional "pretty colors" many are instinctively drawn to.

Finally, we discussed the need for centralized logging as well as a few tools that might help us debug issues discovered through alerts. For that, we evaluated Papertrail, AWS CloudWatch, GCP Stackdriver, Azure Log Analytics, and the Elasticsearch-Fluentd-Kibana (EFK) stack.

We went beyond common Kubernetes operations and managed to make our clusters more robust and more reliable. We made a step forward towards mostly autonomous self-adaptive systems that require human intervention only in exceptional cases that cannot be resolved automatically. When we do need to intervene, we'll do that equipped with all the necessary information required to quickly deduce the cause of the issue and perform corrective actions that will restore our cluster to the desired state.

# Contributions

Like the previous books, this one was also a collaboration effort. Many helped shape this book through discussions, notes, and bug reports. I was swarmed with comments through *DevOps20* (http://slack.devops20toolkit.com/) Slack (often private) messages and emails. The conversations I had with the readers of the early editions of the book influenced the end result significantly. I'm grateful to have such a great community behind me. **Thank you for helping me make this book great.**

A few rose above the crowd.

**Vadim Gusev** helped to proofread and discuss book structure from the novice point of view.

In his own words...

*Vadim is a young IT specialist that started his career as a network engineer but was so fascinated by the idea of clouds and containers, that he decided to switch his career path to DevOps. He works in a small startup and leads it to bright containerized future, guided mostly by Viktor's books. In his free time, he likes to work out, play drums and procrastinate on purpose.*

**Prageeth Warnak** was continually sending pull requests with corrections and suggestions. He made this book much clearer than it would be if I had to rely on my, often incorrect, assumptions of what readers expect.

In his own words...

*Prageeth is a seasoned IT professional currently working as the lead software architect for Australian telco giant Telstra. He enjoys working with new technologies, and he likes spending his leisure time reading books (especially those written by Viktor), powerlifting (he can do 180kg dead lifts), watching Netflix and Fox news(yes he is an originalist and a conservative). He lives in Melbourne with his family. He is fascinated by getting Microservices and DevOps done right.*

# Other Books You May Enjoy

If you enjoyed this book, you may be interested in these other books by Packt:

**DevOps Paradox**

Viktor Farcic

ISBN: 978-1-78913-363-9

Expert opinions on:

- Introducing DevOps into real-world, chaotic business environments
- Deciding between adopting cutting edge tools or sticking with tried-and-tested methods
- Initiating necessary business change without positional power
- Managing and overcoming fear of change in DevOps implementations
- Anticipating future trends in DevOps and how to prepare for them
- Getting the most from Kubernetes, Docker, Puppet, Chef, and Ansible
- Creating the right incentives for DevOps success across an organization
- The impact of new techniques, such as Lambda, serverless, and schedulers, on DevOps practice

Continuous Deployment
To Kubernetes

## The DevOps 2.4 Toolkit
Viktor Farcic

ISBN: 978-1-83864-354-6

- Gain an understanding of continuous deployment
- Learn how to build, test, and deploy applications into Kubernetes
- Execute continuous integration inside containers

# Leave a review - let other readers know what you think

Please share your thoughts on this book with others by leaving a review on the site that you bought it from. If you purchased the book from Amazon, please leave us an honest review on this book's Amazon page. This is vital so that other potential readers can see and use your unbiased opinion to make purchasing decisions, we can understand what our customers think about our products, and our authors can see your feedback on the title that they have worked with Packt to create. It will only take a few minutes of your time, but is valuable to other potential customers, our authors, and Packt. Thank you!

# Index

Metric Server data, combining with 223, 224

Prometheus
  about  69, 70, 71, 72, 73, 74, 75, 76, 77, 78,
    79, 81, 82, 84, 85, 86, 87, 88, 89
  reference link  184
  URL  68, 183

# R

Regular expression
  reference link  104

# S

saturation-related issues
  alerts  120, 122, 123, 124, 125, 126, 127, 128,
    129, 130, 131, 132, 133, 134, 136, 138, 139,
    140, 141, 142, 143
scaling
  considerations  60, 61
Scalyr
  URL  266
semaphore dashboards
  creating  249, 250, 252, 253, 254
semaphores
  versus Grafana notifications  258, 259, 260
  versus graph alerts  258, 259, 260

versus Prometheus alerts  258, 259, 260
Site Reliability Engineers (SREs)  90
Solr
  URL  267
Splunk
  URL  266
StatefulSets
  replicas  32, 33, 36, 37, 38
storing metrics
  Elasticsearch, switching for  294, 295
sumo logic
  URL  266

# T

traffic-related issues
  alerts  106, 107, 109, 111, 112, 114, 115

# U

unschedulable pods
  alerts  143, 144, 146, 147, 148, 149, 150

# W

Webhooks
  URL  87

www.ingramcontent.com/pod-product-compliance
Lightning Source LLC
LaVergne TN
LVHW081516050326
832903LV00025B/1512